# HIPPIE FOOD

# HIPPIE FOOD

How Back-to-the-Landers,

Longhairs, and Revolutionaries

Changed the Way We Eat

## JONATHAN KAUFFMAN

*WM*

WILLIAM MORROW

*An Imprint of* HarperCollins*Publishers*

Poem on pages 40–41 courtesy of Gypsy Boots, LLC.

HIPPIE FOOD. Copyright © 2018 by Jonathan Kauffman. All rights reserved.
Printed in the United States of America. No part of this book may be used or
reproduced in any manner whatsoever without written permission except in the
case of brief quotations embodied in critical articles and reviews. For information
address HarperCollins Publishers, 195 Broadway, New York, NY 10007.

HarperCollins books may be purchased for educational, business, or sales
promotional use. For information please e-mail the Special Markets Department at
SPsales@harpercollins.com.

FIRST EDITION

*Designed by Bonni Leon-Berman*

Library of Congress Cataloging-in-Publication Data has been applied for.

ISBN 978-0-06-243730-3

18  19  20  21    LSC    10  9  8  7  6  5  4  3  2

To Linda and Sandy Kauffman, who have nourished me in ways I appreciate more with every day

# CONTENTS

..................................

# INTRODUCTION

THE SUNLIGHT CAFE, SEATTLE'S OLDEST-SURVIVING VEGETARIAN restaurant, has been around for so long now that my lunch there is as familiar as it is a target for ridicule.

Cubes of sweet potato and Us of celery bob on the surface of a chunky "Mexican bean fiesta soup," the scent of cumin surfing on the steam rising off its surface. Alfalfa sprouts jut out of an avocado-havarti sandwich as if its toasted whole-wheat shell were a squashed-on hat. A side salad is drizzled with tahini-lemon dressing and speckled with sunflower and sesame seeds. Tack on a slice of nutloaf, and you'd have a complete 1970s feast, the antithesis of all-American meat and potatoes, the kind of food that would still be associated with hippies even fifty years after San Francisco's Summer of Love.

The Sunlight Cafe, opened in 1977, doesn't deny its hippie heritage. Although Seattle's climate often renders its name aspirational, when the sunlight does arrive, it floods the brightly colored room. Native American paintings hang above the wooden booths, and solid-looking whole-wheat cookies and muffins lurk in the pastry case. The sign on the men's restroom depicts a stringy-haired, bell-bottomed dude. I share the same scuffed wood table with several white guys in their sixties reading the *Seattle Times* over their huevos rancheros and a group of stout, fleece-clad women debating whether they're going to order the tempeh or the tofu burger because both sound "soooo good."

These are my people. This is the food I have been surrounded by all my life.

For those of you who didn't grow up eating lentil-and-brown-rice casseroles, it may be hard to recognize what came to be called "hippie food." That's because so many of the ingredients that the counterculture of the 1960s and 1970s adopted, defying the suspicion and disgust of the rest of the country, have become foods many of us eat every day.

The organic chard you bought at Kroger last week? In the early 1970s, farming organically was considered a delusional act. The granola-yogurt parfait your coworker just picked up at Starbucks? In 1971, both granola and yogurt were foreign substances, their reputation as tied to long-haired peaceniks as pour-over coffee is to lumberjack beards and high-waisted jeans. Back then, whole-wheat bread had disappeared from grocery stores. Hummus wasn't a childhood staple but a dish only spotted in Middle Eastern markets and vegetarian cafés.

The cuisine that the counterculture took to in the late 1960s, and then helped introduce to the mainstream in the 1970s, embraced whole grains and legumes; organic, fresh vegetables; soy foods like tofu and tempeh; nutrition boosters like wheat germ and sprouted grains; and flavors from Eastern European, Asian, and Latin American cuisines. The food young bohemians concocted with all these ingredients was often vegetarian, sometimes macrobiotic, and occasionally inedible.

Forty years on, people who didn't live in that era might assume that hippie food could only be found in big cities and rural communes, but that wasn't the case. I grew up in the 1970s, in a Mennonite community in Elkhart, Indiana. We only ate the traditional Pennsylvania Dutch fare of our grandparents—sauerkraut, funnel cakes, shoofly pie—once or twice a year. At my parents' house, dinner was likely to be stir-fried tofu and broccoli one night, lentil stew the next.

Ultraliberal Mennonites like my parents were hardly Plattdeutsch-speaking, covering-wearing Amish. Yet the community I was raised in was no commune, either. My dad did sport lush sideburns, and my parents' politics were left of George McGovern's, but even the leftiest Mennonites raised their kids on hymns and social justice activism rather than "Sympathy for the Devil" and key parties.

In 1976 a Pennsylvanian named Doris Janzen Longacre changed the diet of my parents, their friends, and all my Sunday school class-mates with the publication of the *More-with-Less Cookbook*. Informed by Frances Moore Lappé's 1971 *Diet for a Small Planet,* as well as the experience of Mennonite contributors who had volunteered around the world, recipes in the *More-with-Less Cookbook* combined whole-grain ingredients with African, Asian, and Central American flavors, gar-nished with earnest discussions of how to live on a planet with limited resources.

I was five when my mother bought her copy of *More-with-Less*. She was no purist. Yet for the next decade Velveeta cheese and Frosted Flakes disappeared from our pantry, to be replaced by a host of strange brown substances.

Much of what my friends and I grew up eating in the 1970s had all the characteristics that still define hippie food to me, like oatmeal whole-wheat bread, homemade yogurt sweetened with a spoonful of my mother's own jam, date-pecan granola, West African ground-nut stew, and vegeta-bles pulled from our garden—grown without pesticides or herbicides, of course.

My parents, like many of their generation, eased up on the restric-tiveness of the *More-with-Less* diet as their careers accelerated and their children grew more persuasive. Yet the consciousness around food that the cookbook inspired—of the political significance of what we were eating, of the sense that no cuisine is truly foreign, of the goodness of whole-wheat flour and honey—remained. In fact, it has colored my entire career in food.

So I ask with all earnestness: How can you not love an avocado-havarti sandwich? The gush of the ripe avocado. The crunch of the toasted bread. The intense green flavor of the alfalfa sprouts, which smell as if a field of grass were having sex. To me, lunch at the Sunlight Cafe evokes the same warm-blanket comfort that macaroni and cheese does for other Americans. Lunch here isn't satisfying in the same way that a well-charred steak is. But it's satisfying just the same: earthy, fresh, and straightforward.

A decade ago, over a meal of steamed vegetables and brown rice with tahini sauce at the Sunlight Cafe, a thought caught hold: *Why didn't I accept hippie food as a unique, self-contained cuisine? Why did I treat it as an outdated curiosity, instead of giving it the same respect and attention I did Vietnamese pho shops and French bistros?* As I mulled the idea over, two more questions arose: Why *did* the counterculture start eating foods like brown rice, tofu, granola, and whole-wheat bread in the 1960s and 1970s? And how did this cuisine spread across the country, reaching a tiny city like Elkhart, Indiana, in a matter of just a few years?

FIFTY YEARS ON, it may seem inconceivable how revolutionary a stir-fry of tofu and vegetables over brown rice could have been in 1967 and how alienating a havarti-and-avocado sandwich on whole-wheat bread would have seemed to most Americans.

Just for comparison, I picked up a copy of the 1963 *Good Housekeeping Cookbook* at a used-book store. It contained 166 pages devoted to meat dishes and 138 pages of desserts, compared to just 79 pages for salads and vegetables. Adventurous cooks could make Shish Kebabs and Transylvanian Goulash, but the most-stained recipes in my used copy were Scalloped Potatoes, Pot Roast, Deviled Eggs, and Chicken Cacciatore. The majority of recipes relied on boxes and tins: Turkey Cashew Casserole, for example, called for canned meat and condensed cream-of-mushroom soup. A dessert called Rice Chantilly was made with vanilla pudding mix, precooked rice, and heavy cream.[1]

Although the nineteenth century and early twentieth century saw the invention of canning, freezing, and other methods of processing food, World War II marked a turning point in American manufacturers' ability to manipulate our food into forms never seen in nature. Out of the war came the technological processes to produce dried soup powders and pudding mixes, salad oils, canned fruit juices, and ready-to-eat meals. Out of the war, too, came sixty-five approved pesticides, including DDT, invented by scientists researching nerve gases—a fortuitous accident, you might say.[2]

Those advances merely set the stage for a postwar boom in agriculture, food manufacturing, and retail. In the 1950s, the so-called green revolution took hold, led by American scientists who bred higher-yielding strains of staples like corn and rice, whose growth was turbocharged by chemical fertilizers, herbicides, and pesticides. American farms produced 60 percent more in 1959 than they had at the start of the war. Fertilizer use doubled over the course of the 1960s.[3]

The American diet changed drastically as well. Per capita meat consumption rose by a third between 1950 and 1965, and chicken, pork, and beef replaced eggs, dairy, and grains on the plate.[4] Supermarkets took over from small family-run markets, and the majority of new foods introduced in the 1950s and 1960s were tailored to these humongous new stores. Grocery chains added rows and rows of shelves to fill with boxes, bags, and cans.

Middle-class Americans could pile their wheeled grocery carts high: the average wage was rising even as food was getting cheaper. Between

1960 and 1972, household spending on food dropped from 24 percent to
19 percent, and it would drop to 15 percent by the 1980s.[5]

As packaged, industrially engineered foods multiplied, close to four
hundred new food additives were developed during the 1950s alone.
Newly affluent workers invested in refrigerators and freezers, and by
1959, frozen foods had become a 2.7-billion-dollar business.[6] As *Life*
magazine pointed out in 1962, "The food industry will spend more than
$100 million this year inventing and developing new products, two
times what it spent five years ago." Food manufacturers' marketing budgets skyrocketed, too, their core message to consumers: processed foods
are more convenient.

The authors of the 1963 *Good Housekeeping Cookbook* certainly bought
the message. For instance, the "Dining Deck Supper," one of one hundred suggested menus for homemakers, begins with Bouillon on the
Rocks (canned condensed bouillon and a squirt of lemon juice) and
Shrimp with Spicy Dunk Sauce (chili sauce, horseradish, meat sauce, and
spices). The feast segues into Lamb Shanks with Parsley Pockets (with
a sauce of orange juice concentrate, butter, and lemon juice) and Quick
French Bread (two rolls of canned biscuits pressed into a long loaf).

The cookbook does contain a recipe for whole-wheat bread, and
glancing mentions of brown rice and soybeans, but they're novelties,
with no mention of their health or ecological benefits. You won't find
tofu, yogurt, or tahini, let alone nutritional yeast or carob. Seasonings
such as cumin, garam masala, and soy sauce are all but absent. Kale
merits a vague mention or two.

The food Americans were eating in the mid-1960s resembled nothing
that any civilization on Earth had ever eaten before. The United States
outright manufactured a meal like the Dining Deck Supper—through
innovations in farming, food processing, flavoring, packaging, and, yes,
marketing, as well as a queer eagerness to abandon the culinary wisdom
of the generations that preceded them.

The same might be said of 1970s hippie food.

It is impossible to talk about this Esperanto of a cuisine without talking about the conversation *around* food that shaped it. In the late 1960s and early 1970s, food came to mirror the fears of a generation of young Americans as well as their idealism. Hippie food was a rejection—of all the forces that created the Dining Deck Supper—as much as it was an embrace of new ingredients and new flavors. Eating brown rice was a political act, just as wearing your hair long or refusing to shave your armpits could subject you to ridicule and harassment.

The food the counterculture embraced had to be grown differently, sourced differently, cooked differently. Like a sestina, perhaps, the series of strictures cooks had to observe—no pesticides, no flavorings, no packages, no refined sugars or grains, and for some, no meat—was more important, at first, than the taste of the meal. Ingredients had to arrive in the kitchen looking like they were pulled out of the fields, not a package.

Young Americans wanted to strip their cuisine back to its preindustrial roots. And then, as they tried to figure out what they should eat instead of military-industrial trash, a reactionary generation sought counsel from the fringes. They found it in health-food faddists, rogue nutritionists, mystical German farmers, Japanese dietary prophets, and nameless cooks from countries their parents had barely dreamed of visiting. That Harvard nutritionists or newspaper journalists thought these sources were all bunkum only validated that the counterculture was on the right track.

Something happened around 1969 and 1970 to draw the counterculture's attention to food. I have interviewed more than a hundred members of the baby boom generation since I began research on this book—bakers, cooks, restaurant owners, cookbook authors, waiters, co-op workers—and asked each of them the same question: Why did you start eating this way? *It was just in the air,* many of them said. Some

told me about LSD trips and spiritual awakenings. Others mentioned
books that had inspired them or cited their belief that food could help
them change the world.

But the answer that came up most often: America had betrayed their
trust.


IMAGINE THAT IT is 1970 and that you are twenty-two years old and white
(more on this in a few pages).

Even as you grew up with the Cold War, nuclear bomb drills, and
canned dinners, the greatness of the United States was impressed upon
you. Your entire childhood was basted with stories of the Bold, Brave
Country that had won World War II, saved Europe, and was now sending out missionaries, Hollywood stars and Peace Corps members alike,
to teach our way of life to the rest of the world. American industry was
great. American values were great.

Then, just as you entered adolescence, you became aware of America's violent, repressive side.

Even as you studied civics in junior high, you came across articles
about African American college students holding sit-ins in restaurants
and entering the "wrong" section of segregated highway rest stops, only
to be beaten and arrested for the audacity of claiming the liberty and
equality your teachers told you were America's great gift to the world.
At the age of fifteen, in 1963, you heard news of the March on Washington led by Martin Luther King Jr.—perhaps you saw King give one of
the most iconic speeches the modern world has ever heard—and then
the assassination of your president. The year you earned your driver's
license, President Lyndon Johnson signed the Civil Rights Act into law,
and you realized that protest could change the world.

You entered your junior year in high school in 1965, the year the
United States began sending troops to a tiny country in Southeast Asia

that barely registered in your elementary school geography classes. Then it was sending more and more. The choices that graduation would soon thrust upon you and your friends became pregnant with peril: College? Job? Marriage? Army?

By 1967, if you were lucky enough to defer the draft by making it to college, the news grew bloodier. More than 160 riots broke out in African American neighborhoods all over the country, killing dozens, black and white. The rhetoric coming out of the country's two largest student activist groups—Students for a Democratic Society (SCS) and the Student Nonviolent Coordinating Committee (SNCC)—became more dire, accelerated by the charismatic urgency of the Black Panther Party. Your friends were listening to a clutch of bands coming out of San Francisco, like the Grateful Dead and Jefferson Airplane, as well as the Beatles' psychedelic new songs on *Sgt. Pepper's Lonely Hearts Club Band*. You grew your hair out and donned harlequin clothes that evoked both cowboys and Indians (Asian *and* Native American). At the same time, friends murmured of government crackdowns, FBI informants, and even, in the case of the Panthers, outright assassinations.

In 1968, the country careened toward disintegration. The photos and news stories from Vietnam grew ever more horrific, and the antiwar protests crescendoed in volume and number. The campuses of Columbia University in New York and San Francisco State revolted. Martin Luther King Jr. was assassinated. Robert F. Kennedy was assassinated. Paris broke out in revolts. The Czechs attempted to separate from the Soviet Union, an uprising quelled by the arrival of Russian tanks in Prague. At the Democratic National Convention in Chicago, the police whaled on thousands of protesters who looked just like you and your friends. No matter how hard the New Left fought, the conservative Republican candidate, Richard Nixon, won the presidency. And talk entered the news of a draft lottery that would scoop up more young men and send them to kill . . . for what?

The talk among your friends turned toward revolution, whether that meant dropping out and detonating their psyches into a kaleidoscope of color, love, and music, or hunkering down, preparing for the government to send in its own people to suppress lasting social change. The speed at which the country was going to hell horrified and confused your parents, who became obdurate and defensive about what was happening. Maybe you were indignant. Maybe you were thrilled. Maybe you were stoned.

And so here comes 1970. Nixon is now president—not *your* president, the president of "Amerikkka." The rhetoric of the activists among your friends grows even more militant and paranoid. At the same time, many more movement fighters are giving in, disgusted, and saying that if we can't win the rigged game of politics, and we can't stop the war, maybe the system is too fucked to redeem.

You talk of ecology, of women's liberation, of Afrocentrist black power. What we have to do, many of you say, is build a new America in the decaying shell of the old. We need to take all those new values that this country has impressed upon us from childhood—the liberty and equality, of course, plus peace, love, and personal liberation, too—and build a society around them. The revolution has to come from within.

That's when you go over to dinner at a friend's commune, and they set out bowls of brown rice and some quickly fried vegetables tossed with something they're calling "tamari." With the meal comes some rap about how your hosts are effecting real, personal change in their life through this very dinner plate.

That might make sense, you think, and you tentatively take your first bite.

FROM THE PERSPECTIVE of fifty years on, it's convenient to lump everyone who wore a peasant blouse or a pair of flared jeans in 1970 as a "hippie," but in truth, that word still sets some people in the counter-culture aback, prefaced as it was at the time with the word *dirty, stinky,* or *lazy.*

The real hippies, the ones who flowed up and down Haight Street in 1966 and smoked joints in Golden Gate Park, didn't care much about food, to be frank, or at least the natural foods that came to be called "hippie food" in the 1970s and 1980s. The Haight Street freaks, too, with their penchant for mysticism and tie-dye, acid rock and acid, were only a small segment of a much larger counterculture, one that en-compassed leftist radicals plotting the overthrow of the state in smoky basements, community organizers knocking on doors in poor urban neighborhoods, overalls-clad farmers living on communal homesteads, gauzily robed acolytes of Indian and Japanese gurus, and many, many people in their twenties living on the cheap and trying to make a life beyond oppressive jobs and marriages.

The hippie food of this book actually emerged in the late 1960s and then took off, among the counterculture, in 1970 and 1971, part of a much larger shift from the turbulent political activity of the 1960s to the more gentle cultural change of the 1970s.

As members of the Rainbow Party (formerly known as the White Panthers) wrote in the *Ann Arbor Sun* in 1972:

> More and more people are realizing that the industry that is in control of providing food for the people is in fact ripping them off. The food industry is one small part of the larger corporate structure whose only interest is in making money. The deadly chemicals that are put into virtually every food on the market shelf to make the foods last longer, taste better, or look better according to their honky, death-like values are in fact destroy-ing your body and its energy. . . . Food is *naturally* far out. If properly prepared, good clean food gets you high and helps you

stay high by giving your body all the life-giving energy that you need![7]

The burgeoning food movement did not impress everyone in the counterculture. In 1973, one Minneapolis journalist wrote a cynical takedown of what the revolution had become.

Non-involvement seems to be a returning tendency among people who think these days. After the 1972 election, how can anyone avoid feeling helpless? Calculated ignorance brings some degree of false optimism, and no one worries about the bomb anymore and the Dow Jones is up, so who cares? Get out of the city and onto a farm. Peace marches are down to cops and kids, playing parts in a television play, wearing glamorous armbands and shouting ostentatiously to one another to "watch out for provocateurs." There's nothing for a liberal to do these days, peace and ecology are old hat, and the blacks, women, and homosexuals have thrown everyone else out of their movements.[8]

Another, equally patronizing perspective came from a university professor in Iowa City: "At the University of Iowa, last year's window busters are this year's baby sitters, vegetable gardeners, and abortion counselors," he wrote in the *New York Times*. The university was infiltrated with a

new kind of radical who is convinced that the revolution is in fact going beautifully, with a whole new set of issues. These are not national issues, for the radicals believe that they have failed at political action and must now turn inward to more real and personal projects. "You can take care of

your own life and liberate yourself," [student] Debbie Bayer
says. "When you read *The Whole Earth Catalog* you know it.
We have to live our politics now, like the Women's Center
and day care."[9]

Food *was* safe, especially compared to bombs and billy clubs. Food
was under your control. Food was personal, both intimate and communal, at the same time a universal need. Every twenty-two-year-old
who was trying to forge some life outside the dead architecture of their
parents' society had to eat, cheaply and well. So did shoemakers in Ma-
harashtra, bus drivers in Pittsburgh, and Maoist farmers in the Sichuan
countryside.

The counterculture thus embroidered the ubiquitous, populist subject
of food with all the other ideas of how life should be: how people should
be treating the earth, what their bodies needed, how they should engage
in work.

Because income wasn't as important as intention, and because the
economy was still flush and the cost of living was so much lower, millions of young Americans gave their time and their bodies to build a new
infrastructure for growing and selling this good food. Over the course
of the 1970s, the freaks and back-to-the-landers introduced this food to
Americans far outside the counterculture, too. It turned out that radicals weren't the only ones concerned about pesticides on their carrots,
breakfast cereals rimed with sugar, and bread so pallid and squishy that
it hardly seemed like food.

It is possible, however, to overstate the impact that hippie food was
having on America at the time. One of the uncomfortable, even painful, inadequacies of this movement, which became clear to me with each
new chapter I researched, was how *white* it was. A generation of activists
inspired by the civil rights movement to change the world was rarely
able to change it—or at least their food—in ways that invited Latinos,

African Americans, Native Americans, and a tiny but swelling group of Asian Americans to join them.

The health-food movement of the 1950s that preceded hippie food was largely white. The macrobiotic movement, despite its Japanese origins, barely extended outside white circles in the 1960s and 1970s. The communes and the back-to-the-land movement were almost exclusively white. The members of natural-foods co-ops focused on "pure" food were largely white and middle class, while urban groups who worked to obtain inexpensive necessities were working class and much more racially inclusive. Over and over again, counterculture publications would ask: Why aren't we reaching nonwhite audiences? Many groups would make a cursory appeal and give up, or settle for one or two token members.

Some of this failure could be attributed to the broad social segregation of the time, and the fact that the U.S. population was 87 percent non-Hispanic white in 1970. To me, however, the natural-foods movement was stunted by the same problems that hobble the sustainable-food movement fifty years on: longhair circles were almost exclusively white, which left people of color with the burden of adapting to the majority's terms, beliefs, and unconscious prejudices to join. Most food co-ops opened in white or rapidly gentrifying neighborhoods. The back-to-the-land movement took hippies to rural areas hostile to African Americans in particular. Plus, the food movement was characterized by a pervasive nostalgia—a preindustrial romanticism—that was disconcerting and painful to anyone whose ancestors, in that preindustrial era, were slaves.

To some degree, there were parallel conversations around food happening in African American circles, and obvious crossover between the spheres of white counterculture and African American activists, and I'll reference them as I can. But most of the movement I ended up tracing in the 1960s and 1970s took place in white homes, farms, and businesses.

HOW *DO* YOU cover a grassroots movement that had no geographic center and few leaders? This movement was taking place, simultaneously, in every state of the land. Of course, big cities such as San Francisco, Seattle, Boston, Los Angeles, Chicago, and Minneapolis, famous for their hippie enclaves, were home to businesses and publications that reached the entire country.

Smaller college towns were vortexes of influence, too, culinary paradises if you had certain tastes in food. Take, for instance, Ann Arbor, home of the University of Michigan. By 1977, a section of its downtown housed the People's Food Co-op, an herb and spice collective, the whole-grains Wildflour Bakery (which also housed the Grainola Collective), and the Soy Plant. Nearby was Eden Foods, a macrobiotic wholesaler and retail store. Vegetarian restaurants like Indian Summer and Seva both thrived close to campus. Many of these enterprises were getting wholesale goods from the collectively run People's Wherehouse and its collectively operated grain mill. And if you showed up at the Ann Arbor Farmers' Market on a weekend, you'd spot Frog Holler Farm, a tribe of back-to-the-landers who were calling their vegetables and greens "organic."

The scene wasn't much different in Buffalo and Ithaca, New York; Madison, Wisconsin; Fayetteville, Arkansas; Burlington, Vermont; Iowa City, Iowa; Eugene, Oregon; Tempe, Arizona; Boulder, Colorado; and Austin, Texas.

But the movement expanded, almost instantly, beyond those cultural hubs. Homesteads five miles from the nearest house were taking to brown rice and yogurt as quickly as twenty-person communes in Manhattan. And by the end of the 1970s, so were white-haired members of food co-ops in Tallahassee and Mennonite social workers in Elkhart, Indiana. In fact, many of these foods made their way to kitchens in Stuttgart, London, and Montreal—in my attempts to corral a narrative that threatened to bolt in every direction every time I found a new source of information, I limited the scope of this book to the United States.

Tracing just how these fringe ideas and ingredients spread to so many communities felt like an impossible task, fifty years later. When I would ask former hippies why they thought natural foods had taken off all over the country at the same time, swear to god, half a dozen of them answered, "Magic." Then I would start talking to them about what they themselves were doing during those years, and the real answer emerged: travel.

"I see a vision of a great rucksack revolution thousands or even millions of young Americans wandering around with rucksacks, going up to mountains to pray, making children laugh and old men glad, making young girls happy and old girls happier, all of 'em Zen Lunatics who go about writing poems that happen to appear in their heads for no reason," Jack Kerouac wrote in *The Dharma Bums*, one of the canonical books of the counterculture.

Millions of young Americans obliged. Make-work jobs were easy to come by, work in hip circles even easier to take leave from. Hitchhiking cost almost nothing, and couches were everywhere. Communards in Vermont would leave the farm in January to stay with friends in Berkeley. Macrobiotic students would pay pilgrimages to Boston and Chico. The co-op circuit was particularly well established: someone would drive from Austin to Minneapolis for a conference, spend a few weeks visiting other co-ops and staying with the people they'd met, then invite all her hosts to Texas, offering them places to crash.

Longhairs didn't need the Internet. They had word of mouth. Reared on protests and community organizing, schooled on political discourse, committed to the consensus decision making that would turn every meeting into a four-hour debate, they talked and talked and talked and talked. Articles about food from underground newspapers and pamphlets slipped into packages of whole-wheat bread were simply the blooms that sprouted from this vast and fast-growing patch of ideas, not its roots and runners.

So, instead of telling the story of hippie food with an academic's omniscience, I took a journalist's approach, following chains of influence as they wound through the personal stories of the people I interviewed. Some of the people I profile in the book are well known—the figures who galvanized their generation to act—but, just as often, they're bakers or tofu makers or co-op workers whose names didn't show up in Google searches. Their stories were distinctive and yet not unique. More significantly, few acted alone. This movement was collective in both its spirit and its structure. For every person I named, another eight or one hundred people worked alongside him or her: an army of millet-loving cooks.

I'D DIVIDE THE story of hippie food into three eras. The first is the prehistory, the years before 1968. The period from 1968 through 1974 I'd call the revolutionary era, when the prospect of dramatic, instantaneous political change felt imminent and food was going to fuel it. As the Vietnam War ended, in late 1975, and the early baby boom generation looked at the prospect of turning thirty, revolution gave way to lifestyle changes. Most of the counterculture adherents turned their efforts away from protest and created institutions, businesses, and cookbooks that brought the food movement to a much broader audience.

The first three chapters of *Hippie Food* largely focus on the prehistory and attempt to answer the question "Where did hippie food come from?" Looking for the deep history of this new cuisine takes us to Los Angeles in the 1950s and Boston in the early 1960s, then turns back to century-old strains of resistance to the industrialization of food. Each of these chapters traces specific influences—health food, macrobiotics, whole foods—and talks about how these concepts evolved in the kitchens of young baby boomers.

The following chapters cover the second and third eras in the development of hippie food, looking at how the counterculture created this new cuisine and introduced it to the mainstream. The book follows tofu makers as they travel from Tokyo to rural Tennessee, documents a historic meeting on a hilltop in southern Vermont, examines how a generation's wanderlust influenced a restaurant in the heart of Minneapolis, and burrows into the warren of food cooperatives in Austin and Ann Arbor, Michigan. Each of these stories is specific to its place and the people involved, yet mirrors what was happening in hundreds of other cities and towns.

One last caveat: Since the 1960s people have tended to talk about countercultural staples like organic kale or brown rice in one of two ways. Either these foods are going to save our planet and our souls, or they're the equivalent of a cod-liver-oil gargle, prim and repellent.

To me, the story of hippie food became so much more interesting once I shook off both the rhetoric and the reactionary disgust. Although I have been a fan of tofu since the age of eight, I have no interest in telling you why *you* should be eating it. Rather, I want to know why so many other people did.

# 1

# Fruits, Seeds, and (Health) Nuts in Southern California

IN 1958, JOSEPH MCCARTHY'S RED SCARE was petering out, its instigator discredited. The newly formed National Aeronautics and Space Administration was sending space probes out beyond Earth's atmosphere. The oldest members of the baby boom generation were just taking to hula hoops and pompadours. And the Aware Inn and the Health Hut opened in Los Angeles.

The Aware Inn and the Health Hut were located two miles apart from each other, two now-forgotten health-food restaurants in a city that had seen dozens come and go. The two restaurants couldn't have been more different. And yet, within a dozen years, their founders would help shape the diets of a younger generation.

The Aware Inn, located on the Sunset Strip, was close and enveloping, with rose walls hand-painted with an art nouveau leaf motif, booths that pulled you close to your date and pushed the world away, lights just dim enough to make everyone a little ruddier, a little more beautiful. Up a set of stairs was an even smaller dining room with five tables and a bank of windows overlooking the Strip.

The proprietors, Jim and Elaine Baker, were the kind of couple that

Hollywood seems to conjure out of sunshine and free-floating molecules of celebrity. Elaine, a willowy blond artist in her thirties, was running the kitchen in back. Jim, who watched over the dining room, was six foot three, powerfully built, with light brown hair and a snub-nosed, square-jawed, deep-dimpled appeal. The Bakers hadn't come from money, but they had that cool confidence that wealth and ambition convey.

When you and your date cracked the Aware Inn's stiff, leather-clad menu open, your first scan of the menu would have picked out any number of dishes common to tony restaurants in the 1950s, like shrimp scampi and veal Marsala. But then, as you glanced back, you might see bold, intricate salads, a hamburger whose patty was studded with melted pockets of cheese and chopped vegetables—vegetables in a hamburger?—and vegetarian dishes like mushroom rice pilaf served as main courses, not sides. Even the restaurant's signature dessert, cheese-cake, was a bit queer, made with honey and unrefined sugar. The Aware Inn was one of the very first restaurants in the country to print *organic* on its menu. If you asked what that word meant, the Bakers would explain that their vegetables and fruits were grown without chemicals. They cared as much about the provenance of the ingredients as they did the way the dishes were put together.

Decor and soft music be damned, if it all seemed too foreign—as it did for quite a few customers in those early days—and you got up to leave, the burly owner would corner you. "I'll make a deal with you," Jim would tell you. "Try the food and if you don't like it, you don't have to pay for it. But at least try it."[1] It usually worked.

The Aware Inn at least looked inviting to newcomers. By contrast, most of Los Angeles wouldn't even have entered the Health Hut, on Beverly Boulevard near La Cienega, unless they were seeking thrills or carrot juice. The menu proclaimed the restaurant "a haven for movie moguls, folk singers, fire-walkers, fan dancers, phrenologists, philos-ophers, psychologists, soothsayers, saints, showmen, space-people, professors, poets, phony wrestlers, oppressed quiz show contestants, anthropologists, astrologers, alchemists, yogis, artists, bongo & balalaika virtuosos, tree-dwellers, zeros, radical intellectuals, Venusians and utopians."[2]

Every Saturday night at the Health Hut was Back to Nature Luau night. Guests would pack into the tiny, grotty restaurant, which had three rows of shelves selling vitamin supplements and specialty groceries, or more often, they would spill out into the fenced-in patio. There, they'd perch on apple crates and picnic tables where Beverly Hills matrons and soon-to-be-famous ingenues like Angie Dickinson pressed up against beatniks and glassblowers.

Co-owner Lois Bootzin, a red-haired ballet teacher, would shimmy through the crowd toward the stage at the center of the patio, delivering glasses of papaya juice and "moonshine-whiches" (sprouts and avocado on soya bread), while back in the kitchen, a cook named Joyce would use a couple of hibachis to reheat bizarre fare like soybean-and-tomato casseroles.

Grass skirts were never absent from the Health Hut, and when Joyce needed a break from the stove, she'd don one and launch into a rather suspect hula. Also stepping onto the stage might be a white-blond giant named Emile Zimmerman, whose guitar would lead the guests in raucous sing-alongs, or George Liberace (Lee's brother) swaying away at the violin.

But always at the center of the chaos would be Lois Bootzin's husband, the overabundantly bearded Gypsy Boots, shaking his maracas and riling up the crowd, half cheer-squad leader, half generalissimo.

The Aware Inn and the Health Hut were the gallery exhibit and the graffitied wall of health food in Los Angeles in 1958: the one reaching for bourgeois legitimacy, the other a populist bohemia. Yet only a city like Los Angeles could have produced both. Over the course of the twentieth century, certain ideas about nutrition had coalesced in

Southern California, some of them eccentric in the extreme. Los Ange-les also gave rise to health-minded missionaries and self-made experts who spread these notions to tiny storefronts and bookshelves across the country, where young Americans would encounter them in the form of strange vitamin pills, fresh vegetable juices, alfalfa sprouts, carob, wheat germ, and salads.

The owners of the Aware Inn and the Health Hut became missionar-ies in their own right, too, who would help introduce health food, Los Angeles—style, to the psychedelic era.

BY 1958, LOS Angeles had been a mecca for health seekers, beautiful peo-ple, spiritual radicals, and not a few hucksters for three-quarters of a century.

The Southern Pacific Railroad arrived in the West Coast backwater in 1876, the Santa Fe Railroad in 1885. The railroad made it possible to travel from the East Coast to Los Angeles in a week, compared to months aboard wagon trains.[3] Suddenly, a small coastal town gained access to the rest of America, and the rest of America—not to mention Mexico, China, Japan, and the Philippines—poured in.

In those last decades of the nineteenth century, when Los Angeles was doubling its population every five to ten years, the rush brought tens of thousands of invalids who were drawn to the hot, dry climate by pamphlets and promotional books. "The California Cure," the coughers of blood called it, and for a spell the city was almost as well known for its sanatoriums as for its orange groves.[4]

Even after the city turned away from openly recruiting consump-tives—they had too much of a tendency to croak to give rise to the metropolis the city's boosters envisioned—the pursuit of health was etched into the life of the city. And with the ill came the doctors: not just practitioners of what was then called "allopathic" or "regular" medicine, but doctors prescribing all manner of what we now call "alternative medicine."

Los Angeles became one of the nation's centers for "drugless healers" such as chiropractors and naprapaths. Some might be practicing the water cure, wrapping bodies in wet sheets and subjecting them to endless showers. Masters of iridology would stand patients in front of lights whose colors were picked to correspond to the disease. The infirm and the robust alike could seek treatments with massage artists, naturopaths, and yogis. There were vibrating chairs and stretching machines and herbal teas. So prevalent was this interest in healing that in 1899 the *Los Angeles Times* inaugurated a weekly naturopathic medicine column called "Care of the Body." It ran, with few interruptions, for more than forty years.

Twentieth-century allopathic doctors prized the rigors of the scientific method, with its hypotheses and double-blind studies. The germ theory of disease—the realization that microscopic organisms were responsible for a host of infectious diseases—had changed medicine just a few decades before, validating the medical profession in the eyes of the public more than its previous reliance on purgatives, bloodletting, and etherless, antibiotic-less surgery had.

In contrast, naturopaths, chiropractors, iridologists, and the similarly inclined put faith in the evidence of their senses: if they observed a treatment working, it clearly worked. If there was a theme to their advice, one that would carry through to health promoters of every stripe outside the medical establishment, it was that a body in optimum health would resist any illness, whether physical, mental, or spiritual.[5] While they didn't discount the virulence of germs, they argued that germs only affected some people and spared others. The difference between the two groups must be optimum health.

Obtaining optimum health meant putting one's trust in the perfection of nature: engaging in copious amounts of exercise; avoiding toxins, poisons, and drugs in their many forms; eating nutritious foods; and making sure the digestive system eliminated waste at peak efficiency so that undigested food didn't get blocked up there and rot the body from the inside out.

Many of the health reformers and naturopaths of the early twentieth century fixated on living foods because they were still impregnated with that critical quality of "vitality." Cooked food was "devitalized," an adjective that came to be applied to refined flour, sugar, even salt. A body didn't just consume a carrot or a few grains of rice and convert it into fuel, as early-twentieth-century nutrition science was positing; a living being sucked out the vitality of its food, vampirelike, transmuting the life force into its own flesh.

Needless to say, the devout health seeker needed to be eating the most vital of foods: fresh, unprocessed, still charged with their life force. Raw, or "unfired," foods enjoyed a surge of interest in the first few decades of the twentieth century. For the first time in America, such a diet was now feasible, thanks to California's mild climate and robust agricultural industry, which was sending railcars of fruits and vegetables across the country at all months of the year.

To this day, Californians enrage and bewitch North Americans from snowier states with their smug insistence that gorgeous local produce should be accessible year-round. Is it any surprise that raw foodists concentrated in Los Angeles? By the late 1920s, the *Los Angeles Tribune*'s health columnist, Philip Lovell, talked up a local "Health Cafeteria" and the even more appealingly named "Corrective Eating Cafeteria," both of which served vital nourishment, as well as two locations of the Eutropheon, one of the first raw-foods restaurants in the United States.

Eutropheon owners John and Vera Richter, who had opened their first location in 1917 and stayed in business until 1940, were serving what Lovell raved were "tasty salad combinations of every conceivable type and description," as well as crushed-fruit pies with sunbaked crusts made from ground raisins and whole wheat.[6] Vera Richter's 1925 *Mrs. Richter's Cook-Less Book* contained recipes for such delights as Cabbage-Cocoanut Salad, Avocado Soup, and Carob Fruit Cake (well, "cake"). As she wrote in the introduction:

> An alert, clear-headed, springy feeling is . . . the reward of the followers of nature's diet, and since one cannot readily over-eat, the super-abundant fat cells that make life a burden and induce disease need not be feared. If disease is already upon the consumer of fired foods, the way out is plain—eat what nature produced for your food, and eat it as nature made it ready for you. Unfired food does not produce disease, because it contains no inorganic sugar, soluble starch, and partly decomposed protein; neither inorganic salts to irritate the nerves; nor does it readily decay and ferment in the alimentary canals and so produce toxic elements. It has true remedial value for curing disease by supplying the proper food elements in organic form.[7]

In the early twentieth century, a group of writers and freethinkers from German-speaking countries introduced Southern California to the ideas of the *lebensreform* (life reform) movement, which embraced nudism, vegetarian diets, and drugless medicine. In several spots in German-speaking Europe, long-haired, bearded *naturmenschen* (natural men and women) clothed in free-form peasant dress were gathering into intentional communities where they absented themselves from capitalism, practiced free love, and embraced a spirituality that combined Germanic myth and Rousseauian nature worship.[8]

One of them was Arnold Ehret, inventor of the "mucusless diet." Ehret, born in 1866, had left his position as a drawing instructor to operate a clinic in a radical commune in Switzerland. There, he claimed to have discovered his diet after curing himself of Bright's disease, a chronic inflammation of the kidney. He immigrated to Los Angeles in 1914 and, soon after, began writing in English.

In Ehret's two best-known books, *Rational Fasting* and *Mucusless Diet Healing System: Scientific Method of Eating Your Way to Health*, the author took the naturopath's horror over the decaying contents of the intestines to an extreme. "I maintain that in all diseases without exception there exists a tendency by the organism to secrete mucus, and in case of a more advanced stage—pus (decomposed blood)," he wrote.[9] The mucus that dripped from one's nose during a cold was only the overflow from a vast lake of the sticky, repellent gunk that clung to the organs and thickened the blood. The veins clogged up with mucus, the intestines were a swamp of it—or its slightly more solid counterpart, feces. As a writer, Ehret was a poet of putrescence, who took delight in wading into the bogs of effluvia he decried.

The optimal, mucusless diet for humans, he argued, was one that other scientists might have prescribed for lorikeets and arboreal sloths: stewed fruits, salads with simple lemon-and-oil dressings, greens, and plain boiled or steamed vegetables.[10] Occasionally, the mucusless eater could eat a slice of toasted whole-grain bread (toasting prevented it from turning into phlegm in the stomach). But ridding the body of mucus was not merely a matter of abandoning putrefying foods. No! The moment a person stopped eating mashed potatoes and pork chops, his body revolted by throwing off all the mucus it had been storing since birth. Unchecked mucus would coat the tongue and the stomach lining and flow out into the urine. One could, in fact, drown in one's own mucus.

The secret to scouring the mucus from one's viscera without killing oneself was to transform one's diet slowly and to fast frequently, aided by regular doses of an herbal laxative Ehret concocted called Inner-Clean.[11] Sadly, he was unable to prove to the world how long a perfectly mucus-free body might live; he died in 1922 at the age of fifty-six, when he fell and fractured his skull. Nevertheless, his books remained in print for more than ninety years.[12]

ARNOLD EHRET, THE Richters, and their generation of nutrition experts were succeeded by a pair of showier figures who built on the dubious wisdom of their predecessors to become Southern California's greatest dietary evangelists of the 1930s, 1940s, and 1950s: Paul Chappuis Bragg and Gayelord Hauser. Where Ehret spoke the language of illness and health, poison and purity, Bragg and Hauser added another dimension to their message: the confluence of health and beauty.

By the late 1920s, when both men had arrived in Southern California, the motion picture industry had started drawing beautiful people to Hollywood. Within just eleven years of 1911, when Centaur Film Company set up the first film studio in Los Angeles, 85 percent of all U.S. films were coming out of Los Angeles.[13] Reliable weather and cheap land aided the proliferation of studios. By 1923, the Hollywood Chamber of Commerce complained to the *New York Times* that ten thousand young men and women were arriving in Los Angeles each month, desperate to become stars.[14]

As the concept of a movie star crystallized in the 1920s, so did the idea of a movie star as being young and acutely fine-boned or dashing and well muscled. Fan magazines began chronicling the plight of actresses who were dieting to lose weight, having discovered that the camera added ten pounds to their figures.

Hollywood took to health food—particularly its promises of vitality and eternal youth—with a seriousness of intent that can still be found in Gwyneth Paltrow's cookbooks. And in fact, the bran breads, bright salads, and light entrées that health-food experts recommended were far more likely to produce a glow than Lawry's Diamond Jim Brady Cut prime rib and baked potatoes.

Paul Bragg moved to Los Angeles in the early 1920s after working in New York for the best-known health advocate of the time: Bernarr Macfadden, a bodybuilder, vegetarian activist, and publisher of *Physical Culture* and *True Detective* magazines. Bragg supplemented his work experience by claiming bona fides including several naturopathic degrees and titles (which some online detectives have gone to great lengths to disprove).[15]

In his early Los Angeles years, Bragg taught physical education classes at the YMCA and organized a club called the "Wanderlusters" that led hikes up and down the hills surrounding the city. He also founded a health center where he gave lectures; the center's cafeteria, endorsed by the *Los Angeles Times*'s health columnist, claimed in its advertisements to serve "mucusless" foods.

In his earliest cookbook, 1930's *Live Food Cook Book*, Bragg described the people who attended his lectures as being desperate for some way to regain their health after medical doctors and drugs had failed them. "I have helped thousands of hopeless sufferers back to new life and health by teaching them the cause of all disease—a poisoned blood stream resulting from the popular diet of unnatural, demineralized, devitalized, foodless foods," he wrote.

The diet the book recommended was vegan and relied heavily on the recipes of the Richters and other Los Angeles health-food proselytizers of their time. The reason for the absence of animal products, Bragg wrote, was that meat was the ultimate devitalized food: bury a cow and all it does is decompose, he offered as evidence supporting his claim, while a buried peach can yield an orchard. A quarter of the recipes in his early cookbooks were for salads, while another quarter gave instructions for baking, steaming, and boiling vegetables without devitalized salt or spices. He included a few recipes for whole-grain breads but, in honor of Arnold Ehret, cautioned that they should be "thoroughly toasted, dried out, and dextrated" before being consumed.

Bragg eventually softened his stance on meat and dairy as his fame, as well as his bibliography, grew. Bragg's home base remained in Los Angeles for many years, but he acquired a reputation akin to a traveling evangelist. He called his peripatetic talks "the Bragg Crusades."

"Old Age is not a matter of years," states a 1930 advertisement for a Bragg lecture in Oakland, California. "It is a matter of the poisons in your tissues. . . . Learn how to eat vitality giving foods, foods nearer the natural diet of mankind, foods that do not store up waste poisons in your tissues and produce Old Age in your body."[16]

In the ad, Bragg promised to show up in athletic costume to show off his "remarkable physique." Paul Bragg's muscles may not have been as finely etched as those of Bernarr Macfadden or fellow Macfadden protégé Charles Atlas, but his torso was as strong as his jaw; he bared his chest at every photo op well into his middle years, flexing his muscles like a call to victory and showing off an almost maniacal vitality in his two-foot smile. His followers may have come to the lectures desperate for medical cures, but Bragg promised them that the rewards of optimum vitality were so much greater than good health: vitality could be awfully sexy, too.

In Oakland, the Bragg Crusades sold one notable convert on the beauty of good health. A French American teenager named Jack LaLanne, who later described himself as a pimply weakling at the time, was convinced to change his diet and lift weights. By the time he reached his twenties, he had bulked up into a V-shaped hunk with a Hollywood jaw and a body built for bikini briefs. LaLanne would open gyms in Oakland and Los Angeles, invent "trimnastics," and in the 1950s become daytime television's biggest fitness instructor.

A teenager named Jim Baker—future owner of the Aware Inn—claimed, too, to have attended a Bragg lecture on another Crusade stop in Cincinnati, privately consulting the gut-health guru afterward about a persistent case of hemorrhoids. Bragg, Baker would tell his followers three decades later, was the reason he devoted the next few decades of his life to health food and exercise.

By the 1950s, juicing also had taken hold in Southern California, the base of the nation's fruit bowl. Patricia Bragg, whom Paul adopted as his daughter in the 1950s after she divorced his son, claims her father was the first person to import hand-cranked juicers from Europe in 1937. Magazines like *California Health News*, *Prevention*, and *Let's Live*, Southern California's own health-food magazine, soon advertised dozens of fruit and vegetable juicers.[17]

Bragg used his physical beauty to sell a message of good health. For Gayelord Hauser, beauty *was* the message. Born in Germany in 1895, Hauser immigrated to the States as a teenager, studied naturopathy and chiropractic, and moved to Los Angeles in the late 1920s. The city became the base for his cross-Atlantic lecture tours and, later, radio shows, and he published several bestselling books.

Hauser looked like a cross between Dirk Bogarde and Humphrey Bogart. His friendships with Greta Garbo—he played Rock Hudson to her Doris Day—and the Duchess of Windsor were reported in celebrity magazines and newspapers alike, which helped endear him to his core audience of middle-aged women.[18]

"I believe you are as young as your diet," Hauser would tell his followers, whom he called his capital-P "People." Much of his fountain-of-youth diet—centering on lean meats and vital fruits and vegetables—was in line with Paul Bragg's. Hauser also liked to hold elaborate parties where he would serve glasses of vegetable cocktails instead of martinis and daiquiris. In his books *Eat and Grow Beautiful* (1936) and the bestselling *Look Younger, Live Longer* (1950), Hauser supplemented this diet with copious doses of his five "wonder foods": brewer's yeast, blackstrap molasses, yogurt, wheat germ, and powdered skim milk.[19]

Naturopaths and health-food-store owners alike had already revered these five foods, though few sold them with as much panache as Hauser.

Brewer's yeast and wheat germ, for example, had first been used to produce vitamin B extracts in the 1920s and 1930s, when the general public was becoming aware of the power of vitamins to pump up their vim and vigor.[20] By the 1950s, manufacturers were able to chemically synthesize these vitamins, but the aura of health still clung to their natural sources. Molasses was reported to be a great source of iron and trace minerals. Powdered skim milk provided protein and vitamins while keeping the figure trim. Health foodists took to yogurt after discovering Elie Metchnikoff's 1907 study of soured milk's supposed life-lengthening effects on Bulgarian peasants, who were rumored to hit the century mark with astounding frequency. Hauser also touted yogurt's vitamins and protein, giving a polite nod to the mysterious and possibly beneficial bacteria that made it tart.[21]

BY THE 1950S, Hauser and Bragg had both realized that their traveling lectures and books weren't the only way to reach health-conscious Americans. As scores of health-food stores popped up, the two experts also turned their message into merchandise.

Los Angeles was particularly rife with outlets. Lindberg Nutrition stores, vitamin and supplement shops with lunch counters, had been set up in communities across the Southland, and stores such as Organicville, Foods for Life, the Health Pantry, and Full O' Life offered the health seeker enough means for chasing vitality to electrify Frankenstein's monster into life.

Vitamins were certainly the primary currency of these stores, and the popularity of the multivitamin was reaching its peak in the late 1950s and 1960s, but health-food stores offered far more than shelves of pill bottles. They were the League of Justice headquarters for Gayelord Hauser's superfoods and advertised special products for the diabetic, the allergic, the starch restricted, and the obese.

Alfalfa and desiccated liver tablets shared shelves with Arnold Ehret's Innerclean laxative and "vegetal salts" (as opposed to devitalized
mineral salt). Lecithin—purportedly for emulsifying fat and removing
it from the bloodstream—was sold by the tub. Some stores also stocked
Southern Californian foods like Alta Dena raw milk, El Molino stone-
ground wheat, Hain Pure Foods safflower seed oil, and whatever "organic" vegetables they could buy from farms that eschewed pesticides
and fertilizers. Some sold fresh-pressed juices as well.[22]

The health-food marketplace grew so self-aware that stores all over
the country banded together to form the American Health Food Association in 1936, later known as the Natural Nutritional Foods Association. The association held conferences starting in the 1930s; by the
1950s and 1960s, it was battling crackdowns by the U.S. Food and Drug
Administration over the many untested claims the health-food industry
generated.

The American Medical Association and public-interest groups joined
the FDA in attacking health-food-store owners and writers like Paul
Bragg and Gayelord Hauser. The battlefield: the press, congressional
hearings, and occasionally the courts. Their weapons: disdain and outrage. Health-food gurus were called "food faddists" when a critic was
being polite and "quacks" when he or she wasn't. Experts from Harvard
and Cornell, the Food and Drug Administration, and the Department of
Agriculture took to the nation's general-interest magazines and newspapers to fight the rise in food faddism.

A typical salvo, from *Science Digest* in 1952:

> No matter what the food faddists say, there is no such thing as
> the "perfect" food. Yogurt and wheat germ and brewer's yeast
> and blackstrap molasses and a host of more obscure dietary fads
> may not do you any harm—true. But they also won't do you
> any special good.[23]

Or this, in the March 1963 issue of *Better Homes and Gardens:*

> The term [*health food*] is meaningless; all foods contribute
> to health. But it usually refers to a food or food product sold
> through so-called health-food stores on the basis of claims
> about its health-preserving powers. If the food tastes unpleas-
> ant, as it often does, or if its price seems excessively high, so
> much the better for business.[24]

The nutritional establishment characterized shoppers at health-food
stores as "little old ladies in tennis shoes," a cliché that made its way into
story after story about food faddists, though sometimes they exchanged
their sneakers for dungarees. Health-food critics heaped pity on the industry's deluded victims and fury on the deluders; health-food propo-
nents promised the faithful that their illnesses were proof that medical
science was failing millions of people.

Articles pooh-poohing food faddists rarely veered in their tone or
their conclusion: when we eat a regular balanced diet—which might
well include Coca-Cola, T-bones, and canned peas—we get all the
nutrition we need.

The critics didn't slow the growth of the health-food market. By the
mid-1960s the American Medical Association estimated ten million
Americans were spending $500,000 a year on vitamins and nutritional
supplements. Southern California continued to be the industry's capital:
three of the five national groups devoted to promoting health food were
based in Los Angeles.[25]

HEALTH FOOD DIDN'T lure Gypsy Boots, founder of the Back to Nature
Health Hut, or Jim Baker, co-owner of the Aware Inn, to Los Angeles.
One wafted there in his lifelong flight from convention; the other fled

there to gamble on fame and only found it after he gave up. For both men, spectacular health was their birthright, their entry into health-food circles, and a currency they used to pay their way in the world.

Robert Bootzin—Boots's legal name—was born in San Francisco in 1915, the son of Russian Jews. His father was an itinerant door-to-door broom seller, his mother an iconoclastic vegetarian who would dress the children in coat-of-many-colors outfits and lead them into the orchards of Sonoma County to pick fruit for extra cash.

From his teenage years on, Bootzin possessed an untamable energy. It is hard to imagine how one body could vibrate at so high a pitch. He had the cheekbones of Errol Flynn and the physique of Channing Tatum, but the zigzagging mania of Tigger. He spoke as if he'd been plugged into the biggest amplifier a cock-rocking stadium act could buy. His body exuded kinetic feedback at every turn. It's not surprising that school could not contain him. No one job could contain him. A state as big as California could barely contain him.

What little sense of conformity he might have retained dissipated after tuberculosis killed his older brother, a barber, at the age of twenty-two.[26] In mourning, Bootzin slipped out of the habit of cutting his hair and beard. He dropped out of school and claimed to have lived in the wilds of San Francisco's Golden Gate Park for a spell, then began roaming with the picking season, hitchhiking the length of the state.[27] "I lived for twenty years in caves and under trees and on top of trees," he later told Groucho Marx.[28] During the summer, he'd head north of San Francisco to pick apricots and berries in Sonoma, travel south through its coastal vineyards and Central Valley almond orchards to the date palms of the high desert and the citrus groves of Orange County. He subsisted on nuts, cheese, and fruits, supplemented by foraged watercress from the streambeds and alfalfa from the fields.

The backdrop to Bootzin's vagabond youth was the Depression and World War II, when young men circumambulating the state, hitching rides from farm job to farm job, were hardly rare. It was no crime then for him to set up a fruit stand along the side of the road, dealing oranges from a stack of crates until there was nothing left to sell, nor to camp in the wild lands that still covered much of Southern California when he had amassed enough money to buy food for a few weeks.

Along the way, Bootzin picked up the name "Gypsy Boots" (for a few years he was called "Figaro," from a song he'd belt out when peddling figs). He also joined up with a band of similar-minded, similarly hirsute men who came to be called the "Nature Boys."

Among them was Maximilian Sikinger, a strapping blond German who settled in the Santa Monica Mountains in the 1940s to practice massage and teach yoga, as well as Bob Wallace, who looked so much like Jesus that everyone called him that.[29] Then there was the ethereal eden ahbez, one of Boots's closest comrades in the Nature Boys for a time. ahbez was so humble he forswore capital letters in his assumed name, dressed even more Christlike than Bob Jesus in robe and sandals, and spent his days meditating and composing songs with equal intensity. In 1947, ahbez managed to slip Nat King Cole a few songs he had written after a concert, and Cole took to "Nature Boy," recording the song—with its Eastern harmonies and lingering melancholy—in 1948. The song became such a hit that it earned ahbez tens of thousands of dollars, as well as profiles in newspapers and major magazines like *Time*.[30]

The Nature Boys orbited one another rather than traveling as a pack, taking on itinerant farm work like Boots did and sometimes assembling at a raw-food store in Los Angeles that would employ them from time to time (one source suggested it was the Richters' Eutropheon). They would pile into the seats of Gypsy's Jeep—he ripped off the canvas top and slung bananas over the bars—and drive to Tahquitz Canyon near Palm Springs or Topanga Canyon just west of Los Angeles, where they would spend weeks living in the caves.

Other times, the Nature Boys would roam down to Muscle Beach in

Santa Monica, just as tan and athletic as the bodybuilders who gathered
there in the late 1940s and 1950s. There, bikini-clad women and melon-
biceped men, so clean-cut you could barely spot a hair on their chests,
put on gymnastic shows for the gawkers. The Boys would join them to
hand out fruits and nuts or even give lectures on the sand about the awe-
some powers of raw vegetables.[31]

The Nature Boys' hair and beards may have been repellent to the
straights of the time, their vegetarian and fruit-focused diet almost in-
comprehensible. Boots, who traveled with his tambourine, was the
group's clown and troubadour. With every performance he espoused a
way of life far outside the norm of postwar America: no possessions, no
status, a reverence for the natural world that blended the spiritual and
the dietary. As ahbez's hit song proclaimed, "The greatest thing you'll
ever learn / Is just to love and be loved in return."[32]

In the early 1950s, Boots migrated back to San Francisco, pursuing an
improbable courtship with an Indiana immigrant named Lois Bloemker,
who had studied at UC Berkeley and was then working in a department
store. They wed in 1953, scandalizing her family, and Alex, the oldest of
their three boys, came along soon after.

Lois remained Boots's straight man, so to speak, for more than forty
years. In the early years, the two traveled up and down the state, but
several years after Alex was born, they returned to Los Angeles for
good. Boots took jobs as a traveling salesman, as an opener for novelty
act Spike Jones and His City Slickers, as a chauffeur and a tree trim-
mer's assistant—most of which he was fired from for being, well, Gypsy
Boots.

In 1958, just after the couple gave birth to a second child and needed
to settle down, a relative loaned them just enough money to rent a
restaurant on La Cienega. The Back to Nature Health Hut and its nutty
luaus brought Boots to the attention of Hollywood's more bohemian
stars, like Red Buttons and Gloria Swanson, as well as the bodybuilders

the Nature Boys had befriended on Muscle Beach. The restaurant also attracted television cameras. On one local show, host Jack Linkletter circles the yard, quizzing the guests on why they don't eat meat, before making his way to a bare-chested Boots, who rips into an alfalfa-sprout sandwich like a cheetah devouring a gazelle. Then Lois dances sinuously across the screen, and five-year-old Alex, wearing a turban, pretends to meditate so hard he doesn't notice the microphone under his nose.[33]

Unfortunately for the world, the luaus would not last very long.

BEFORE THE AWARE Inn opened, Jim and Elaine Baker had never run a restaurant, either. In fact, at the age of thirty-six, Jim was embarking on perhaps his third career, having already lived enough lives to wring the vitality out of most men.[34]

Baker was born in Cincinnati in 1922, raised by a single mother and converted to the cause of exercise and diet by Paul Bragg. He married at the age of nineteen, then rushed into World War II. Baker served in the Marines as a sergeant for three years, earned a Silver Star for bravery at Guadalcanal, and trained in the service as a judo instructor, where he befriended another muscle-bound soldier and Bragg convert named Jack LaLanne. Like his friend, when Baker returned to Cincinnati, he ran a fitness studio for a half dozen years.[35]

Yet it was then that the restlessness that would plague and inspire Baker for the rest of his life first set in. At the age of thirty, that fear of claustrophobic boredom compelled him to leave his wife and young daughter for Los Angeles. Like many immigrants to the land of the beautiful, Baker came west to audition for Hollywood: a new Tarzan movie. The part went to another actor, but he ended up staying.

Part of the reason was that he met up with Elaine Ross. The two met on a double date, accompanying other people, and hit it off so electrically that halfway through dinner the couples swapped.[36] A shared interest in exercise and health food, as much as their beauty, brought them together. Early in their marriage, the Bakers decided that they were not suited to working for other people and plotted together on some business enterprise that would allow them independence. Their pursuit of health and fitness redoubled after the birth of their first son, who was deaf. Not only were they always active, both had also become skilled and enthusiastic cooks.[37]

The couple first settled in the bohemian enclave of Topanga Canyon. Located in the hills east of Malibu, just a few physical miles and a world away from Hollywood, Topanga Canyon was developing a reputation as an enclave for actors and blacklisted artists, and the Nature Boys often circulated through. Baker, who had always been good with his hands, made belts and sandals. Elaine plied her trade as a graphic designer. Together they began studying mystical traditions, attending every Sunday the lectures of Manly Palmer Hall, a Los Angeles spiritualist and collector of arcane teachings from all over the world, who had compiled an occult encyclopedia called *The Secret Teachings of All Ages*.[38]

Topanga Canyon was where Jim Baker was arrested for his first murder in 1955: the Bakers were living on a small campground, and a neighbor who had left his dog in the Bakers' care while he was in prison had gotten into a fight with Baker upon his release. In the fight, reported the *LA Times*, the victim had pulled a knife on him and Baker had countered with a judo throw and a couple of sharp chops. He broke the man's neck. After a few days in jail, the death was ruled justifiable self-defense.

In 1957, a few years after a second son was born, the couple took over a fur shop on the Sunset Strip—a mile-plus length of Sunset Boulevard located just outside the Los Angeles city limits, where laissez-faire police presence had allowed a burgeoning nightlife to flourish. After gutting the space and installing a kitchen in the store's former vault, Elaine painted the walls and Jim built out the booths.

They tested and retested the dishes they'd serve, blending high-end and healthy. Through the health-food store they regularly shopped at, they located a few Southern California farms supplying antibiotic-free meats and vegetables grown without chemicals. Natural-foods bakers supplied them with whole-wheat breads. The couple worked with Rosa Cardini, daughter of the inventor of the Caesar salad, who was running her father's packaged-salad-dressing business, to develop a proprietary lemon-herb vinaigrette. Fervid believers in the evilness of refined sugars, the Bakers concocted desserts using raw sugar or honey.

According to Elaine, the restaurant's first customers were people they'd encountered through the health-food world, as well as Jack LaLanne, who worked out with Jim Baker, and his family.[39] The initial suspicion with which first-timers greeted the restaurant gave way to success. The Aware Inn's mix of health and intimacy, combined with its relatively affordable prices, drew in Hollywood both young and old.

FOR ALL THE money that Angelenos were spending on vitamins and lecithin, brewer's yeast and wheat germ, Gypsy Boots's Health Hut still drew bohemians rather than Betty and Tom Smith from Bakersfield. The restaurant was an anarchic circus, a permanent stage for Gypsy, whose gregarious charm and need to perform bordered on mania. "He had a switch that just turned on," his second son, Dan, says. "If there was anybody around, he was *on*."

As Boots later explained in his autobiography, his almost desperate eagerness to amuse was combined with a sacred veneration of laughter. "People laugh at me," he wrote, "but I don't care. So long as they are laughing. Laughter is the healthiest thing in life."

Gypsy Boots got his chance to be on the biggest stage of his life in 1962. The Health Hut had closed—"I gave away more than I sold and the landlord said I was making too much noise," he admitted[40]—but it introduced Boots to enough people that he segued into selling fruit to a rarefied clientele. He began delivering fruits and nuts, dark breads, avocado-sprout sandwiches, and carob cookies to rich patrons and the beauty salons of Beverly Hills, a job he kept to some degree for much of the rest of his life. Kirk Douglas was a client. So, through the salons, were Natalie Wood and Joan Collins.

Through the salons, too, he met a producer for Steve Allen's nationally syndicated late-night show. The producer was the show's designated "kook-booker," who met Gypsy Boots once and invited him on. Allen loved the element of surprise, so when he announced that his next guest was the "goodwill ambassador of health and happiness," he had no idea what was going to walk out onto the stage. Out from the wings bounded Boots, grinning like a jack-in-the-box head and howling, "Hello, Steve Allen! It sure is good to see you! Boy, am I going to get you healthy!" Boots blended up a banana-soy-milk smoothie for Allen, recited a poem, and charmed his way into stardom.

By this time, the forty-eight-year-old's looks were grizzling over, his beard and long hair striping with gray, but he still had the physique of a young man and all the reserve of a six-month-old puppy. For three years, Boots appeared on the show at least once a month. He might swing in on a vine or lead in a goat that he'd coerce Allen into milking; he decorated a Christmas tree with daikons and kiwis, hopped up and down on sharp rocks to prove his bare feet had become as tough as hiking boots. He dived into the audience or passed out oranges. And every appearance came with a poem or a lecture about his philosophy:

> I feel so fine, I feel so great.
> So let me go open up that gate.
> I just have had a tremendous date
> With a glass of milk and a soy bean cake.
> All my muscles are strong and loose,
> Because I drink lots of mango juice.

For scorns and frowns I have no use,
'Cause I feel wild as a goose.
Life is a game of take and give.
The world is my brother and I love to live.
So what's this living really worth,
If there isn't any peace on earth?[41]

Boots became such a regular character on the show that his appearance would be announced in newspaper television listings across the land, sometimes as the headlining guest. His sons say he began receiving letters from viewers across the country who'd tell him about how much he inspired them to eat more healthfully (or at least to drink juice). Boots even claimed that twenty-five fan clubs had sprung up in cities across America.

It was the peak of his popularity, and Boots made the most of it in the way he knew how: hustling. For a few months in 1963, he traveled around the Southwest with a band, Gypsy Boots and the Hairy Hoots; on the tour he talked to a United Press International journalist about his plans for a "nature nightclub"—only one watercress cocktail per person.[42] He and Lois crashed celebrity parties, and Boots spent a few months as a good-luck mascot for a Dodger player until he got himself kicked out of the stadium for standing on his head in the stands and whipping the crowd into a frenzy.

By 1965, Boots was also hawking his autobiography, *Bare Feet and Good Things to Eat,* as well as WILD MAN T-shirts and bumper stickers. Like all good health-food gurus of the time, he became a brand: he gave his name to an herb tea, a powdered vegetable broth that doubled as a seasoning salt, and a protein powder. His biggest, and longest-lived, success was the Boots Bar, an energy bar made for him by a Hungarian candy maker.[43] The first version of the bar contained carob, brown sugar, and malted crunch, but the second version could have been the blueprint for Clif and Kind bars, a sticky mass of sesame and sunflower seeds, honey, dates, and dried figs.

Adults who entered their twenties in the late 1960s may have remembered Gypsy Boots from their weeknight television watching. If they lived in Southern California, they certainly encountered Boots Bars, which were sold well into the 1980s. His direct influence on the burgeoning counterculture was subtle, perhaps, but direct nonetheless. Gypsy, Lois, and their three sons would spend their Sundays hiking up Griffith Park—"my church," he'd say to them—and hanging out in the trees, where they interacted with Los Angeles's nascent hippie scene. He became such a figure at the weekend gatherings that he recorded a song titled "We're Havin' a Love-In," and made his way onto the program of the Newport Pop Festival, where he was onstage alongside the likes of Jefferson Airplane and the Grateful Dead.[44]

California hippies were drawn to Gypsy Boots not just because he looked like them, but because he embodied their ethos. He shunned wealth and exuded freedom from authority, benevolent chaos, and a universal affection that hinted at a deeper, more universal love. Boots may have had no interest in drugs, and his position on free love was undocumented, but the counterculture gave him his due. The role he played in life was one sacred to them, after all: that of a holy fool, a truly free man.

BY THE TIME Gypsy Boots was teaching Steve Allen to make smoothies, money was good enough for Jim and Elaine Baker to move to a mansion and hire cooks and nannies to take care of their children. The Cardinis were selling the "Aware Inn" dressing in grocery stores, and the Bakers plotted opening a second restaurant called the Old World, a more casual, breakfast-to-dinner place. And Jim Baker, whose charisma seemed to grow with the restaurant's popularity, tumbled into an affair with an actress named Jean Ingram.

Ingram's estranged husband found out and threatened Baker. In January 1963, the threats culminated in another fight in the upstairs dining room of the Aware Inn, the brandishing of another weapon—this time a gun—and another judo-chop killing. This time, the district attorney was less inclined to believe in self-defense, and Jim was convicted of manslaughter. After five months in jail, he was given a second trial, and the conviction was dropped.[45]

The judge's decision allowed the plans for the Old World, located just a few buildings down the street from the Aware Inn, to go ahead. Again, Elaine Baker designed it, taking a large house with a wrap-around porch and modeling the interior after a European farmhouse inn. They furnished the interior almost completely in wood—wood tables, lattice-backed chairs, and wood-paneled booths—and blue-and-white wallpaper resembling Dutch tiles.

The waiters would swing through the Old World's dining room with coffeepots and giant Belgian waffles (made with unbleached flour and soy flour) covered in whipped cream. Diners could order a bowl of yogurt with fresh fruit and wheat germ, or a cheese-walnut loaf, but the crowds were more likely there for big scoops of butter-pecan ice cream, made with raw milk and raw sugar and churned in-house. Again, much of the meat and vegetables were organic, the breads whole grain, and the salads bountiful. The Old World offered an even more appealing, hedonistic vision of what health food could be. And it brought in a new clientele.

In the seven years between the openings of the Aware Inn and the Old World, the crowd on the Sunset Strip changed. Before, the neighborhood was the playground of the New Hollywood and the wealthy who trickled down from the Hollywood Hills, a place with a penchant for louche behavior—high-end call girls, cruising gay men—that only enhanced its appeal to the elegant. Now, on Fridays and Saturdays, the sidewalks were thronged with teenagers, the cars bumper to bumper, simultaneously stalled and teeming.

As *Life* magazine described the scene in 1966:

> The whole Strip is throbbing, wailing, putting out the high tension, the big beat, hundreds of big beats from the engines and radios and wheels and coming from the open bars of clubs and discotheques. . . . There are kids in chrome-plated Nazi helmets, anti-war buttons and Maltese crosses. There are surf kids, kids from poor homes, rich homes and no homes, thousands of kids. Negro boys wear blond wigs. Girls are in boots or their bare feet. Shoulder length hair is for everybody, along with little-old-lady sunglasses, ruffled bell-bottom pants, bullfighter jackets, pirate costumes—the ultimate in rebellious fashion.[46]

Diners had to shoulder their way through the crowd to enter either of the Bakers' restaurants, and then fight their way back out after the meal. The Aware Inn continued to offer an oasis from this madness, but the Old World opened its doors to it. Money came here, but so did singers, artists, and rock-and-rollers.

The hippie kids "were so beautiful, so heavy," Jim Baker would later tell his followers. The new Strip called to him. The kids ignited that old, destructive restlessness. "There I was, miserable, alcoholic, with lots of money, live in a mansion, drive a Rolls-Royce, have an old lady—and bored with it all. I wanted to find out what this new life was."[47]

And he did. Shortly after the Old World opened, the Bakers split: too much infamy, too much stress, too much boozing. Jim offered Elaine whichever of the businesses she preferred, and she took control of the Aware Inn, while he settled for the Old World.

The divorce began what Jim Baker later characterized to his acolytes as four dark years, a midlife crisis as oversized as the life before and after it. Baker, then in his midforties, hooked up with a dark-haired, nineteen-year-old Frenchwoman named Dora Jagla, whom he later married in Mexico. The two embarked on a path to self-destruction in the name of psychedelic exploration. Hallucinogens, speed, booze. He drove a purple Rolls-Royce. He dyed his hair red. He spent less and less time in the restaurant, and, according to several employees, would drop in daily to grab hundreds of dollars out of the cash register.[48]

At some point, one that only Jim Baker knew, he hit bottom and began yet another metamorphosis. Perhaps it was when he found himself on top of a mountain above Jerusalem, blitzed on hash, and realized some force in the universe would take care of him. Perhaps it was after his investors forced him out of the business.[49]

After his return, Baker renewed his spiritual study with new intensity, but what in fact may have saved him was a third restaurant.

He found a little spot with a great patio about a mile down Sunset Boulevard from his two former restaurants—at the intersection of bohemia and power, not too far from where Laurel Canyon emptied out into the flats. He stripped the space down to bare walls and rebuilt it, lovingly, with no money and little help. Without Elaine's eye, the restaurant didn't immediately welcome the first-time visitor, but it reflected the spirit of the psychedelic era. Baker built a brick fireplace and set multicolored candles on top of it that dripped over the mantelpiece. He installed stained-glass windows and hired hippie painters to paint a Manly Palmer Hall–inspired man encased in a pentagram, his body a rainbow. He named it the Source.

At some point during those four dark years, Jim Baker's quest for health turned him into a vegetarian, and he decided to make the Source's menu meat-free. In fact, he went even further: it would be primarily a raw-food restaurant, one that might have impressed Arnold Ehret, in fact. But there was no overt mention of mucus in Baker's new nutritional philosophy. Instead, he modeled his diet after an esoteric Christian book called *The Essene Gospel of Peace*.

The gospel was published by Edmond Bordeaux Szekely, head of a resort just across the Mexican border called Rancho La Puerta and a man whose early life, if his autobiography is to be believed, was almost as epic as Jim Baker's. The French Hungarian Szekely claimed that, as a scholar in Italy in his twenties, he was allowed into the archives of the Vatican and the monastery of Monte Cassino south of Rome. There, he supposedly found both Aramaic and Hebrew writings from the Essenes, an ascetic Jewish sect that hit its peak in the centuries before and after Jesus—writings that were corroborated by an Old Slavonic text Szekely subsequently discovered in Vienna.

After translating this gospel into French, Szekely embarked on the life of a peripatetic scholar, teaching at the University of Cluj (now in Romania) and traveling to Equatorial Africa, Pakistan, and Tahiti. He founded an Essene church in the South of France. He survived a shipwreck in the Caribbean. By the count of the International Biogenic Society, which he founded in 1928, he wrote sixty-eight books over the course of his life. (Many are rather slim.)

In 1938, Szekely founded Rancho La Puerta on a tiny camp in Tecate, Mexico. There, he put the word out that he would offer lectures in spirituality and health based on the teachings of the Essenes, which Szekely had translated into English the year before.[50]

Though *The Essene Gospel of Peace* that Szekely claims to have uncovered intersects here and there with the accepted gospels, it upends pretty much everything the average mainstream Christian knows about Jesus: Jesus, transmitting the wisdom passed to him by both God the Father and the earth our Mother, commands his followers to purify themselves through fasts, water baths, and naked sunbathing. The text's recipe for baking bread by grinding sprouted grains and forming them into cakes to cook in the sun led to the creation of "Essene breads" (now available in every Whole Foods refrigerator case in the country). And Jesus's detailed description of how to hollow out a gourd to self-administer an enema, not to mention the demonic results of such a ritual, is one of the more eye-opening passages in the Christian apocrypha.[51] In 1979, a Swedish academic named Per Beskow attempted to retrace Szekely's research, only to find no evidence of the texts or, indeed, Szekely's visits to the Vatican.[52] Proof did not stop the *Essene Gospels* from being printed and reprinted, possibly hundreds of thousands of times, and their message from being adopted by hippies, holistic health practitioners, and Neo-Essenes around the world.

With the exception of its embrace of acidophilus-cultured milk, Szekely's Essene diet was remarkably similar to the health food Los Angeles had been espousing since Arnold Ehret's day. It was bullish on fasting and heavy on "eliminative foods" such as raw fruits and vegetables. Interpreting the gospel, Szekely advised his patients and followers to avoid all meats and seafood, and to soak or sprout many of the grains and legumes they would eventually cook or consume. If possible, all ingredients should be natural, grown without pesticides or other chemicals, and simply seasoned. Meals should be limited to twice a day.[53]

Whether because Jim Baker adopted the diet and felt its effects or because it was the first practical diet he'd come across that embodied a metaphysical path, Baker modeled the inaugural menu of his newest restaurant on Szekely's gospel.

The Source opened in April 1969. Folk singers, fire-walkers, fan dancers, phrenologists, and philosophers familiar with Jim Baker's previous restaurants showed up. Many others looked at the menu, which was primarily juices and salads, and passed. Dora, Baker's young wife, left him and returned to France. The restaurant flagged, and with it, Baker's will. The sole bright spot: a new relationship with an even more gorgeous nineteen-year-old, named Robin.

At that time, a pair of the Source's first employees, hippies from Minnesota, were taking classes in something called "kundalini yoga" with Yogi Bhajan, a Sikh teacher from India who had just arrived in Los Angeles.[51] Bhajan's classes were both physical and metaphysical. The yogi employed meditation and breathwork to send his young Western students into some sublime states.

After weeks of convincing, Baker went with his young coworkers to Bhajan's class. When he engaged in Bhajan's signature Breath of Fire exercise—a rapid, pulsating inhale-exhale—for the first time he collapsed on the floor, insensate, then began howling from distress, pain, and spiritual ecstasy. The Breath of Fire wrenched Baker out of his last life and delivered him, weeping and shuddering, into the new.[54]

Baker threw himself into Bhajan's Sikhism and into yoga. Yet his discipleship only lasted a year before Baker, too much the alpha to remain a devoted follower, began offering meditation classes on his own. After a three-month trip to India in 1970 with his spiritual teacher—a trip in which it became clear to some followers that some of the spiritual ancestry of Bhajan was concocted—Baker broke with his mentor to become a guru in his own right.[55]

MOST OF THE rhetoric that dominated health-food publications like *Prevention* and *Let's Live* would not play well with the generation that came of age in the late 1960s and 1970s. Most young Americans were not taken with these publications' stories of miracle cures, overreliance on words like *vitality* and *vigor*, more-is-merrier approach to vitamin supplements and other superfoods, or jaunty advice to "Perk up! Slim down!"

Vegetarian cookbook writers of the 1970s and the authors of underground-newspaper food columns rarely counseled readers to consult Gayelord Hauser or Paul Bragg for advice. Arnold Ehret became a cult figure, especially for people who took to fasting (one follower of the mucusless diet: Steve Jobs). However, his ideas about mucus in the blood and intestinal putrefaction filtered into the broader culture in oblique ways, such as through the comedian and civil rights activist Dick Gregory, whose 1974 book *Dick Gregory's Natural Diet for Folks Who Eat* embraced a raw-foods vegetarian diet.[56] Ehret's Southern Californian contemporaries, such as Herbert Shelton, Pietro Rotondi, Otto Carqué, Vera Richter, and Frank McCoy, faded from view. Even Jack LaLanne, the best-known television fitness guru of the 1950s and 1960s, the younger heir to Hauser and Bragg's philosophy of eating, belonged to the suspect pre–World War II generation.

The exception was a nutrition expert from Southern California named Adelle Davis, who believed in both whole wheat and the scientific method. Davis would become one of the main conduits passing an older generation of food faddists' beliefs about natural foods to the granola generation (see page 111).

Yet the influence of the health-food movement on hippie food is undeniable. Certain of its core principles leached into the counterculture, such as the idea that a truly healthy body would not get sick, that fasting exorcised toxins and impurities from the bloodstream, and, most significantly, the belief that refined flours and sugars and processed foods were poison.

Even more evident were all the health-food staples that entered into young Americans' culinary lexicon. The health-food marketplace may not have been big, but it was one of the first sources that young Americans turned to in the 1960s and 1970s when they went searching for clean, natural foods. Tiny vitamin shops, and the proverbial little old ladies in tennis shoes, supplied them with organic potatoes and whole-wheat flour when no other store would carry such bizarre fare. In the process, longhair cooks also learned about blackstrap molasses, wheat germ, yogurt, fertilized eggs, and nutritional yeast.

Many of the foods that became associated with hippies in the 1970s were, in fact, specific to Southern California: vegetable juices, smoothies, herbal teas, dried fruits and nuts, alfalfa sprouts (see page 55), and carob (see page 95), not to mention the Californian love of a ripe avocado. Young kids may never have known that an earlier generation had avoided table salt because it was supposedly "devitalized," but they sprinkled dulse flakes and Bragg's Liquid Aminos on their food anyway.

Once Jim Baker's meditation classes attracted legions of young, beautiful acolytes, they adopted their teacher's diet, honoring its holiness if not its history. And when these young followers turned the Source into one of the most successful vegetarian restaurants on the West Coast, they translated forty years' worth of Southern Californian health-conscious cuisine—the food of the Eutropheon, Arnold Ehret, Paul Bragg, and Edmond Bordeaux Szekely—for all of hip Los Angeles.


IN MAY 1971, when Robert Quinn first set foot in the restaurant, he recognized its owner, even though they had never before met in this lifetime. Before Quinn became Omne Aquarian, before he became a vegetarian cook and a designer of psychedelic rock albums—before, in fact, Jim Baker took Quinn and hundreds of young Californians on a spiritual trip they'd never quite return home from—the twenty-year-old Antioch College student had been bumming around Berkeley and Los Angeles, a searcher in search of a quest.

Quinn had heard of the Source, which was gaining a reputation for being a righteous vegetarian place drawing turbaned Sikhs and Hollywood producers in equal measure. He'd passed by it any number of times, in fact. But he had never encountered Jim Baker.

He had, though, been receiving messages telling him he was traveling toward the man he would come to call "Father Yod" and "Yahowha." There was the time when his grandmother appeared to him in a stoned vision, her being showing through his sister's face, to tell them that he would soon meet his father. Just a few days before that day, he had lain down to nap and instead had been greeted with the luminous, blinding radiance from a being who assured him that what he was seeking was true. The apparition had left him giddy, electrified with anticipation, and it inspired him to paint a watercolor of a great, grandfatherly man in flowing white robes hugging him as a small boy.

The painting, a talisman of the joy Quinn expected to find, accompanied him on the bus to Sunset and Sweetzer, where he descended to walk down the block. The moment he caught sight of Baker, he finally understood who its subject was. "Jim Baker's on the patio sunning himself," Quinn remembers, "and he looks like a lion surrounded by a pride of lionesses. They were all beautiful hippies in white clothes with long hair, wearing American Indian jewelry and feathers in their hair. They're all sitting there entranced, sunbathing."[57]

The man the painting brought to life was still luminously handsome, but at the age of fifty his features were wreathed in an abundant mane the color of his robes. Quinn walked up to Baker and handed him the painting. Baker looked at it, looked back, and Quinn had the sense that he had been recognized just as deeply—on a level that plunged far beyond the contours of his face, even beyond this lifetime.

The next day, Quinn joined Baker's growing family of followers. Some would call it a cult. Its members called themselves the Brotherhood of the Source. In the first years of the 1970s, Baker ushered a following that numbered in the hundreds into six feverish years of meditation and sex magic, ecstatic music, and mind-blowing food.

The Source Family, as they also called themselves, would wake up at 3:15 in the morning and begin a program of exercises and cold baths that would prepare them for the morning meditation at 4 A.M. At that predawn hour they would gather in the common room, all 150 of them, dressed in white flowing robes, and Baker would lead them in chanting, songs, and yogic practices like the Breath of Fire and the Star Exercise.

The spiritual leader would speak to his charges of all the things he had learned and experienced, both in the corporeal world and the realms far beyond. His mystical lessons wove together theosophy, Yogi Bhajan's kundalini yoga, kabbalah, the arcane European traditions Baker had learned from Manly Palmer Hall, and Egyptian cosmology. It was a raucous, fertile blend of gods and energies, and the Brotherhood of the Source, as the spiritual shock troops of the Aquarian Age, dived straight into it.[58] After their meditations, the brothers and sisters would pass around a bowl of rainwater and a bowl of sacred "shim," or marijuana, which they would inhale for six seconds and no more. Then they would begin preparing for their day.

Jim Baker took the name Father Yod and assigned each of his followers a new given name, everyone taking the last name Aquarian. That was how Robert Quinn became Omne Aquarian, living and working alongside brothers and sisters with names such as Isis, Damian, Electricity, Octavius, Mushroom, and Makushla; Jim's legal wife, Robin, became Ahom. Soon after, as Father Yod continued to evolve, Robin/Ahom was forced to share Father Yod with other spiritual wives, who grew in number to fourteen, and whom he eventually dubbed his Council of Women.

For the first three years that Omne was a member of the Source Family, he also joined the family business, the Source Restaurant. The brothers and sisters who put in shifts at the Source worked long, hard hours, the kitchen dominated by men, the women serving the tables. (Not surprising for a religious group centered on a man with fourteen wives, the Source Family fell further and further out of step with women's liberation.) The mornings would be spent prepping vegetables and fruits for all the salads and juices, as well as making soups (vegan split pea, lentil) and Baker's well-loved natural-foods cheesecakes.

The Source's food was nothing like Omne Aquarian had seen in his childhood. Having grown up in a small, blue-collar town on the East

Coast, he knew steak and potatoes, or thanks to a little cross-Catholic-country culinary exchange, lasagna and kielbasa with sauerkraut. Despite the fact that California had become the salad bowl to the country, the scarcity of highways and air transport kept much of the state's bounty on the West Coast. "I did not see my first kiwi, avocado, or papaya until I came to California," he says.

The Source, and the Source Family by extension, bought food from the Los Angeles farmers' markets and from a cadre of hip entrepreneurs who had recruited a few older farmers to grow fruits and vegetables without pesticides or fertilizers. Gypsy Boots, who was by then making a living selling fruits and nuts, would make occasional stops at the Source, and the brothers and sisters would purchase whatever fruit he was hauling around in his station wagon.

They would transform these fruits and vegetables into a diet that was more colorful and vibrant than Ehret's austere mucus-free food and Edmond Bordeaux Szekely's Essene diet, though the Source Family food resembled both in its fetish for raw vegetables and straightforward seasonings. The fare was simpler and cleaner than the health food of Paul Bragg and Gayelord Hauser, too, yet it incorporated their beloved yogurt, wheat germ, brewer's yeast, carob, and alfalfa sprouts.

"The fare at the Source was shockingly simple," Omne now says when he reflects on his diet of those days. "At the time, though, it was refreshingly unique." The menu listed salads upon salads: Timmy's Salad of grated carrots, beets, and sprouts, or the Aware Salad with all that and tomatoes, cucumbers, red cabbage, and pine nuts. The Magic Mushroom combined sautéed mushrooms and onions with steamed seaweed, sprouts, and chard, all topped with grated cheese. The restaurant's best seller, the Source Special, is the one all the family members remember with fondness and longing, because none of them thought to retain the recipe for its key ingredient, Source Dressing, which Rosa Cardini's company continued to manufacture for Baker. They'd spread the lemon-herb vinaigrette onto a slice of whole-wheat bread, then layer on a thick green smear of guacamole, sliced raw mushrooms, tomatoes, and a pouf of alfalfa sprouts. Onto the top would go a few slices of Cheddar cheese, then it'd be slipped under the broiler until the cheese melted.

Some family members today say the food was so good because Baker brought them in contact with the freshest fruits and vegetables, grown in the best possible way. Others say that the flavor was an expression of their devotion. Everything about the Source Restaurant, in fact, was an expression of the Aquarians' devotion—to Father Yod, to one another—and so they'd pour as much positive energy into the food as they could generate in their earthly bodies, and they'd serve it with the kind of beatific smiles that impressed even the most jaded Angelenos. They amplified L.A.'s superficial good vibes and made them sincere.

Gypsy Boots's old friend Steve Allen attended one of Father Yod's morning meditation sessions and remarked on how "the young women, particularly, almost swooned as he smiled and touched their shoulders."[59] In every conversation, whether lecture or casual banter, Father Yod communicated to them that he was their earthly father as well as their spiritual guide. No, even more than that: he was a god, training his children to become gods in their own right. The Aquarian Age was beginning, and it would be theirs to claim.

The Source Restaurant sustained 150 or so of Father Yod's children in a lifestyle that was at once monastic and lavish. Under the aegis of Damian Aquarian, a brother who exhibited intuitive leadership and a tight sense of control over staffing and money, the restaurant was making $500,000 a year in 1974 dollars (the equivalent of $2.5 million in 2015).[60]

Many of its staff worked long hours, with no individual wages—all their possessions, from bank accounts to toothbrushes, belonged to the family. Yet Father Yod housed them in a series of mansions and supplied them with clothing and an abundance of organic food. He funded the construction of a state-of-the-art recording studio where he and a band of brothers made long, psychedelic rock albums. The business paid for Rolls-Royces and vans for their transportation, as well as the fancy meals Father Yod would escort groups of his white-robed children to. It was not a life of deprivation, at least until after the family sold the Source and attempted a move to Hawaii in 1974. The move ushered in a disastrous year that culminated in Father Yod leaving his body—he attempted to hang glide for the first time in his life, and the winds swept him down onto the rocks, battering the life out of him.

While the restaurant was going strong, though, all of Hollywood came to the Source Restaurant to dine with Father Yod and his children. The actors who had followed Jim Baker from the Aware Inn to the Old World were regulars—Charles Bronson, Steve McQueen, Warren Beatty—as well as the suits that made them all world famous. Goldie Hawn was a regular. Ravi Shankar and John Lennon dined there when they were in Los Angeles. The band Yes showed up in separate limos. Woody Allen showed the Source to the world when he filmed his breakup with Diane Keaton's Annie Hall on the restaurant's patio after ordering a plate of mashed yeast. Tally up the reminiscences of the Source Family members, and they'll list enough celebrities to fill up three *Sgt. Pepper's Lonely Hearts Club Band* album covers, all the famous people who came to eat with them when they were young, beautiful, and overflowing with universal love.

## Alfalfa Sprouts

Eating the newest and most fragile of sprouted seeds is an ancient practice. East Asian households have long supplied themselves with fresh vegetables in winter by sprouting soybeans and mung beans. Egyptian women of the pharaonic ages scarfed fenugreek sprouts to make themselves more curvy. Victorian-era

Brits sprouted mustard and cress seeds in clay jars to fill tea sand-wiches. Until the 1970s, though, only Southern Californians ate raw alfalfa sprouts.

The origins of the practice are unclear, but it emerged from the health-food movement. From the 1920s to the 1950s, alfalfa tablets were a B-list tonic in health-food stores. A 1920 advertisement for Sterrett's Alfalfa Compound, for instance, claimed the tablets were "an infallible remedy for Indigestion, Constipation, Neuritis, Rheu-matic pains, and all character of Nerve and Stomach troubles."[61]

Some southerners did sprout alfalfa, but not for eating. The *San Antonio Evening News* reported in 1922 that Texans were drinking a tea made by pouring hot water over alfalfa sprouts; other than that it was "refreshing," the paper didn't mention why.[62] In 1953, supple-ment manufacturer Pavo suggested one use: "Drink it as directed, not only for relief of Arthritis, but to supplement your diet with valuable vitamines [*sic*] and minerals to help maintain that feeling of well-being."[63]

The first mentions of alfalfa sprouts on salads and sandwiches only appeared in Los Angeles newspapers in the late 1950s. Though I haven't been able to identify the person who introduced them to midcentury food faddists, I'd guess that Californians who became familiar with bean sprouts at Chinese and Japanese restaurants had the idea to take alfalfa seeds out of tablets and put them into sprouting jars, seeing them as another source of vital, living nutrients.

In a 1957 advertorial in the *Pasadena Star News* titled "Just Between Girl Shoppers," Betty Harris wrote, "Since one of the newest eating fads is to chomp alfalfa sprouts in soups or salad, Hines [Grocery Store] has these. They look like bean sprouts and are supposed to be especially good for us. They do wonders for cattle, I know."[64] A year later, Gloria Swanson—legendary for her health-food regimens, and a later fan of George Ohsawa and macrobiotics—was telling news reporters that her favorite lunch was alfalfa sprouts, salad, yogurt, and milk.[65] By that time, of course, Gypsy Boots and Lois Bootzin were already serving alfalfa sprout sandwiches to Health Hut customers.

By the early 1970s, alfalfa sprouts were de rigueur on avocado sandwiches and salads all across the country. Grocery stores sold packs of them, but most people grew alfalfa sprouts at home. "Sprouted seeds and grains are cheap, easy, untouched by chemicals, and delicious," the Washington, D.C., *Quicksilver Times* reported in 1971.[66] Mainstream magazines and newspapers ran sprouting guides. Bruford Scott Reynolds's 1973 *How to Survive with Sprouting* appeared in bookstores. You could find sprouting kits in food co-ops and dime stores alike. Alfalfa sprouts were no longer a tonic for arthritis, but as essential to the crunch of a good sandwich as lettuce and pickles.

# 2

# Brown Rice and the Macrobiotic Pioneers

ON OCTOBER 21, 1961, A CURIOUS caravan rolled into the town square of Chico, California.

Dozens of residents circled the square to gawk at twelve suitcase-laden cars that maneuvered into parking spots and disgorged restless children and skinny, cramped-legged adults. If you were just passing through town, you might think that this was a new batch of college kids, arriving to the university town a couple of months too late into the semester. Even in a town of thirty-six thousand, new students wouldn't draw an audience of townspeople, however. Nor should they merit newspaper reporters, television cameras, and klieg lights, as well as Mayor Ross Lawler, who'd prepared a welcome speech to greet the newcomers.

The onlookers had been tipped off to the caravan's not-so-grand entrance by a series of national news stories that had followed the thirty-four travelers since their departure from Long Island three weeks before. Out of the cars stepped Broadway musicians, a Columbia University professor, a couple of Japanese immigrants, a Harvard-educated economist who'd helped formulate the Marshall Plan, and most titillatingly,

Teal Ames, then one of the stars of the popular soap opera *The Edge of Night*.

Were the new arrivals Communists? Cult members? What were they doing here, in *Chico*? "We're searching for simplicity," Ames told reporters. "I got all the excitement out of my system back in New York and discovered it isn't really worth it."[1] This was no publicity stunt: her soap-opera character—and lucrative salary—had just been killed off.

A search for simplicity wasn't why the reporters and townspeople were crowding around this band of pilgrims, however. The news stories all reported the New Yorkers were migrating west to escape the coming nuclear apocalypse. Moreover, they were feeding themselves an exotic diet called "macrobiotics," based on the teachings of a Japanese philosopher named George Ohsawa.

Within a decade, this odd new system of nutrition would shape the diet of the baby boom generation in ways that would perplex and delight George Ohsawa's early, California-bound followers. As macrobiotics entered the counterculture, it would bring young Americans in contact with new foods, ancient traditions, farmers staking their land and reputations to accommodate their tastes—and rice. Organic brown rice, to be exact. Which was the reason the New Yorkers had picked tiny, out-of-the-way Chico as their destination.

ARRIVING IN CHICO with the TV star, the professor, and the economist was a small, brusque trumpeter named Dick Smith, who was driving a German Borgward into which he'd stuffed his brand-new wife, three new stepchildren, and a host of boxes.

Smith had encountered Ohsawa almost two years before, when the world-traveling philosopher—who was also what we'd now call an "alternative medicine practitioner"—made his first trip to the United States to give a series of lectures in New York in the winter of 1959 and 1960.

Word had gone out among New York musicians that this Japanese guy over at the Buddhist Academy was teaching that he could cure cancer. That's what caught the attention of Smith, who was watching cancer devour his father's body, unobstructed by the doctors who had all given up on checking its feast. If Western science wasn't able to cure his father, he thought, why not listen to what Ohsawa had to say? So he went with a friend to a lecture, and then another.

Pictures of Ohsawa from that time show a slim, almost gaunt man whose features were obscured by thick black glasses and a smile that cast ripples all the way up to his forehead. By the age of sixty-six, he'd survived torture and imprisonment at the hands of the Japanese military and parasites that had colonized his body while traveling across Africa. Yet Ohsawa didn't appear to his audience to be physically broken. In fact, he exuded energy. Speaking in disjointed and accented English, his bass voice could shake the walls and vibrate the conviction of his thoughts right into his listeners.

What he was telling them was confusing, intriguing, galvanizing, not a little bizarre. Ohsawa's philosophy and his diet were both based on what he called the Unique Principle: although the universe was a unified whole, he'd repeat, it was ruled by the opposing forces of yin and yang, forces that roiled and intersected and gave birth to the ten thousand things. Yin was expansive, dark, feminine, bitter, purple. Yang was contractive, bright, masculine, salty, red.

Ohsawa taught them about seven principles that governed the order of the universe, which became aphorisms in macrobiotic circles, convenient little explanations to pop out of your pocket when you were fighting with your husband or talking to your macrobiotic fellows about the parking kerfuffle you got into at the store last week:

1. That which has a front has a back.
2. That which has a beginning has an end.

3. There is nothing identical.
4. The bigger the front, the bigger the back.
5. All antagonisms are complementary.
6. Yin and yang are the classifications of all polarizations, and antagonistic and complementary.
7. Yin and yang are the two arms of one (infinity).[2]

"Why are there so many hospitals and sanatoriums, drugs and medicines, so many mental and physical illnesses in Western civilization?" Ohsawa would ask his audiences. "Why is there the need for so many prisons, the great numbers of police, the vast air, sea and land forces? The answer is very simple. We are sick, physiologically and mentally."[3]

The cause, he would tell them, was that we have lost our deep understanding of the ways of nature, and yin and yang have become completely out of balance in our bodies. To remedy the problem, Ohsawa proposed a diet unlike anything any American, no matter his or her ethnic background, was eating: no red meat, no sugar, no alcohol, no dairy, no refined flours, no yeasted breads, and no tropical fruits such as bananas, then omnipresent in elementary school lunch sacks. This diet Ohsawa called *macrobiotics*: *macro* means "great" in ancient Greek, and *bios*, "life."[4] In place of chicken à la king and Salisbury steak, Ohsawa instructed, Dick Smith and his fellow audience members should eat a diet centered around brown rice, which Ohsawa called the Japanese "principal grain."

In fact, Ohsawa claimed, if his listeners would eat nothing but brown rice sprinkled with *gomashio* (salt ground together with toasted sesame seeds) and drink nothing but roasted green tea (*bancha*), they might just rid their bodies of tuberculosis, diabetes, schizophrenia, and even cancer.

The audience, Ohsawa would say, shouldn't just listen to him, but try it themselves! After all, macrobiotics had saved his own life. Growing up in a suburb of Kyoto, Ohsawa—then named Yukikazu Sakurazawa—watched tuberculosis kill off his mother and two younger brothers. In his teenage years, he began coughing up blood, too. Just as the prognosis was looking dire, he discovered the writings of Sagen Ishizuka, a physician in the Imperial Army who had founded an organization called Shoku-Yo Kai (*shoku* means "food" in Japanese; *yo*, "nourishment"; and *kai*, "organization").[5]

Ishizuka was telling the Japanese that they could regain their collective health if they returned to the diet they ate before the arrival of Commodore Matthew Perry's ships in 1854, opening trade between the United States and Japan. Meals should be made up of unpolished rice, fermented soy foods, and vegetables grown without chemical fertilizers. This wasn't reactionary conservatism, Ishizuka would add. Nutritional science—nineteenth-century nutritional science, which had yet to discover vitamins, fiber, or phytonutrients—would back him up. Health, he claimed, stemmed from the proper balance of sodium and potassium in the body. Ishizuka drew up elaborate charts of sodium- and potassium-dominant foods.

The dying teenager tried the Shoku-Yo diet. His health quickly recovered. Within a few decades, he was leading the organization.

Ohsawa's contribution to the Shoku-Yo philosophy was to graft Taoist philosophy onto Ishizuka's scientific-minded theories about health. Chinese and Japanese notions of yin and yang—how foods could be yin or yang, and how to balance these forces in the body—were based on centuries of observation and experience. Ohsawa embraced the general idea, then tossed out the rest. He claimed Western science ignored truths about the nature of health and well-being that formed the base of East Asian medicine, but then sloughed off these ancestral doctors' wisdom, too. Instead, he applied the universal duality to his mentor's nutritional charts: sodium-dominant foods were yang, potassium-dominant ones, yin. Sometimes, Ohsawa's yang and yin foods actually synced up with traditional Chinese dietary prescriptions, in the same way that you sometimes wave to your next-door neighbor when he's coming home from a one-night stand and you're taking your dog out for an early-morning run.

AFTER TAKING IN Ohsawa's lectures, Dick Smith decided to start with the brown rice part. One problem: he couldn't cook. For the first few weeks, he gave up his regular breakfasts of steak and eggs and boozy postperformance feasts in favor of handfuls of raw brown rice, chewing them, as Ohsawa instructed, diligently enough that "you should eat your liquid and drink your food."

Oddly, the raw rice eased the stress of Smith's nightly performances in the pits of Broadway musicals. "Every night when you go to work you got to be perfect," he said years later. "If you made a mistake or cracked a note, it went all over the theater and everybody heard. It put me on edge. After I started eating the rice for seven days, I went to work and I couldn't care less whether I hit a clam and the whole world heard it. I was still playing like I always did, but without the anxiety. So I said, this is pretty good. I'm going to stay with this."[6]

Smith convinced the woman he was courting, a Lindy's hatcheck girl named Penny, to start cooking some of the recipes that Ohsawa's followers were distributing in a slim, mimeographed book that their leader had titled *Zen Macrobiotics* (macrobiotics had nothing to do with Zen Buddhism and everything to do with Ohsawa's recognition that Westerners were showing an interest in Asian religions). The trumpeter even surprised Penny and her three kids one day by rifling through their cupboards, tossing out foods Ohsawa had decreed they shouldn't eat.

He also went to a private consultation with Ohsawa, who many followers agreed had a healer's gift. "George Ohsawa could just look at your face and tell you what's wrong with you, according to your ears, eyes, hands, nose, and the shape of your face," Smith remembered. "He took one look at me and said: Too much vitamin C. No fruit for three years!" (Vitamin C was one of Ohsawa's bugaboos in those days, being extremely yin.)

"It's funny, because I was anemic, and my doctor was telling me to drink a gallon of orange juice a day," Smith added. "But I followed George, and I started getting better. I got rid of the anemia from eating brown rice. Whatever he told me seemed to work." In fact, some long-time sinus problems, to which he'd never given much thought, disappeared along with the anemia, and his weight dropped from a chunky 180 pounds to 135.

Ohsawa had tapped into many of the same fears and aspirations as the American health-food movement: emphasizing vitality and energy, decrying the medical establishment's scalpels and pills, promising a corporeal transcendence over disease. While he couldn't draw the same audiences as a Gayelord Hauser or a Paul Bragg, a community of a few hundred American followers gathered around Ohsawa over the next few years. The master and his wife, Lima, would travel between New York, the community Ohsawa had seeded in France and Belgium in the mid-1950s, and the study center in Japan that he'd established shortly after World War II, which was devoted to the Unique Principle and world peace. The Americans began holding summer camps on Long Island, where Ohsawa lectures alternated with cooking classes.

Ohsawa was a galvanizing presence. He was charming, mercurial, scathing. His followers were wary of his sharp retorts but would still flock around him, magnetized by his energy, eager for instruction or medical advice.

This was a man who'd had the temerity to tell the government of wartime Japan that they'd lose the war unless they stopped feeding their soldiers white rice and sugar (and was tortured and jailed for it), the gall to show up in Albert Schweitzer's camp in Africa to convince the great doctor that he was Schweitzer's kindred spirit, and the persistence to spend decades trying to persuade Europeans about the virtues of brown rice and miso. Ohsawa would get up at six in the morning to scrub the floors of wherever he was staying, his followers later reported, and would bound up the stairs, two at a time. By the time he came to America, he'd written more than two hundred books in Japanese and French, dashing each off like a round of Christmas cards, and began writing just as prolifically in English with the assistance of students who could help translate.

*Zen Macrobiotics*, which evolved from a mimeographed book to a printed paperback, was a good example of Ohsawa's looping, dashed-off prose. He had a lot of ground to cover for his neophyte readers—his own definition of health, his interpretation of Eastern philosophy, Japanese folk cures for innumerable illnesses—and so he did it in seven-league boots. The book is alternately jumpy and florid. Some of its instructions ("If you have few intimate and loyal friends, it would be wise to observe these directions: Take a small spoonful of *gomashio* . . . to neutralize the acidity of your blood") now read as pure kook. Others, such as his endorsement of smoking, even worse.

Many tenets, though, map out today's zeitgeist to a startling degree: "Do not take any fruits and vegetables that are artificially produced with chemical fertilizers and/or insecticides," Ohsawa wrote in 1960. "Do not take any food that comes from any long distance. . . . Do not use any vegetable out of season." It's hard for anyone who owns a copy of *The Omnivore's Dilemma* to read *Zen Macrobiotics* and not see a little Ohsawa in Chez Panisse menus and Jamie Oliver shows.

At the core of the book are two tables. The first describes a hundred or so foods by their degree of yinness or yangness. The second table lists a series of numbered diets ranked by their ability to bring the yin and the yang of the body in balance. Diet number negative three, for instance, the most adulterated of them, is made up of 10 percent grains, 30 percent animal products, 45 percent vegetables and salads, and smaller amounts of soups, fruits, and desserts.

Diet number seven—the one that Ohsawa claimed has the greatest ability to cure illness and bring spiritual clarity—consists of 100 percent whole grains. "To accelerate the macrobiotic cure, you had better drink less . . . enough less so that during a twenty-four hour period, you urinate only twice if you are female and three times if you are male," Ohsawa added. Because the body "decomposes one tenth of our blood cells every day," he would argue, it would take a human on such a radically purifying diet only 10 days to change its entire composition.[7]

THE EARLY MACROBIOTIC community in New York brought together artists and intellectuals as well as health faddists and the desperately ill. They were drawn in by their first encounter with Eastern philosophy— perhaps, too, by the glimpses Ohsawa offered of a culture that had been at war with America just sixteen years before. Ohsawa floated the most intriguing ideas into his writings, applying yin and yang to scientific and philosophical concepts. Early macrobiotic newsletters reprinted arcane articles about blood composition, experiments in transmuting sodium to potassium, and disquisitions on the nature of justice, all interpreted through the lens of the Unique Principle.

While these new converts were following Ohsawa's philosophy to the loftiest of heights, they were learning to prepare vegetables *nituke*-style—by cooking them with a small amount of water and soy sauce—as well as soba noodles, miso soup, and a strange, meaty substance made of wheat gluten that Ohsawa called "seitan," a term he may have coined. They gave up coffee in favor of green tea that they roasted until it filled the house with smoke. They gave up toast for unsweetened oatmeal in the morning and mashed potatoes for brown rice at night. They concocted primitive desserts of agar agar and apples or smashed adzuki beans thickened with kudzu-root starch. The first generation of Ohsawa followers also invented East-West dishes along macrobiotic lines, such as a vegetable pie with a whole-wheat crust, braised root vegetables and cabbage, and a "cream" sauce made of toasted whole-wheat flour and water. Brown, needless to say, predominated.

Just as Ohsawa's American followers were opening their first macrobiotic restaurants and importing staples from Japan like wakame and "tamari"—the name George Ohsawa used for soy sauce fermented the traditional way, instead of enzymatically produced sauces from American companies like La Choy—their teacher addressed his audience's fears about the imminence of thermonuclear war.

These fears may sound hysterical to anyone born after the Cold War, but 1961 was the moment when paranoia over nuclear war escalated into a pandemic. Tensions between the United States and the USSR over the construction of the Berlin Wall strangled foreign relations. The Cuban missile crisis was less than a year away. Everyone was digging a nuclear fallout shelter in his or her backyard.

If anyone would have a concrete sense of the horrors nuclear war could unleash, it'd be a Japanese man born in 1893. Over and over, Ohsawa told the Americans to get out of New York City. Some members of the group took Ohsawa's warnings to heart, forming an emergency committee. Dick Smith recounts that a Columbia professor studied Atomic Energy Commission reports to locate the most fallout-free spots in the country, then recruited a few others to fly to California's Sacramento Valley on a scouting expedition. Driving around the area, the committee zeroed in on Chico, California.

The university town made the perfect site for a new utopia. The city was surrounded by mountains, which would stop any winds blowing radiation north and east from prime targets like San Francisco. Furthermore, temperate, golden Chico was the middle of the most fertile rice-growing region in California. When the bombs hit, the group decided, they'd be assured of having enough of Ohsawa's principal grain.

The group, which eventually numbered thirty-four, prepared themselves for the pilgrimage by "yangizing" their bodies as much as they could, eating strictly according to macrobiotic guidelines. They also agreed to meet up at a camp in Long Island on September 18, 1961, and trek across the country. Dick and Penny got married on the day before the big move, packed up Penny's three kids, and met up with the others to start their new life.

The caravan took its time crossing the country, delighting in the scenery, stopping at campgrounds every night. Smith wasn't the only musician in the group: there were four trumpeters, and they would break out their horns in the evening, playing for hours while the women in the group prepared large pots of rice and vegetables over the campfire.


WITHIN A FEW weeks of the pioneers' arrival in Chico, the media blitz faded away. One year passed, then two, and the macrobiotics found themselves puzzling over what to do in utopia.

Some moved on, while a few members with advanced degrees found work at the university. Those of the community with savings pooled funds to establish the George Ohsawa Macrobiotic Foundation and supply it with a printing press. Teal Ames did find simplicity of a sort, marrying a local and getting pregnant. And after giving up a successful musical career on Broadway, Dick Smith found himself in a new town, with a new wife and three kids to support, and no orchestra within seventy-five miles.

He picked plums and joined a crew cleaning trash off the highways. Although Smith insists he had no problem leaving his old life behind, he spent his weekend nights—for decades, in fact—playing trumpet at local saloons, thrilling the cow-town drinkers with cheesy covers of songs he used to mock in New York.

In his spare time, Smith and another musical macrobiotic, Bob Kennedy—formerly a studio musician at CBS who often played on Jack Paar and Ed Sullivan—started a small food business, assisted by other community members. Kennedy was suave while Smith was terse and blunt. In the early days, they would grind a brown-rice cereal they called "rice cream" in a basement kitchen, yangizing their bodies by chain-smoking until the doctor upstairs would tromp down to complain.

The pair called their new company Chico-San. Funded and staffed by the macrobiotic community, they opened a small retail shop, which they stocked with foodstuffs imported from Ohsawa-affiliated producers in Japan, including miso paste, green tea, pickled plums, seaweed (Smith says Chico-San coined the term *sea vegetables* to make it sound more appealing), and tamari.

They supplied mail orders to macrobiotic followers all over the West Coast, but they aspired to become producers as well. In addition to grinding rice cream, Smith and Kennedy baked one-pound bricks of unleavened whole-wheat and rice bread—Ohsawa had declared that yeasted products were unhealthfully yin—and Smith drove all over Northern California pitching them to health-food stores. They had better luck with a gluten-nut cracker they concocted to fit the restrictions of a proto-Atkins-diet fad called "Calories Don't Count."

Even though they were drafting other members of the macrobiotic community into weekly volunteer stints, Smith and Kennedy weren't exactly papering the walls with dollar bills. That was, until George Ohsawa paid a visit to the fledgling macrobiotic community in 1963. Demonstrating another one of his moments of eccentric, brilliant prescience, Ohsawa suggested Chico-San make *senbei*, round, puffed-rice cakes, a street snack never before seen in America. After he returned to

Japan, Ohsawa sent Chico-San a little electric machine that made one rice cake at a time.

Rice cakes—those Styrofoam-light, crumbly disks that seem to radiate anticalories—proved the making of the business. Customers at the health-food stores Chico-San supplied loved the cakes. Smith says he and Kennedy took long shifts working the machine, spooning soaked brown rice onto a heated round plate, pressing the cover down, and waiting—one, two, three beats—before lifting the lid. Pop! The grains would explode into a puffy, round disk.

The pair may have been holding down two or three jobs, and pressing their families and friends into volunteer service, but they eventually found themselves the owners of a viable business. What they didn't have was a supply of the raw material they most sought—brown rice grown without fertilizers or other chemicals, Ohsawa's "principal grain."[8]

So Bob Kennedy went looking for it.


STRANDED IN CAMBRIDGE, Massachusetts, a victim of a broken motorcycle, Evan Root first encountered brown rice in 1965 as if it were a muezzin's song calling him to prayer.

The twenty-one-year-old was seated around the table with some friends, a giant bowl of spaghetti at its center, when two of the guests started gossiping about a couple they knew who were eating unpolished rice to expand their consciousness.

Having never tasted brown rice—in 1964, even the high priests of health food treated it as a vaguely benevolent gesture for one's body, far less effective than yogurt or brewer's yeast—Root found the idea of connecting with the cosmos more appealing than the rice itself. "I had done some peyote," Root says, "and I had my eyes open to more than one level of consciousness." Hallucinogens only opened the doorways of perception. They didn't furnish a room where a man could live. If you could ingest a mushroom and look on different planes of existence, he wondered, what if other, everyday foods had subtler, more pervasive properties?

The idea lodged itself in the base of his brain, teasing him with possibility, all through that free-floating summer. Root had meant to be on a months-long motorcycle trip around the country, girlfriend clutching his back, before the actor—with his high forehead, square jaw, and measured bass voice, he still resembles a lawyer in a courtroom drama—had to return to the Hartford Stage Company for the winter season. But the bike had foiled their plans. The motorcycle-repair shops were too clannish to help out a young couple more interested in Cambridge's folk-music scene than carburetors and piston rings. So they crashed with an eccentric friend who spent the summer pretending he was the couple's infant son.

A few weeks after the party, Root finally ran into the subject of that dinner-party gossip and quizzed him for details. "He gave me the low-down," Root says, "but I didn't understand anything of it." He did pick up a copy of *Zen Macrobiotics* and read it closely, tantalized by the thought that he could find a way to tap into the true order of the universe.

That summer, Root worked hard to locate the odd ingredients he was supposed to be eating to connect with this larger self. Like peyote or hash, they were impossible to find through normal channels. He asked a friend, who asked another friend, and soon Root found himself at a karate dojo buying a few pounds of brown rice. Another guy in Cambridge became a macrobiotic dealer, amassing a stash of *kudzu*-root starch, *umeboshi* (salted plum) paste, miso, and tamari to sell to those in the know.

In the summer of 1965, Root quit the troupe and moved to New York, where he auditioned here and there, found a job as a fact-checker at the *New Yorker*, and tried to practice macrobiotics more seriously. He attempted diet number seven, which mostly meant eating toasted brown rice out of a pouch that he attached to his belt.

"When I was eating diet number seven I felt pretty wasted," he says. "But I had a job, and I wasn't going to let anything get in my way. No matter how fagged out I felt, I insisted on taking the stairs two steps at a time, and I was determined that macrobiotics was going to work." He lost a lot of weight and set his parents worrying.

No matter how hard they fretted, nor how tired he felt, nothing could convince Root to stop pursuing a sense of oneness with the cosmos through brown rice.

EVAN ROOT WASN'T the only New Yorker in his twenties who found the transcendental possibilities of macrobiotics compelling. The young and adventurous were finding copies of *Zen Macrobiotics* in esoteric bookshops and attending lectures that Ohsawa and his followers were giving. Never press-shy, Ohsawa caused a sensation when a young *New York Herald Tribune* reporter named Tom Wolfe interviewed him, and the teacher predicted John F. Kennedy's death three months before that fateful Dallas trip.[9]

The exotic, ascetic appeal of Ohsawa's diet number seven in particular called to a generation whose penchant for flinging themselves far out into the far-out was just beginning to crescendo.

The first of these extremists to make national news was Beth Ann Simon. A reedy, charming West Village painter, Beth Ann and her husband, Charlie, found themselves in 1965 seeking a remedy for Charlie's migraines, not to mention a way to rid their systems of pot, LSD, heroin, and all the other drugs they'd been doing.[10]

The headache-dispelling effects of one teaspoon of *gomashio* convinced the couple to dive all in. They began studying Ohsawa's writings and eating nothing but brown rice, heavily seasoned with *gomashio*, and restricting their liquids to a few cups of roasted green tea a day. Soon they became thin. Then skeletal. As sores appeared on their legs—

scurvy—Beth Ann became convinced that the cure for her ills was to double down on the diet, though the Simons did write to Ohsawa in Japan for advice.

In late October 1965, Beth Ann's parents attempted an intervention. She told them, "I am going to get well, and when I get rid of all these poisons in my body I will be well for the rest of my life." Three weeks later, she died.

Today, we might be more likely to view her death as a form of anorexia nervosa. Beth Ann's father blamed macrobiotics, launching an outcry that made the national news. A grand jury in Passaic, New Jersey, investigated the death and released a report in 1966 condemning the dangers of macrobiotics, citing three other malnutrition-related deaths. The *Harvard Crimson* reported, anecdotally, about another student who'd sought a cure in diet number seven after doing too much LSD— dangerously yin—and died in much the same fashion.

Suddenly, the wry, gently mocking tone that colored news reports on this diet veered into the alarmist. The police raided the macrobiotic foundation in New York where Root was buying his food supplies, shutting it down and hauling away pamphlets and bags of whole grains (not life-threatening, they later determined). In California, the FDA ordered Chico-San to stop making any health claims about its food and to break all financial ties between the for-profit business and the nonprofit George Ohsawa Macrobiotic Foundation.

Ohsawa, in Japan at the time the scandal broke, dashed off a letter to the foundation's newsletter warning his students that too many of them misunderstood what macrobiotics was. Macrobiotics didn't equal brown rice—it was a much larger way of "transmuting the comprehension of each individual . . . by means of a biological, physiological, and medical re-education."[11] He expressed dismay over Simon's death, and a few sentences later complained that he'd received her letter too late to respond in time, primarily because the couple had forgotten to enclose return postage.

The master didn't have much more of a chance to help his students ford the flood of criticism. On April 24, 1966, Ohsawa, then in Tokyo, died of a heart attack. He was seventy-two.

EVAN ROOT DIDN'T develop scurvy or faint from malnutrition, despite his most sincere efforts. Instead, he moved back from New York to Boston.

By 1966, Root had given up auditioning and was casting about for a way to get more involved in macrobiotics. He was helping a friend set up a restaurant on the Upper East Side when word filtered south from Brookline, Massachusetts, that Michio and Aveline Kushi, two of Ohsawa's Japanese disciples, were moving and needed some help.

He had first attended a lecture Michio gave in New York the year before and was awed. "Michio had a lot of energy to communicate, a lot of *chi* in his delivery," Evan says. "He could talk about the most mundane thing, like what was on your plate, and he could somehow take it out to the infinite universe and by the end of the weekend, bring it back down to the food on your plate. I was as high as a kite after listening to him."

The Kushis had begun studying with Ohsawa in Japan more than a decade before he finally conquered—if that's the appropriate word here—the West. Michio, a student of political science at the University of Tokyo, became active in the world federalist movement in the late 1940s, through which he encountered Ohsawa's Student World Government Association, then located outside Tokyo. There, the master was attracting idealistic youth with lectures offering the Unique Principle as a vehicle for world peace.

After a few years, Ohsawa sent some of his acolytes out into the world, too. In 1949, Ohsawa helped Michio secure a visa to study at Columbia University, one of the first in a fleet of Japanese disciples dispatched to North America, South America, and Europe. Though he soon dropped out of school, his English too rudimentary at the time to follow lectures, Michio's letters back to Japan would be read aloud to the students there. His words inspired Tomoko "Aveline" Yokoyama,[12] a young woman from a Christian family, to immigrate to New York two years later. The two shared an apartment, and soon, a marriage and family.

They settled in New York, along with another couple, Herman and Cornellia Aihara, whose path to America—student visa, epistolary romance—resembled theirs. All through the 1950s, until George Ohsawa's arrival in New York in 1960, the Kushis and Aiharas served as macrobiotic sleeper agents. They ran a Japanese gift shop for a spell and worked other odd jobs, their legal status as immigrants somewhat tenuous. In the late 1950s, Michio became a vice president at Takashimaya, the Tokyo-based department store, and helped it establish a branch on Fifth Avenue.

The close allegiance between the two families ended in 1961, when the Aiharas immigrated to Chico with the caravan, where they eventually ran the George Ohsawa Macrobiotic Foundation.

The Kushis balked at leaving for California. Yet they decided to escape New York, too.

In 1964, Aveline moved the children up to Martha's Vineyard; Michio followed her north a year later. In 1965, they settled in Cambridge, and not much later moved to Wellesley. Trouble followed them to each city: In Cambridge, where one of his students died of malnutrition, Michio reportedly was charged with practicing medicine without a license for displaying acupuncture needles at one of his lectures; the charge was dropped once he agreed to leave town.[13] The staid suburb of Wellesley, where they moved next, didn't know what to make of Aveline, who would wander around the neighborhood in a kimono. In 1966, the authorities in Wellesley, too, grew alarmed by the young longhairs coalescing around the Kushis' house and pressured the couple to leave yet another town. The small following they'd attracted dissipated. That's when the Kushis started phoning around, looking for a volunteer to help them relocate to Brookline.

Root didn't spend much time dithering over a decision. He quit his *New Yorker* job, packed up his things, and traveled up to Brookline, moving in with the Kushis and their five children.

Just before his arrival, Aveline had set up a small basement storefront on Newbury Street, not far from the Boston Public Library. The name she gave the store, Erewhon, came from an 1872 novel written by Samuel Butler. (*Erewhon* is *nowhere* with phonemes reversed.) In Butler's *Erewhon*, criminals were seen as having an illness, while those who became physically sick were guilty of disobeying the laws of the universe: a proto-macrobiotic allegory, George Ohsawa had proclaimed.[14]

Aveline Kushi put Root in charge of the store. In those early days, Erewhon was barely more than a buying club. There were sacks of brown rice and other grains piled around the dim room, shelves stocked with dried seaweed and beans, and, on the floor, a large keg of tamari. Root spent his days behind the cash register, eager to engage anyone who entered in long conversations, selling copies of *Zen Macrobiotics* and a few bags of goods here and there. Frankly, the work was dull, animated by Root's zeal for macrobiotics and the weekly lectures that Michio would give in the storeroom.

Michio was hardly a charismatic prophet in the Ohsawa mold: built like a greyhound, he had the retiring demeanor and measured speech of the law professor he might have become. As former student and macrobiotic historian Ronald Kotzsch later described him, "[With] a high and broad brow over dark owl-eye glasses, a perennial black three-piece suit, and a cigarette poised toward the heavens, Kushi was an impressive and mysterious figure."[15] Where Ohsawa was likely to meet students' questions with challenges and derision, Michio would respond with, "Ah, yes," or "Beautiful, beautiful." He called his teaching style yin, compared to Ohsawa's yang ways.

Nevertheless, word trickled out from Boston, accelerated by Michio's traveling lectures, that this guy was plumbing the infinite depths of a philosophy only sketched out in Ohsawa's jumbled writings. At the same time, *Zen Macrobiotics* and another Ohsawa translation, called *You Are All Sanpaku*, published in 1965 by Billie Holiday biographer William Dufty, were being passed from hand to hand in Minneapolis and Chicago and Los Angeles, read by the same people giving Zen, tarot, and kabbalah a go.[16]

This wasn't Dick Smith and Bob Kennedy's generation of macrobiotics, who were still reeling from Ohsawa's death. Younger seekers weren't so concerned about preventing cancer as they were, like Root, attuning themselves to the forces that governed the cosmos. They were hunting for anyone who could point the way to other ways of being in the world that weren't prescribed by parents, church, and media. They were also looking for other pathways than the easy hedonism of the prevailing counterculture, which by the late 1960s was beginning to show itself hollow, even destructive.

In 1967 and 1968, they began road-tripping to Boston, showing up at Erewhon or at Michio and Aveline's house in Brookline. Audiences at Michio's lectures grew from eight to thirty to one hundred—Michio moved them to a nearby church—and the Kushis were faced with what to do with this informal, campus-free university.

At first the Kushis took them in, just as they had Root, but the house filled up quickly. So Aveline began renting out giant houses around Brookline that, in the pre-condo, post-domestic-servant era, were languishing on the rental market. These "study houses," as they came to be called, modeled themselves after the Kushis' own. A married couple would serve as the dorm parents—often the man would teach classes on philosophy or shiatsu, while the woman would lead cooking classes.

A head cook, similar to a *tenzo* at a Buddhist monastery, would be appointed, and other residents might take charge of specific meals. It was amazing how many people could fit into a mansion: everyone shared a room, and privacy was immaterial. (The houses were zoned as single-family dwellings, so if the authorities came to inspect, beds would be hidden, people would scatter, and the heads of household would invent elaborate family trees to describe the bodies who remained.)

While Michio Kushi was the electrifying force, the one these young converts were traveling to be near, Aveline was the motor chugging beneath the community and propelling it forward. She was more soft-spoken than Michio, with cheekbones like two ripe peaches swelling beneath dark, teasing eyes. But George Ohsawa had nicknamed Aveline "the Axe" for her determination. She may have walked around Boston in traditional Japanese garb, but she'd also jump on the back of Root's motorcycle when given a chance. Aveline was the one who moved the family up to Boston, who opened up the businesses, who tended to the legions of rudderless arrivals amid her own family duties, teaching them how to cook and sew.[17]

Just as the Summer of Love was crescendoing in San Francisco, in Boston Root grew bored of tending the store and cooking at Aveline Kushi's elbow. He decided he'd rather open the city's first macrobiotic restaurant and knew she was the one he had to convince. The arrival of a San Franciscan named Paul Hawken gave him the leverage he needed to make his case.

Hawken, who'd been mounting psychedelic light shows when he came across *Zen Macrobiotics* and moved east to meet Michio Kushi, proved to have a real curiosity about the mechanics of the food business—as Evan says, "not only how to sell the beans but where they might come from." Root urged Aveline to let Hawken take over Erewhon. The two men took a West Coast road trip together, Root giving lectures on macrobiotics at their stops, and by the time they returned to Boston, Aveline had leased the space for the restaurant and agreed to the transfer.

In February 1968, Sanae, named after George Ohsawa's wife, opened.

The food that Root cooked at Sanae was typical of the macrobiotic cuisine crystallizing among the new generation of macrobiotics, in homes as well as hip macrobiotic restaurants like the Osoba Noodle Nook and the brown-rice food cart (Berkeley), the Wayfarer (Portland, Oregon), the Paradox (New York City), and Yes! (Washington, D.C.). "There was never a recipe book," he says, "but there was a formula: Brown rice every day. An alternative grain—millet, buckwheat, barley—every day. Then there was a vegetable of the day, a bean of the day, seaweed of the day, plus miso soup and a soup du jour. We'd do short-order stuff, too, like fried rice, fried noodles, tempura, broiled fish, and homemade sourdough bread." It wasn't so different from what diners still eat at macrobiotic restaurants fifty years later: Japanese peasant food, sparely seasoned and cooked with whole grains, simplified even further by being transplanted in foreign soil. Nevertheless, within six months, people were lining up outside Sanae on weeknights, waiting for tables.

Diet number seven, with its bewitching promise to clarify the spirit and put a body right with the world, was still most young people's introduction to macrobiotic cooking. However, in the wake of the Beth Ann Simon debacle and other malnutrition episodes, Michio and Aveline tried to wean their students away from dietary zealotry. Over the following decade, they developed what came to be called the "Standard Macrobiotic Diet."

According to the 1985 *Aveline Kushi's Complete Guide to Macrobiotic Cooking*, 50 to 60 percent of one's diet should be whole grains. (This could include, to a minimal extent, breads, noodles, and flaked grains.) Brown rice was the great staple, of course, but millet, barley, and oats were also acceptable. Another quarter of the meal should be made up of vegetables, getting a balance of "root, round, and leafy green vegetables," at least two-thirds of them cooked. Bursts of protein were allowed in the form of beans and soybean products—another 10 percent of daily meals—and though the Kushis didn't restrict liquids like Ohsawa had, they recommended macrobiotic practitioners drink one to two bowls of soy- or miso-flavored broths a day.

Given that herbs and spices were verboten, garlic suspect, and seasonings limited to a few Japanese staples, what was a macrobiotic eater to do for excitement? Add small amounts of sea vegetables, pickles, seeds and nuts, in-season fruits, and the occasional piece of fish or bowl of clams.

It's hard to overemphasize how different the diet was from the four-food-groups approach—meat, milk, grains, and produce—the Kushis' young American followers were taught from kindergarten. But through young Americans, macrobiotics introduced some radical changes into the diet of the counterculture. It knocked two of the USDA's four food groups off the plate, introduced legions of young cooks to Asian ingredients, helped bring stir-frying and steaming to the masses, and gave the first shape to an emerging cuisine built on the foundations of eating seasonally, organically, and often locally. Macrobiotics helped fuel the prejudice against refined sugars and flours that swelled and contracted and swelled again as the decades passed. And, of course, macrobiotic food fed the impression that the food of the counterculture was earthy, brown, and bland.

THE ALTERNATIVE PRESS, made of hundreds of newspapers based on college campuses and in hip communities across the country, took off in 1967 and 1968. Early on, its lifestyle coverage was largely limited to art, rock, and drugs. Food appeared several years later, some newspapers running the occasional essay or recipe collection, others launching regular columns on cooking and nutrition. The columnists' new nutrition, especially in the earliest years, was always based on macrobiotics.

You can see macrobiotics hit the zeitgeist, for example, in the *San Francisco Express Times*, which rebranded itself as *Good Times* in 1969 and ran from 1968 to 1972. In 1968 and 1969, a series of simple illustrated recipes—potatoes with dill, Russian borscht, yogurt pie—titled "Alice's Restaurant"[18] gave way to a column called "Eat and Enjoy," whose rotating columnists surveyed food markets and dropped random recipes for chicken gizzards, Hippy-Go-Bake Cake (spice cake with raisins), and even peyote chips.[19]

In January 1970, the playfully eclectic tone shifted toward the proscriptive when a new columnist, named Mary Schooner, joined the lineup. Her opening salvo:

> Most people think macrobiotics is some kind of strange vegetarian diet. Straight people think it is eating nothing but brown rice and getting scurvy. Heads think it's health foods, honey instead of white sugar, and good quality dope. [*San Francisco Chronicle* columnist] Herb Caen wrote that the cast of *Hair* was on the "orgiastic" macrobiotic because they gave an opening party where no liquor was served, only fruit juice. Actually, the diet avoids honey as well as sugar, peanuts, and dairy products as well as meat . . . and they don't get sick very much. Since I started the diet a year and a half ago I've had four colds and some headaches, most caused by eating things that were too yin, and that's it.[20]

For the next year, more epicurean writers alternated recipes with Schooner's macrobiotic basics: Caraway-Scented Goulash one week, buckwheat patties the next. In one issue, Schooner even attacked Marrakesh Lil, one of the epicureans, for having dared print a recipe for cooking brown rice that didn't maximize the grain's chewy, yang nature. The macrobiotic lessons continued until December 1970, when Schooner announced she was moving to Boston to study with Michio Kushi.

Similarly, in September 1969, the *Los Angeles Free Press* introduced a

column called "Food for Thought," by Mick Wheelock and Lini Lieberman, which was later titled "Ecological Cookery." Mick had already
announced his dietary allegiance a few months before, in an Ohsawa-
fueled diatribe about how the Viet Cong's simple diet of brown rice and
vegetables was nutritionally superior to that of American soldiers.[21]

In their weekly columns, Mick and Lini offered recipes for unyeasted
whole-wheat breads and muffins, disparaged the dubious claims of
health-food stores, ranted about pesticides, and introduced readers to
millet, seitan, and other macrobiotic staples. "A simple diet of natural,
unrefined food produces the strongest, healthiest and most enlightened
people," they wrote in June 1970. "A rich diet of chemicalized food, animal products, refined foods and sugar eventually brings ill health and
decay to any people or nation."[22]

Mick and Lini became the counterculture's first hip dieticians, their
columns syndicated in other underground newspapers. *Mother Earth
News,* which launched in January 1970, assembled Mick and Lini's published work into a series on macrobiotics that ran through the magazine's
first year. *Kaleidoscope,* Milwaukee's underground newspaper, then re-
purposed the *Mother Earth News* articles into a ten-part feature titled
"Food Thing." "*Kaleidoscope* is happy to be able to present, beginning
with this issue, a complete rundown on food—what to eat, why, and
how to fix it all," the editors gushed in the preface to the first installment.
"Food Thing, which runs below, is by far the best single piece we've
seen done on the subject."[23]

LIFE IN THE Kushi study houses was intensely social. Intense, period:
dozens of young migrants from around the country, packed into rambling houses, each of them pushing themselves to mirror the devotion
they saw in their fellow students.

Some of the female students dressed in kimonos and men in short *happi* coats. As one older student later described, a core group of young men around Michio "dressed like Michio, talked like Michio, and smoked like Michio." When you look at pictures of the Boston community, it's striking how conventional they look, with hair that barely scraped their ear tips, skinny ties and stovepipe pants, and a remarkable absence of paisley or stripes. They were encouraged to give up drugs and alcohol— disastrously yin—with the exception of scotch, Michio Kushi's spirit of choice, which he declared was somewhere in the yang zone.

The residents of the study houses were always heading out to their fellow houses for constant parties, or piling into cars to head down to Boston for Michio's lectures, or grabbing a snack at Sanae and the fancier Seventh Heaven, which opened several years later. They worked for Erewhon, or a short-lived macrobiotic bookstore, or the *East West Journal*, a magazine the Kushis started in 1970. They studied Japanese martial arts like kendo and aikido, shiatsu (Japanese massage), acupuncture, and ikebana (flower arranging). There was always someone new arriving in town, or visiting from Japan, who had to be welcomed. Always someone to send off to Chicago or Minneapolis or Seattle, eager to open a grocery store or study house there.

Root remembers time and time again getting off work at eleven, still keyed up from the dinner rush at Sanae, and returning to the Kushis' house in Brookline to find the dining table ringed with people. They'd be talking over ideas that Michio had brought up or macrobiotic interpretations of the events of the day. Most nights, their night-owl teacher was there, too, and if the discussion continued after midnight, Aveline might appear out of her bedroom, drift into the kitchen, and quietly make noodles.

There was so much to discuss. Michio took the intuitive, rambling structure that Ohsawa had drafted—the Unique Principle—and redesigned it as a Gothic cathedral. As Kushi later summarized in his 1977 masterwork, *The Book of Macrobiotics:*

> [Yin and yang] are the eternal laws governing all phenomena, vis-
> ible and invisible, individual and group, part and whole, past and
> future. . . . They are the highest understanding mankind has ever
> had, and they are the native genuine intuitive wisdom in every-
> one. They are the key to realize all possible dreams. By knowing
> them, we can turn sickness into health, war into peace, conflicts
> into harmony, chaos into order, and misery into happiness.[24]

The young Americans, galvanized by psychedelics and disillusion-
ment with Christianity, may have initially been drawn to the Japanese
trappings of macrobiotics and its shadings of Taoism, Buddhism, and
traditional Chinese medicine. However, the philosophy proved relatively free of mysticism. In fact, macrobiotics was downright practical. While the goal was long life and world peace, its primary practice
seemed to be eating.

As frequent Kushi collaborator Alex Jack explains today, "There's a
correspondence between personal illness and conflict and war in society.
In other words, there's a macrocosm and a microcosm. In order to have a
healthy, peaceful world, we must be able to govern ourselves and maintain
our own health—physical, mental, emotional, spiritual. It spirals out from
the individual to the family to the community to the state and the world."
In short, macrobiotics promised not just good health but social transformation through an ever-widening spiral, Kushi would say, of influence.

Such a big responsibility residing in each pot of brown rice. And so
much promise, too. "With a sense of the possibility of world transformation simmering in their hearts," Root says, "people took this message
seriously as well as happily. We were changing the world!"

But the details—the details!—could swallow a man or woman up.
Yin and yang could be applied to electrons and protons, as well as the
solar winds and the spiral of the Milky Way. To ingest the kind of food
that would put scholars of macrobiotics in harmonic balance with the

universe, they approached the Talmudic in the degree to which they sifted out the yinness and yangness of things and phenomena.

Short-grain brown rice, for example, was more yang than long-grain rice, and pressure-cooking it yangized it even more effectively than steaming it. A carrot was more yang than an onion by a few degrees, but it wasn't merely yang: each root had a yin end and a yang end. When you cut the carrot, you had to take that into account, as well as what you were going to cook the carrot with, to ensure you balanced yin and yang in the meal.[25] In addition, you shouldn't peel the carrot, for fear of wasting vital nutrients, and when you cooked the carrot, you should do it with a calm, happy spirit, understanding that you were broadcasting your mood to your dining companions through the food.[26]

Of course, as George Ohsawa himself articulated, everything that has a front has a back, and the bigger the front, the bigger the back. The macrobiotic community saw itself as devoted and idealistic. Others saw them as puritanical know-it-alls.

Even within the macrobiotic community, the days of scurvy faded, but they gave rise to the problem of sneaking. You and your housemates might share oatmeal and miso soup for breakfast, soba noodle soup for lunch, and millet and stir-fried vegetables for dinner, but accusations would float around that some were sneaking out to a diner for eggs and forbidden hash browns (potatoes!). Enter your room without warning, and you might find your closet door open with your roommate inside, cramming spoonfuls of sesame butter into his mouth. Root admits that his own weakness was citrus fruit. "I can remember the first grapefruit I ever had," he says. "It was as if I'd smoked a joint, it was so expansive." No surprise—it may have been the biggest hit of fructose he'd taken in months.

GIVEN THAT EATING was the spiritual practice of macrobiotics, its code of honor, its badge of membership, one of the Boston community's greatest—and most unheralded—contributions may have been to the business of selling food. At the core of that legacy was Erewhon, the tiny food market that Evan Root handed control of to Paul Hawken in 1968.

Passionate, far-seeing, by all accounts brilliant, and by some accounts prickly, Hawken cared about where the foods came from, how to display them, and how to sell them to other like-minded eaters. The light-show artist had a line on the tastes of his generation and wasn't dollar-shy the way so many of its anticapitalist, SDS-inspired members were. Within a year or two, he turned the ramshackle little basement shop into a proper store, then much more.

As Hawken explained in a 1973 article he wrote for the *East West Journal,* the Kushi community's cultural magazine, his drive to expand Erewhon far beyond a macrobiotic buying club came from a brown-rice fast that he undertook in 1969. Five weeks of diet number seven produced a vision less hallucinatory than intellectual and spiritual:

> I slowly began to relate the biological pattern of life before me to the fabric of my life. Past incidences and cellular manifestations became as one. Before me flashed the childhood diseases, the thousands of pills and tablets, the chemicals eaten intentionally or unknowingly, the fat or stringy steaks, the sugar and cigarettes, coffee and Cokes. . . . It was as though each cell in my body had accumulated the essence of every substance that it had come in contact with. . . .
>
> But, I wondered, what were these small and tiny parts of my cell glowing with a strong and pure light? Why were these different? . . . Then I knew that these small areas were the manifestation of the limited but pure foods I had been eating for a short while. In writing this for you, it sounds corny, but in experiencing this, it was simply a stunner.[27]

Hawken wrote that he made it his mission to expand those areas of light by locating foods grown in clean soils and ensuring that they were sold still fresh and ripe with life force. "Erewhon was not merely to be a 'corner store' acting as a middleman between various food processors and a consumer," he concluded. "For those seeking the unveiling of the spirit, Erewhon would attempt to provide the renewing and cleansing power of the earth."

Erewhon's growing staff of young Kushi followers—all of them earning room, board, and a too-small stipend—soon moved into a larger storefront down the street. Hawken began traveling around the country, hunting down farmers who could grow grains, beans, and other supplies to the pesticide- and fertilizer-free standards that Ohsawa had first advocated.

Some, like Frank Ford of Arrowhead Mills in Deaf Smith County, Texas, had been converted to this vision in the preceding decade; Arrowhead Mills was on the path to becoming an important distributor. Others were simply farming the way their great-grandfathers had, suspicious of the chemicals the USDA and their neighbors had taken to so readily. The Erewhon staffers convinced these holdouts that they never need make the switch to "conventional" agriculture, selling to the natural-foods market instead.

Just a few years after the days when Root was knocking on the door of a karate dojo to score a bag of brown rice, food co-ops and natural-foods stores began opening, each operating as islands unto themselves, relying on rumor and word of mouth to source the products they stocked their shelves with. Distributors selling natural or organic products were few and scattered. Erewhon's young staff, sensing the zeitgeist rumbling toward them, flung themselves into wholesale distribution. In late 1969, the company moved into a ten-thousand-square-foot warehouse and printed up its first catalogs.

Their timing couldn't have been better. Erewhon's supply network was in place when the natural-foods boom took off in the early 1970s. Erewhon—and the larger macrobiotic community—helped determine what products would make it onto the shelves of these stores. The company proselytized with every shipment, printing macrobiotic recipes on its packages, including stacks of educational flyers with its shipments, and designing folksy, handcrafted-looking packaging that would be replicated by a thousand producers to come.

By August 1970, when *Organic Gardening and Farming* magazine ran a profile of Erewhon, wholesale business had exploded: in just one year, the company had gone from supplying two or three stores to supplying one hundred fifty. Organic vegetables were coming from nearby farms as well as California. The company was locating new sources of unfertilized, unsprayed, whole foods.

The one product missing from Erewhon's first catalogs was the one it sought the most fiercely: organic brown rice, the cornerstone of the macrobiotic diet, George Ohsawa's principal grain.

BOB KENNEDY HAD the lock on that.

By 1968, Chico-San was importing dozens of products from Japan to supply its mail-order business, and an Ohsawa student named Junsei Yamazaki had come to Chico to brew giant vats of soy sauce, cure miso by the barrel, and concoct "Yinnies" brown-rice syrup, which the macrobiotic community permitted itself to use to sweeten desserts. The company had funded a small distribution company as well as a tiny macrobiotic café and market in Berkeley called the Osoba Noodle Nook, with the never-realized goal of turning it into a national franchise.

That said, rice cakes were becoming Chico-San's top seller. The company had built an automated machine that could pop out eight cakes at a time, and almost every day, it seemed, cakes would leave the factory by the truckload. Yet Kennedy and Dick Smith couldn't find a farmer—in the heart of rice country, no less—who was willing to grow brown rice for them using farming principles of the sort outlined by George Ohsawa and J. I. Rodale's influential *Organic Gardening and Farming* magazine. Kennedy approached more than a hundred fifty rice farmers in the region, with no success.[28] Until his accountant introduced him to the Lundberg brothers.

Eldon, Wendell, Harlan, and Homer Lundberg certainly looked like the other farmers tending swaths of flat, clay-rich soils fed by the Sacramento River. Their Scandinavian-blue eyes, fine blond hair, and round cheekbones marked them as a set. The four were farming the land purchased by their parents, Albert and Frances Lundberg, who had moved to Richvale, California, from Nebraska in 1937, when overfarming and drought turned the topsoil into clouds of fine, gray dust that devoured the prairie.

Albert became an active member of the Butte County Rice Growers' Association, a co-op that gathered and milled the rice grown in the surrounding area, selling it on the commodities market. In the 1950s, he divvied the property he had acquired among his sons, the youngest of whom was in high school at the time. The boys went to college, served in the military, and reunited in Richvale, where they took over for their father when he retired.

By the late 1960s, though, the brothers had become aware that their rice-growing methods were diverging from the rest of the Rice Growers' Association—in fact, from the standard ag college approach as well.

"I can remember agriculture classes," says Homer Lundberg, the youngest of the brothers, "where the professors came out and said, 'Soil is just a medium to hold the roots of the plants you want to grow so we can feed them the chemicals they need.' Our idea was, [soil is] that all right, but a whole lot more. We've just scratched the surface in the complexity in soil nutrition and human nutrition."[29]

Guided in part by Albert's memories of the Dust Bowl, the Lundbergs had begun rotating their crops more often to give the land more time to recover between plantings and had reduced the chemical fertilizer they used. But they were still selling their rice to the Butte County Rice Growers' Association. "We were growing a food product from a different perspective than our neighbors were," Homer says, "but once we got it through the harvester and into the truck to be hauled in to the drying and storage facility, it was all dumped and commingled with the rest of the rice."

Third-eldest brother Harlan heard about Chico-San's quest to find a source of organic brown rice for its rice cakes. The two parties began to talk. The reason hundreds of farmers had turned Bob Kennedy down to date was that the risk was considerable. Reducing one's fertilizer use as the Lundbergs had begun doing was one thing, but no one in California had tried growing 100 percent organically on a commercial scale. What if it produced only a pittance of their normal yields? What if this experiment put four families out of business?

Chico-San agreed to shoulder the risk for the Lundbergs, paying them a minimum rate no matter how much rice they produced, which would shrink if yields increased. In exchange, the Lundbergs would have to give Chico-San exclusive rights to sell this organic brown rice for five years.

The brothers planted seventy-six acres in the spring of 1969. They learned to control water grasses and sedges by first drowning the land and then draining it. The technique stressed the rice plants but killed off all the competition.

Growing a few acres of a test plot didn't just involve running an agricultural experiment. The Lundbergs began backing out of the Butte County Rice Growers' Association, a move that caused a rift in their close-knit rural community. They also discovered that no commercial rice mill could take on such small amounts and process them separately, so they had to import parts from Japan and construct their own mill.

Nevertheless, the brothers delivered their first organic brown rice crop to Chico-San in February 1970. It wasn't the largest of crops—roughly half the standard yield—but it was big enough that neither farmer nor customer was ruined. To the contrary, it convinced both sides that they could make a go of organic rice farming.

Chico-San fulfilled its side of the agreement, packaging and marketing the rice. Kennedy and Smith put out notices in the West Coast macrobiotic newsletter and produced pamphlets describing the agreement. *Organic Gardening and Farming* published a major article about Chico-San and the Lundbergs in 1971, publicizing both names to more than a half million readers looking for sources of organic brown rice.[30]

The company quickly sold out of the Lundbergs' 1969 crop, and in the spring of 1970, the Lundberg brothers devoted three hundred acres—almost five times the original plot size—to organic production. That one sold out, too, albeit more slowly. Chico-San played enforcer as well as marketer, sending samples of the rice to a lab every few months to test for fumigants or other chemicals.

Now that they had backed away from the Rice Growers' Association, the Lundbergs were ever more eager to divert their crop from the commodity market. They began selling rice grown on chemically fertilized but unsprayed fields to Paul Hawken at Erewhon, who marketed it as everything-but-organic, and at lower prices than Chico-San. Hawken didn't stop looking for organic rice, and in 1970, he found a willing farmer in Arkansas.

The appearance of a competitor ratcheted up the pressure on Chico-San to sell. In 1971, the Lundbergs doubled their organic acreage again. But Chico-San's rice-cake production and wholesale business were unable to keep up with this exponential growth. By the time the 1972 crop was almost ready to harvest, Chico-San was far behind in its sales—Homer says the company had only sold 25 percent of his previous year's crop.

Then disaster hit.

In August 1972, Smith was working on Chico-San's automated rice-cake machine when one of the hydraulic oil pressure lines broke, spraying oil all over the machine's heating elements. It burst into flame. "The fire was moving so fast that when this flame shot in my face, my arms went up," he says, making the sign of cross in front of his face to illustrate, "so I didn't get any in my eyes. If I had inhaled, I . . . I got away lucky. It just burned my arms. Burned me pretty good." Though Smith was pulled away to safety, the blaze whipped itself into an inferno, leaping from the production building to the warehouse to the office. Within a few hours, most of Chico-San had burned to the ground.

The only casualty: the company's exclusive agreement with the Lundbergs.

The brothers had taken out huge crop loans in order to quickly expand their organic efforts, and even before the fire, Kennedy had told the farmers that they should just hold on to the 1971 rice until he could sell it. But you can't hold on to organic brown rice indefinitely, Homer Lundberg says. Not only do the oils in brown rice make it spoil more quickly than white rice, the rice wasn't sprayed with insecticides. They'd already had to spray small amounts of their crop with insecticide to ward off an infestation and then sell it on the commodity market—at a huge loss. "We were seeing the thing spin out of control," he adds.

Within days of the fire, eldest brother Eldon Lundberg, fretting over the incoming harvest, approached Kennedy and demanded that he break the contract, freeing the Lundbergs to sell their rice to all the other stores and distributors who had been wanting access to it. Cornered, Kennedy complied.

DICK SMITH WOULD simmer about the betrayal for the next four decades. In terms of the availability of organic brown rice, the broken agreement was the puff of breath that caused the dandelion to disintegrate, sending its feathery seeds spinning across the country.

Even now that the Lundbergs were able to ship their organic rice anywhere they chose, the family farm faced a precarious decade, growing a mix of conventional and organic rice in order to feed four families. But the brothers forged forward with their agricultural experimentation, and in 1973 helped to found the California Certified Organic Farmers to assemble other farmers, old and young, who felt the same way they did.

Long-haired kids from tiny co-ops and natural-foods stores around Northern California drove their VW vans to the farm in search of the Lundbergs' righteous rice. "We identified with the hippies right off the bat," Homer says. "We were pretty square, I guess, but we did try to think outside the box, and they did, too." The brothers would load up each van until the engine was practically scraping the road, and extend the visitors just enough credit to return for another load.

The brothers recognized that their image—principled, authentic— was a big part of the appeal of their rice. Even as they sold their rice farther and farther from home, and their name became synonymous in the natural-foods market with brown rice, the Lundbergs stuck to the open-door policy they maintain to this day: if anyone drove to Richvale, they'd show them around the fields and talk to them about how the rice is grown.

As for Chico-San, the double blow of the fire and the Lundberg Farm's desertion did not flatten the business. Bob Kennedy and Dick Smith were able to rebuild their factory in a new site within two months, and the rice-cake business boomed once again, with mainstream grocery stores placing larger and larger orders.[31]

Erewhon quickly bought up more and more of the Lundbergs' organic brown rice, selling it across the Eastern Seaboard and wherever the company expanded in those early natural-foods-boom days. And the 1970s saw Erewhon—and macrobiotics in general—hitting its peak.

The permanent Boston community grew to several hundred strong, flourishing until Aveline and Michio moved to the Berkshires to found the Kushi Institute in 1985. Even more significantly, their young, mobile students migrated around the country, taking their zeal and their brown-rice-centric diet with them. Study houses and communities erupted in Minneapolis, San Francisco, Seattle, Chicago, New Hampshire. Macrobiotic sections appeared in almost every natural-foods store, and macrobiotic plates on menus in college towns around the country.

The circulation of Boston's *East West Journal,* which featured stories as disparate as profiles of poets and sharp critiques of McDonald's marketing practices, grew to sixty-five thousand, reaching far beyond the boundaries of the devoted. Michio and Aveline drew not just idealistic kids but celebrities to the cause of macrobiotics, the most prominent being John Denver and John Lennon and Yoko Ono, counterculture royalty.

Erewhon expanded to Los Angeles in the early 1970s, when Aveline moved there for a few years, seeking medical treatment for an ill son. The two branches' sales grew, and grew, and grew—beyond the organizational capabilities of the young staff, in fact.[32] Erewhon's employees and imitators dispersed across the continent over the course of the early 1970s, opening grocery stores and natural-foods distributorships modeled on Paul Hawken's "points of light." Eden Foods in Michigan, Bread and Circus in Boston (later swallowed up by Whole Foods), Essene in Philadelphia, Laurelbrook in Maryland, The Well in San Jose, and dozens of smaller businesses would all trace their origins back to George Ohsawa.[31]

The ranks of the faithful, those who balanced yang and yin at every turn and numbered their diets, never ballooned into a great Unique Principle corps. Macrobiotics proved too austere to enter the mainstream. But brown rice, well, that became a totemic food of the counterculture, as much a symbol of worldview as throwing the peace sign, eclipsed in importance only by another staple: whole-wheat bread.

## Carob

"Care for a carob pod? I'm undulated with an overabundant sur-plus," the *Los Angeles Times*'s one-named humorist, Abercrom-bie, wrote in 1945. "If you know any carob pod fanciers who prize them things please infer them to me. Or have 'em send me a self-addressed piano crate and they can have the whole kaboodle."[34]

Carob, the ersatz chocolate with the waxy, insipid taste that traumatized so many children in the 1970s (ahem), wasn't yet carob in 1945. In Los Angeles, carob was an altogether different kind of nuisance.

*Ceratonia siliqua* trees are indigenous to the Mediterranean, and have long been cultivated north and south of the sea for their six-inch, lumpy brown pods. High in carbohydrates and sugars, the pods could be fed to camels or boiled down into a thick syrup that, much like sorghum, is used as a sweetener. Rumors that John the Baptist had lived on carob pods during his desert exile gave the pods their alternate name, St. John's bread.

In the 1910s, government agriculturalists planted test plots of carob around Southern California, as well as arid regions of Ne-vada, Arizona, Washington, and New Mexico. "The day may come when the deserts will be extensive forests of carob trees," Santa Barbara horticultural commissioner C. W. Beers told the *Los Ange-les Times*. Forecasting a boom, in the 1920s, a few entrepreneurs in the Los Angeles area set up factories for refining carob pods into sugar. None of their efforts succeeded, and for most Southern Californians, carob was just another ornamental tree spewing its pods over sidewalks and lawns.[35]

Around the same time, however, Southern Californian health-food faddists cottoned to carob's unique flavor. Chocolate, as well as coffee and sugar, had fallen out of favor with the faddists because it was overly stimulating. In 1932, the *Los Angeles Times*'s health column, "The Care of the Body," advised the health-conscious mother to con her children's sweet tooth with "scores and scores of wholesome confections made of figs, nuts, prunes, honey, dates, raisins, and carob meal."[36] By the 1950s, one article called carob "the chocolate tree," mentioning that soda fountains were already stretching the cocoa powder in their chocolate malteds with carob.[37]

It's not clear how the counterculture grew convinced that carob was healthier than chocolate. Most likely, they were repeating the nutritional wisdom that health-food-store clerks passed along, but man, did this generation ever take to carob.

"Carob satisfies your desire for a deep chocolatey taste without filling you with insatiable greed as does chocolate," wrote *Wings of Life* author Julie Jordan in 1976 in the headnotes to her recipe for whole-wheat Carob-Date Bread ("delicious with butter or cream cheese and honey").[38]

By the late 1970s, shoppers could find carob chips, carob milk, and carob bars in food co-ops, but no one could best the whole-grain bakeries of the time when it came to creative uses for carob. One whole-grain baking book included several dozen recipes: Carob Chip Bars with Sunflower Seeds, Carob Halvah, Carob and Peanut Butter Tofu Bars, Carob Coconut Brownies.[39]

Not everyone bought the message. "I found that [carob] took a while to get used to," confessed Maureen Goldsmith in 1972's *The Organic Yenta*, "and I must admit I do sneak out for chocolate every once in a while."[40]

# 3

# Brown Bread and the Pursuit of Wholesomeness

RICE MAY HAVE BEEN GEORGE OHSAWA'S principal grain, and the counterculture's first totemic food. But as the 1960s segued into the 1970s, whole-wheat bread took on a larger importance for young Americans, becoming as much symbol as sustenance.

As a symbol, it had the power to soak up meaning the way that a leather car seat does August sunlight. For the radical edge of the Love Generation, tripping their way through Golden Gate Park, whole-wheat bread was an act of guerrilla theater. For others, it was a rejection of modernity, a search for older, healthier ways. Loving the taste of whole-wheat bread took determination. Making it was a statement of *self*-determination. To bakers across the country, it offered, with perhaps a bit of melodrama, a means of wresting control from the power structures that encircled them.

Most of the twenty-two-year-olds who peered over dough-clumped forearms at a recipe they'd tacked to the table had no idea that they were joining a hundred-year fight against factory food in America. Groups on the edges of society had been trying to keep bread brown ever since white flour became the norm, even taking their arguments to the government, with no success. By the 1960s, whole-wheat bread was a curiosity—something you'd have to seek out. Its elusiveness made it all the more appealing.

Sure, learning to bake bread daunted first-timers, but the alternative— consuming the bagged loaves of fluffy white bread stacked into square-edged walls on store shelves—was even more frightening, if everything the baby boom generation was reading was true.

ONE OF THE first times the counterculture transubstantiated whole-wheat bread into a symbol was, appropriately, in San Francisco during the Summer of Love.

By the summer of 1967, the Haight-Ashbury neighborhood hadn't just become the biggest street scene in San Francisco. It was setting the tone for the cultural revolution. Around the turn of the twentieth century, this small, central neighborhood had filled in with ornate three-story Victorian houses, later divvied up into giant flats. Sixty years on, the curlicues and columns on the elaborately painted structures were flayed by time and neglect, and Haight Street between Divisadero Street and Golden Gate Park resembled a small town that had lost its station on the main railroad line. Gay men had taken to the Upper Haight, as many San Franciscans called the neighborhood. So had students at San Francisco State University, who could split a three-bedroom flat for $175 a month.

After Ron and Jay Thelin's Psychedelic Shop opened on Haight and Ashbury in January 1966, selling bongs, Indian fabrics, and books about Rosicrucians and Zen monks, the concentration of young men and women in Edwardian frippery and fringed leather jackets hanging about intensified. Mod boutiques appeared. So did Far-Fetched Foods, a health-food store, and cafés catering to the new bohemia such as the Drogstore and I and Thou.[1]

With the shops and the students came the bands that were beginning to play at the great ballrooms—the Fillmore, the Avalon—over a backdrop of swirling light shows. And, of course, the drugs. Enough young people traveled down the coast to supply the neighborhood with Mexican marijuana, and a local named Owsley Stanley, a chemist with an aptitude for psychedelic proselytization, contributed thousands of pounds of LSD at prices that any starving student could afford. The Haight's psychedelic-influenced residents called themselves the New Community. Others threw the word *hippie* at them, a diminutive of "hipster."

A few folks at the Haight-Ashbury were beginning to pass around copies of George Ohsawa's *Zen Macrobiotics*, but food wasn't much on people's minds. The revolution was. The war was. Racism and inequality and the fucking pigs were, and so were drugs and music and this new mod-meets-Edwardian-meets-Indian-meets-Jesus-and-Mary aesthetic. If you were going to drop out and be free, you were going to eat whenever you could, as cheaply or as well as you could, not stopping to consider every ingredient or its effect on your body.

The New Community was home to many of the artists who belonged to the San Francisco Mime Troupe. The Mime Troupe—whose members, incidentally, pronounce its name "meem"—was not a pride of white-faced actors collectively flailing their way out of an invisible box. When the troupe was founded in 1959, director Ronnie Davis, who had studied with famed mime Etienne Decroux in France, combined pantomime, dance, music, and visual spectacle, infusing them with politics that grew more radical as the 1960s progressed.

The troupe's performances were sharp and fearless. In 1965, it traveled the country performing a minstrel show that savaged racism, African American and white actors alike in blackface. That same year, the City of San Francisco rescinded the company's permit to perform one of its plays in a public park, arguing that the performance was obscene.

When the troupe appeared in Lafayette Park, anyway, the play turned into another kind of performance altogether: a public arrest.

A group of Mime Troupe members, spearheaded by actor Emmett Grogan, his childhood friend Billy Murcott, and playwright Peter Berg, were inspired by the arrest in quite another way. That act—reenvisioning the arrest as the performance, not the play—helped them realize that they could fuse art and life, spectacle and politics, in the street. In Berg's words, they could become "life-actors."[2] A life-actor's performance was meant to embroil the audience in the spectacle of a new life, a new way of seeing the world; you weren't telling people the world could be different, you were showing it to them—acting as a culture grenade that would blast through their mental shields.

Grogan, whose Irish features looked as if they had been shaped in long swipes of a carpenter's plane and whose clipped speech was 100 percent Brooklyn, was a quintessential trickster, blessed with both charisma and possibly a little sociopathy. He began circulating flyers he typed up, a blend of poetry and polemic. The flyers excoriated both the status quo and the Haight-Ashbury's psychedelic scene, which he argued was politically complacent and dominated by hip merchants who were out to make money instead of changing the world. Grogan signed each flyer "the diggers."[3]

As fellow actors learned the source of the flyers, they split from the Mime Troupe to join Grogan, Murcott, and Berg in spontaneous street performances that Berg named "guerrilla theater," which would ensnare the audience and often the authorities as well.

"The Diggers represent the gap between radical political thought and psychedelia," one unnamed representative—they were all unnamed in the press, by choice—told the *San Francisco Chronicle*.[4]

In October 1966, just a few weeks after LSD was outlawed in California, Grogan got it into his head that the Diggers should blur the lines between performance and life even further. A sense of urgency was building, he felt, for the Haight-Ashbury community to respond to all the young people who were showing up on the street, sniffing out rumors of the psychedelic scene or news stories they'd seen in *Life* and *Time*. Some of the arrivals were college grads, some were high school runaways. They stepped out from their hitchhiked rides or off the Greyhound, with no money or employable skills, to a world where drugs were plentiful and people were willing to take advantage of the uninitiated.

Grogan and Murcott took a pickup to the San Francisco Wholesale Produce Market early in the morning and charmed the workers into giving them boxes of fruits and vegetables. They liberated a couple of giant milk containers from a dairy and took everything over to one of the Digger apartments to cook. Meanwhile, Murcott dashed off another mimeographed flyer and began handing it around:

## FREE FOOD

GOOD HOT STEW
RIPE TOMATOES
FRESH FRUIT

BRING A BOWL AND SPOON TO
THE PANHANDLE AT ASHBURY STREET
4 PM 4 PM 4 PM 4 PM

FREE FOOD EVERYDAY FREE FOOD
IT'S FREE BECAUSE IT'S YOURS!
THE DIGGERS.

And the people showed up.

The free food became a daily ritual, publicized in the underground newspapers, chronicled in the mainstream press, and depended on by the Haight-Ashbury hippies.

Jane Lapiner and David Simpson joined the effort to feed the masses along with their fellow Mime Troupe friends. Lapiner was a dancer who had moved to Berkeley in the early 1960s with her then husband, an academic. After the couple had a daughter and split up, Lapiner migrated to the Upper Haight, where she began teaching dance classes and performing with the troupe, living with another member in a crash pad. She and her daughter moved out of the house after Lapiner fell in love with Simpson, an actor who'd washed ashore in San Francisco after serving a few years in the Coast Guard and had joined the troupe before its minstrel show tour.

To Lapiner and Simpson, the food was the act that demonstrated the weird genius of the Diggers. The daily meal had no leaders, no staffing rotations, and yet it got done. "Nobody got stuck with the job long," Simpson says now. "People would do it for a few days, a few weeks, then they would pass it on to other people informally, who would take it up."

"There was no structure, there was no leader," Digger member Peter Coyote explained to French filmmakers in 1998. "There was no ideology except do your thing. Do it anonymously and do it for free."[5]

In their respective memoirs, Grogan and Coyote wrote that the Digger women took on more of the job of cooking than the men, who were too busy arguing over Marcuse and being aimlessly radical. Early in the mornings, a crew of people, usually including pretty young women, would make the rounds of the Wholesale Produce Market district in the industrial southeast end of town. *Anything you can't sell?* they'd ask. *Any extras we could have?* They'd load up the truck with spotted lettuce and soft tomatoes.

Lapiner got roped into the prep. She remembers, one morning, walking out of her bedroom to find a dozen or so roosters in the kitchen, pecking and crowing. Someone had stolen them from the wholesale market, and Grogan was preparing to slaughter them for soup, even though none of them had killed a chicken before.

The free food did not keep the Diggers too occupied to engage in guerrilla theater. Emphasizing that the meals were as much performance as they were a social benefit, they constructed a twelve-foot-by-twelve-foot wood frame, which they painted bright yellow. They'd drag the frame to the Panhandle, the block-wide stretch of green that juts out from the east end of Golden Gate Park, and set it up next to the pot where they would dish out stew. Anyone showing up with a spoon and a bowl would have to step through the "frame of reference" to eat, as potent and direct a metaphor for the transformative intent of the Diggers as anything Grogan published in a flyer.[6]

As the Diggers established "crash pads" for homeless kids and set up a Free Store where everything was for the taking, they accepted help from the outside, provided it didn't come with restrictions. Father Leon Harris, pastor of the All Saints Episcopal Church, a block off Haight, recognized that the need among the incoming flower children was growing extreme and offered the church's kitchen to cook free lunch in.

The sixteen-year-olds who appeared in the Haight could eat, at least, he figured. First soup, and soon bread. The bread baking began on June 24, 1967, when a research engineer named Walt Reynolds—who, in the spirit of those days, appeared out of nowhere and faded out of history just as quietly—held a massive, daylong baking session in the kitchen.

Reynolds, a big Dutchman with silvering temples and an Amish beard, was nothing like a hippie, but he claimed that he had a mission to teach people to make whole-wheat bread. "Commercially baked bread is a joke," he told the San Francisco Chronicle in 1968. "It tastes like wet Kleenex."[7] He showed up that morning with four hundred pounds of whole-wheat flour, butter, jam, tea, and stacks and stacks of one-gallon coffee cans. He began mixing dough and roped in any of the Diggers at the church, as well as any of the divinity students who passed by, to bake with him. They baked 166 loaves of bread that day—shaped by the coffee tins into big, domed cylinders—then sliced them warm and took them out to the street, inviting anyone who wanted more back to the church for jam and tea.[8]

The Diggers were inspired by this kindred spirit and returned to the kitchen the next Saturday to bake bread, with Reynolds as an adviser. Within a few weeks, they settled into a regular schedule on Tuesdays and Fridays, often baking late into the night. The bread wasn't always great—the quality always depended on who was baking it, and the crust could be as tough as a sheet of fiberglass—but it was free, and yours![9]

Like the soup, the free bread the Diggers distributed was a nonhallucinogenic tab. It communicated to anyone who chose to think about it—really think about it, not just nod at their raw and noble rhetoric—that he or she was not bound by the laws of labor and wages, success and failure, rich and poor, criminal and upstanding citizen. All they had to do was realize: The bread was free. They were free. The whole universe was free.

After the Summer of Love, Haight Street began emptying of youngsters, the drugs got harder, and the Diggers threw a massive "Death of the Hippy" parade and renamed themselves the Free Family. The meals in the park grew spotty, yet free bread continued, its production moving up to a commune in Marin County, where the bakers set up an outdoor oven next to a swimming pool and spent their days baking, everyone topless, diving into the water to wash off the flour.

The recipe for coffee-can bread, which the Diggers printed on leaflets and distributed, made its way out into the world. Information, like bread, was free, too. And because it was royalty-free, too, the recipe would be reprinted, verbatim, in other publications, including the first, January 1970, issue of *Mother Earth News*.

At one point before the baking sessions petered out, Simpson joined the rounds of the Wholesale Produce Market in the early mornings, looking for flour. The warehouseman, it seemed, had come to respect what the Diggers were doing. The volunteer cooks no longer had to feel like they had to flirt for every last grain. "We were always trying to qualify what *free* meant, because *free* was such an important word," Simpson says now. "My motto is 'Free is when nobody else wants it.' There was such a vast supply of waste, it was politically an eye-opener. Thousands could live on the garbage of the poor."

That didn't mean they would use whatever came their way. The Diggers insisted on whole-wheat flour. "We had already developed a critique of white bread," Simpson says.


WHAT THE DIGGERS didn't yet know was that they were far from the first Americans to develop a critique of white bread. In fact, as a nation, we have been critiquing white bread since long before the appearance of the industrial mills that produced the fine, white, nutritionally deficient flour that most of us now buy in five-pound bags.

Kernels of wheat have three main parts: the papery, firm outer bran that surrounds each kernel; the oily germ, embryo of the seed; and the endosperm, basically the fuel source for the seed as it sprouts, which is primarily made up of starch and protein. The difference between white and whole-wheat flour is that the former is made from the endosperm alone.

Traditional gristmills—the kind memorialized in state parks and Thomas Kinkade paintings—used water or animal power to grind wheat kernels between massive, grooved stones. From this relatively coarse gray-brown flour, the darker, heavier bits could be sifted out ("bolted"), a laborious process usually undertaken only for the elite. The elites, in fact, had been demanding white flour since ancient Greece.

After the 1880s, when roller mills replaced gristmills and flour became a commodity trucked across the country, everyone could eat like the king of Crete. Roller mills crush the grains between steel rollers, automatically separating the endosperm from the germ and bran at railroad-telegraph-shuttle-loom speeds. This process has the advantage of producing an elegant flour that not only can be turned into airy, delicate breads and pastries, it can also be stored for longer; the oils in the bran and germ quickly go rancid, and bugs seem to have little interest in it (a point that would become, strangely, described as a virtue ninety years later). The problem, of course, is that many of the other nutrients besides protein and starch remain with the discarded germ and bran.

In the 1830s, when the finest of bolted flour was still flecked with gray bran, a lecturer on the temperance circuit named Sylvester Graham began proselytizing about vegetarianism and the horrors of commercial "white" bread.[10]

An ordained Presbyterian minister, Graham had a reputation for being a prickly, self-important scold who could alienate even staunch supporters, but as a speaker he possessed a suave confidence that, for a decade, captured the imagination of thousands of listeners up and down the East Coast.

Influenced by the writings of a contemporary French physician named François Broussais, Graham argued that the body was a finely tuned system that connected the intestines to all the organs and was easily thrown out of whack.[11] What a person ate had the greatest effect on his or her health, Graham argued, but it was not the only factor. Staying healthy meant eschewing overstimulation, which would cause the system to be inflamed and agitated, producing disease. And what stimulated the nervous system to a dangerous degree? Sexual excitement, alcohol, coffee and tea, tobacco, meat, sugar, spices—and white bread.

Of the foods that had the power to excite or regulate such a jumpy, delicate system, bread had the greatest, Graham argued:

In all civilized nations, and particularly in civic life, bread . . . is far the most important article of food which is artificially prepared; and in our country and climate, it is the most important article that enters into the diet of man; and therefore it is of the first consideration, that its character should, in every respect, be as nearly as possible, consistent with the laws of constitution and relation established in our nature; or with the anatomical construction and vital properties and powers and interest of our systems.[12]

The problem with white bread was twofold. For one, at the dawn of the industrial age, it was increasingly made by large commercial enterprises, who may or may not be personally known to the person buying their breads. These unknown bakers, Graham testified, were likely to adulterate it with "alum, sulphate of zinc, sub-carbonate of magnesia, sub-carbonate of ammonia, sulphate of copper, and several other substances."[13] The argument didn't make Graham terribly popular with bakers, who once rioted outside a lecture hall where he was speaking.

The second problem was that white bread was *too* nutritious. Just like masturbation and steak, Graham would argue, white flour could stimulate the system to the point of debility. By contrast, whole-grain bread had a proportion of "innutritious matter" in it that was perfectly calibrated to the natural balance of our bodies. (A century later, Graham's innutritious matter would be known as dietary fiber.)

In his 1837 *Treatise on Bread and Bread-Making*, Graham spelled out the qualities of good, healthy bread in obsessive detail. It should be made with good wheat, preferably from "virgin" soil (unadulterated by manure and other fertilizers, though the reference to sexual purity was no mistake). It should be ground by millstones into none-too-fine flour, leaving the "branny" in the mix. This flour should be mixed with water and a good, sweet yeast, baked and fully cooled before consuming. And the only person in the household who should make bread was the matron of the house, not her servants and certainly not a faceless merchant. Bread was the cornerstone of good health, after all, an expression of the love and care a mother gave her family.

The popularity of Grahamism was due, in part, to the fact that he was one of the first health lecturers to convince his listeners that maintaining good health was in their power, and illness was preventable, not a burden that a cruel and whimsical God inflicted upon their bodies. Considering that medical treatment at the time was dominated by bloodletting and emetics, just as likely to kill as cure the patient, subsisting on brown bread and water seemed the lesser of evils, at least until one grew tired of the regimen. Considering also that the average American's daily diet was dominated by cornmeal, salt pork, and beans, and that dinner in nineteenth-century America tended to resemble a Nathan's hot dog contest, all grabbing and gorging, it's not surprising that those who embarked on Graham's ascetic diet of whole-grain bread, overcooked vegetables, and water actually felt better.

Graham's lecturing career—widely pilloried in the press from start to finish—only lasted ten years before he faded from public view. His strain of vegetarianism endured, however, most notably in the diets of the Seventh-day Adventists (see chapter 6). Even longer lasting was Graham's name. You can still find coarse "graham flour" in the bulk bins of many food co-ops. Up to the early twentieth century, cookbooks included recipes for "Graham Bread" and "Graham Gems" (muffins). And of course, most one-year-olds are weaned on graham crackers, a now-sugary cookie invented years after their namesake's death.


EVEN AS COMMERCIALLY milled white flour eclipsed stone-ground whole wheat in the early decades of the twentieth century, suspicion of white bread never faded away. But whole-wheat advocates drifted further and further into the fringe.

By the 1930s, only 10 percent of bread was baked at home, up from 90 percent just a few decades before. Small bakeries gave way to giant factories that could produce a hundred thousand loaves a day, or even more. Some even advertised that their bread was untouched by human hands—the machines could slice the loaf, too, before slipping it into a cellophane bag. Store-bought white bread was convenient, hygienic, and cheap. Its square, even edges helped it stack neatly on supermarket shelves. Sure, it didn't have much flavor, and it could double as a spare pillow if extra guests showed up for the night, but the crumb was so white and so even: a modern bread for a modern age.[14]

The health-food movement never let whole-wheat bread die. Seventh-day Adventist cookbooks, in the Grahamist tradition, included recipes for pies, cakes, breads, and cookies out of graham flour. Body-building health guru Bernarr Macfadden regularly called white bread the "staff of death" in the 1910s, a charge echoed by his Southern Californian protégé, Paul Bragg, in the 1930s. Bragg incorporated numerous whole-wheat recipes into his own cookbooks, and many of the early health-food stores of the 1920s and 1930s primarily sold whole-grain cereals and whole-wheat baked goods, as well as unrefined sugars, dried fruits, and herbs; some even had their own mills.[15]

Every few years, one of the mainstream magazines or major news-papers would publicize a new study suggesting whole-wheat bread was more nutritious than the squeezable new white breads, and the health-food press parroted these studies with malicious glee.

The critique of white bread, however, changed. In fact, it inverted Sylvester Graham's idea that white bread was more nutritive than whole-wheat bread. The shift occurred because of a revolution in nutrition that took place in the first two decades of the twentieth century: the discovery of vitamins.

In 1900, scientists believed that food was composed of six kinds of substances, five of them capable of being absorbed by the body: proteins, fats, carbohydrates, minerals, water, and refuse (bones, eggshells, and the like).[16] As long as a body consumed enough calories and grams of protein, it would thrive.

By the 1920s, scientists had identified four more substances, vitamins, essential for survival: A, B (an understanding of the complex of B vitamins would come within the next decade), C, and D. These would be found by searching for the causes of diseases we now know to be nutritional deficiencies: scurvy (vitamin C deficiency) among sailors who had little access to fresh fruits and certain pickles, beriberi (vitamin B1 deficiency) among eaters of milled rice, pellagra (niacin or B3 deficiency) in poor southern sharecroppers whose diet was dominated by corn, and rickets (vitamin D deficiency) in the urban poor.[17]

By the start of World War II, the growing field of nutrition had not only developed a notion of the amounts of vitamins humans should consume to stay healthy—the national Food and Nutrition Board published the first recommended daily allowances (RDAs) for vitamins in 1941—scientists had also determined that the standard American diet didn't include enough of them. One major factor, some began to argue, was that milling, canning, and other forms of processing were removing vitamins from the diet.[18]

A robust debate over what to do about nutritionally bankrupt milled flour stretched from the discovery of the vitamin B complex to the war years. The debate pitted the food industry against nutritionists, who were overwhelmingly convinced that Americans should switch back to whole-grain flours. By that time, only 3 percent of bread sold was whole wheat.[19] As evidence of widespread vitamin B complex deficiencies piled up, and the war in Europe began to look like it would require American fighters by the legion and that they be fit to fight, the American Medical Association finally backed the idea of vitamin enrichment. Conveniently, lab techniques for manufacturing B complex vitamins became inexpensive at right about the same time.[20]

In 1941, the FDA reached an agreement with flour milling and baking trade associations to enrich flour with thiamine, riboflavin, niacin, and iron. The agreement placated millers and bakers, who recognized it would only cost them fifty cents a barrel, and pennies more a loaf, to add these new chemicals to their flour, and they could now market their product as vitamin packed.[21] The War Food Administration made enrichment compulsory in 1943. With the agreement, white bread became healthy again.[22]


MILLERS MAY HAVE embraced the shift, but Adelle Davis didn't.

Born in 1904, Davis studied nutrition at UC Berkeley and the University of Southern California School of Medicine, where she obtained her master's in biochemistry in 1939. She spent most of her career as an independent nutrition counselor, but as the years progressed she wrote and reissued a series of books that the mainstream and the counterculture alike—though not her peers in the medical world—treated as textbooks on vitamins, minerals, and good health.

The most famous of these were *Let's Eat Right to Keep Fit* (1954), *Let's Cook It Right* (1947), and *Let's Have Healthy Children* (1951), books whose popularity snowballed with each new edition. A year before her 1974 death from cancer, the *New York Times* reported that she had sold more than 2.5 million hardcover books and 7 million in paperback.[23] Davis went on marathon lecture tours and became a familiar face on television, with an imperious, steel-gray bun and the cadences of a high school drama coach. She was dubbed the "high priestess of nutrition" by *Time* and "Earth Mother to the Foodists" by *Life*.

Davis's first passion was for vitamins: defining them, chronicling their benefits, analyzing Americans' daily diet for nooks and gaps where a few extra vitamins should be squeezed in. Her approach was based on extrapolation: if animals that ate a diet deficient in inositol or PABA lost color in their hair, well, then, by eating extra B vitamins you could keep your youthful hair color—or even restore it.[24] Davis's own recommended daily allowances for vitamins and minerals could be as much as four times higher than the federal government's.[25] Her methods—poring over thousands of nutritional studies and interpreting them for the general public—exposed her to significant criticism; several researchers found her books riddled with inaccuracies and misinterpretations.

While Davis recommended vitamin supplements by the fistful, she also believed in getting much of one's nutrition from natural foods and organic vegetables. She bridged the gap between health-food faddists like Paul Bragg and Gayelord Hauser and readers who put more trust in scientific lingo. Davis's dietary recommendations included prodigious amounts of raw milk and fertile eggs, which supposedly had extra B vitamins and hormones, supercharged with Hauser staples such as desiccated liver powder, nutritional yeast, wheat germ, and yogurt. She often added superfoods to recipes with an enthusiasm that could defy good taste.[26]

In addition, Davis was a great public critic of processed foods and of the companies that suckered us all into thinking they were good for us. "Health in America is controlled by the refined-food industrialists who support a multimillion-dollar business," she told Johnny Carson in 1972.[27]

Not surprisingly, she was no fan of fortified white bread. "'Enriched' flour is one of the most misleading terms ever used," she wrote in *Let's Cook It Right*.[28] "It would be as logical to consider yourself enriched by a burglar who ransacked your home but left you a few possessions." She frequently sang the joys, as well as the virtues, of baking bread:

Whenever anyone asks me how to build up the health of a growing child, a convalescent, or an invalid, how to add more protein, calcium, iron, or B vitamins to the diet, how to work more wheat germ, brewer's yeast, or blackstrap molasses into foods, or simply how to have fun at cooking, my answer is "Make your own bread." There are many excellent whole-wheat breads on the market, but none can compare in nutritive value or, to my way of thinking, in flavor with those which you can make at home.[29]

Many baby boomers say they baked their first loaves of whole-wheat bread after consulting Adelle Davis's cookbooks, and her quotes on baking frequently appear in hippie recipes for whole-wheat bread. (There is even a story told in Digger circles that Davis donated money to Free Family bakers to buy a load of whole-wheat flour.)[30]

But the counterculture critique of white bread that emerged in the late 1960s took on an even darker cast than Davis's. This critique magnified Sylvester Graham's paranoia over the chalk or sawdust commercial bakers might slip into their bread and brought it into the chemical age: fear of what chemical manufacturers were slipping into our food.

In the mid-1950s, and accelerating into the early 1970s, a growing body of books warned innocent diners about the dangers of fertilizers, pesticides, and food additives. By 1972, you could collect a large enough stack of alarmist books to dwarf Stephen King's lifelong output. Read your way through Leonard Wickenden's *Our Daily Poison* (1956), William Longgood's *The Poisons in Your Food* (1960), Booth Mooney's *The Hidden Assassins* (1965), Jim Turner's *The Chemical Feast* (1970), Beatrice Trum Hunter's *Consumer Beware! Your Food and What's Been Done to It* (1972), and Gene Marine and Judith Van Allen's *Food Pollution: The Violation of Our Inner Ecology* (1972), and you might be afraid to open your refrigerator at night.

The mainstream press could talk about innovation in the food world in optimistic World of Tomorrow terms. For instance, in 1968 the *Buffalo Evening News* reported in a story about the "revolution in food": "An exciting aspect of this effort is the studies by researchers here and abroad to produce proteins from petroleum through a fermentation process. Imagine a single oil well fueling a man and his car!"[31]

Meanwhile, William Longgood's *The Poisons in Your Food* saw the revolution in a different light:

> Virtually every bite of food you eat has been treated with some chemical somewhere along the line: dyes, bleaches, emulsifiers, antioxidants, preservatives, flavors, buffers, noxious sprays, acidifiers, alkalizers, deodorants, moisteners, drying agents, gases, extenders, thickeners, disinfectants, defoliants, fungicides, neutralizers, sweeteners, anticaking and antifoaming agents, conditioners, curers, hydrolizers [*sic*], hydrogenators, maturers, fortifiers, and many others.[32]

In 1965 alone, Gene Marine and Judith Van Allen reported in *Food Pollution: The Violation of Our Inner Ecology,* food manufacturers used 661 million pounds of additives. The authors analyzed a list of these chemicals published in a 1965 report by the National Research Council–National Academy of Science's Food Protection Committee, and they counted 1,622 additives, including 720 synthetic flavoring agents, 357 "natural" flavoring agents, 35 coloring agents, and 30 preservatives.[33] The fact that the FDA had classified most as "generally recognized as safe (GRAS)" did not reassure them at all.

No one knew what long-term exposure to all these chemicals—even in small doses, even generally regarded as safe—would do to our bodies. Books like Marine and Van Allen's horrified readers by describing the effects of DDT, both before and after Rachel Carson's 1962 *Silent*

*Spring* would galvanize the ecological movement. The food-pollution writers also informed their readers that the class of pesticides known as organophosphates were originally invented by the Nazis as a nerve gas, which a generation of Vietnam War protesters interpreted as an omen.

Some of the stories in these books are, in fact, still horrifying, like the fact that farmers were implanting diethylstilbestrol (DES) pellets in the necks of roosters to hormonally castrate them, producing "caponettes," and in cattle to fatten them up. The endocrine disruptor, which was often still traceable in the meat, was shown in 1971 to cause cancer in the women who took it, not to mention genital anomalies in babies exposed to DES in the womb. Or the fact that from 1930 to 1955, white flour was bleached with nitrogen trichloride gas, which was proven in 1946 to cause canine "hysteria"; the FDA considered the replacement, chlorine dioxide, a poison that was "probably safe as normally used."[34]

Writers like Longgood and Marine and Van Allen piled on to Adelle Davis's charge that enriched white bread was nutritionally empty—they listed all the fertilizers, pesticides, bleaches, emulsifiers, dough conditioners, and other chemicals that could make their way through every fluffy, bland slice into our bodies.

The average American didn't have to read a stack of books to stoke their worries over the toxins hidden on every grocery-store shelf. All a consumer had to do was watch the news.

In 1958, the controversial Food Additives Amendment (which contained the "Delaney Clause," named after U.S. Representative James Delaney) was added to the Food, Drug, and Cosmetic Act, ruling that "no additive shall be deemed to be safe if it has been found to induce cancer when ingested by man or animal," provoking a new concern over carcinogens. The Delaney Clause was followed by national scandals over chemical poisoning. In 1959, the U.S. Food and Drug Administration announced a recall of cranberries contaminated with aminotriazole, a weed killer that had been found to be carcinogenic. In 1969, cyclamate, one of the most common artificial sweeteners used in sodas and other sugar-free treats, was recalled after a study found that rats fed a cyclamate-saccharin mix were more likely to develop bladder cancer. In December 1970, studies found unacceptably high levels of mercury in canned tuna, a scandal that the FDA shook its head at until an independent researcher called them out.

The government, most muckrakers assumed, was not on the public's side.

ANOTHER CRITIQUE OF white bread was coming out of the Nation of Islam. In the late 1960s, Elijah Muhammad, leader of the Black Muslim group from World War II to his death in 1975, published two volumes of dietary advice for his followers. The Qur'an forbade pork, of course, but Muhammad's dietary proscriptions went much further: catfish, potatoes, black-eyed peas and lima beans, soy flour, and cornbread were all verboten. He emphasized a diet high in raw, fresh vegetables, fresh meat, and whole-wheat bread, though the latter should be toasted or eaten a day after it was baked. (Shades of Arnold Ehret? Hard to tell.)

Muhammad scorned processed food as well as many of the southern staples becoming known in the 1960s as "soul food." The white race had thrust both cuisines upon African Americans, he wrote. "The scientists of this world (the white race), failing to gain the confidence of the people, ran a race of commercialization between each other," he wrote in the first volume of *How to Eat to Live*. "This commercializing of foods has put forbidden, divinely forbidden, and poison foods on the market for human consumption."[35]

Malcolm X took Muhammad's rhetoric a step further, racializing the dark-versus-white bread divide in a 1963 *Playboy* interview with *Roots* author Alex Haley:

Anyone who has studied the genetic phase of biology knows that white is considered recessive and black is considered dominant. When you want strong coffee, you ask for black coffee. If you want it light, you want it weak, integrated with white milk. Just like these Negroes who weaken themselves and their race by this integrating and intermixing with whites. If you want bread with no nutritional value, you ask for white bread. All the good that was in it has been bleached out of it, and it will constipate you. If you want pure flour, you ask for dark flour, whole-wheat flour. If you want pure sugar, you want dark sugar.[36]

In the late 1960s and early 1970s, the Nation of Islam opened collectively run Shabazz Bakeries in Washington, D.C.; Chicago; San Francisco; Baltimore; and other cities. The bakeries avoided white flour, preservatives, and refined sugars. Muslims were far from the only customers to buy their breads, whole-wheat doughnuts, bean pies with whole-meal crusts, and "Eat to Live" gingerbread. Brother John 36X told the *Washington Post* in 1973 that the D.C. bakery's goal was not just to follow the teachings of Elijah Muhammad but to become 100 percent independent from the white economy. "It might be tomorrow," he said. "It might be in two years. But we don't plan to wait too long."[37]

WHETHER ECHOING ELIJAH Muhammad, Adelle Davis, or both, the white counterculture made stark differentiations between dark and light foods. "Only in America could people want their food bleached before they eat it," wrote one anonymous commentator in Milwaukee's *Kaleidoscope* newspaper in 1971. "Flour, sugar, rice—all bleached out. In their mania for cleanliness, American consumers ignore the fact that bleaching removes the vitamins and nutrients which make food worth eating in the first place."[38]

For counterculture types, though, the difference between brown and white wasn't racial. It was "natural" versus "plastic." And by natural, they meant "real."[39]

"Plastic bread," the counterculture began calling the fluffy white stuff they'd grown up with, to them identical whether it was Wonder or Taystee or Tip Top. It was the only bread they knew. American kids at the time grew up being scolded for tearing the crusts off the slice of bread on their plate and squishing it into marble-sized pellets perfect with which to pelt a younger sister.

As adults, the claylike appeal of white bread appeared more ominous. "Revolt against plastic food in a plastic culture is in full swing," began the introduction to muckraker and natural-foods advocate Beatrice Trum Hunter's 1972 *Whole-Grain Baking Sampler*, "and commercial white bread has become the target for justified spoofing."[40]

An unnamed writer in Durham, North Carolina, introduced his or her recipe for "Spirit of Love Bread" by repeating a study that had become more or less an urban legend:

> If your background is similar to mine you probably grew up on plastik [*sic*] enriched builds strong bodies 12 ways white bread. Three quarters of a group of laboratory rats fed bread like that died from malnutrition in 90 days. Those days are over for me now. There is an old folk saying that bread not baked with love is useless for it only feeds the body and not the spirit. So bake bread with a spirit of love for the people who will eat it.[41]

"Plastic" became the shorthand for commercial food, and the antithesis of what was natural. Plastic meant lab-manufactured, factory-made, chemically flavored and colored and preserved. Plastic food was wrapped in plastic bags and stacked on plastic shelves in great, impersonal, modern supermarkets. It looked created, not grown or made by human hands. It tasted like plastic—or rather, it tasted like nothing that came from fields, forests, and waters.

In January 1970, Mick Wheelock and Lini Lieberman, syndicated alternative-press nutritionists, ran a three-part series on bread that would be echoed in recipe headnotes and counterculture diatribes throughout the decade. "The quality of store-bought bread has decreased to the point where it looks and tastes like foam rubber," they wrote. "As soon as you put a piece of it in your mouth it dissolves without giving you time to chew, taste, or enjoy it. It would go moldy in a few days if it wasn't full of preservatives."

The pair then spelled out their argument in favor of whole-wheat bread, in which you can read inadvertent echoes of Graham and the overt influence of Davis and Longgood:

> The kernel of wheat did not occur in Nature for some arbitrary reason. It was specifically designed by Nature to be a *whole* nutritional package [emphasis author's]. The schizoid approach that Western civilization has towards Nature and food is both ignorant and exceedingly dangerous. . . . The manufacturers of white bread can offer no explanation for their use of white flour other than their claim that the loaves are "more aesthetically pleasing." Yet they readily admit that this milling process robs the flour of much of its nutritional value.[42]

Nature had made the flavor of the wheat berry perfect, too, and we had let ourselves become swindled by marketers and manufacturers into believing nature was wrong. To eat natural foods meant stripping away the fertilizers, flavorings, and preservatives. In the same spirit as Sylvester Graham, it meant short-circuiting a civilization that prized profits over health and returning to a time when food wasn't multisyllabic and toxic. We couldn't trust Dow Chemical, but we could trust a kernel of wheat.

The opposite of plastic bread, as Ita Jones described in her syndicated column, "Grub Bag," was a bread that had the power to change her life the moment she first bit into it. "It was dark bread, like the earth and birds' shadows," she wrote. "Thick, brown-crusted, with a taste I remembered for days."[43]

Brown bread looked nothing like store-bought, and to watch the dough swelling in the bowl, and smell it coming out of the oven, gave twenty-year-olds who had never grown up with home bakers a thrill. "Fresh-baked bread made with freshly ground whole wheat is so potently alive and real that it is somehow shrouded in mystery and magic," another author gushed.[44]

The way to stop poisoning your body with plastic bread, they all argued, was to bake it yourself.

BUT HOW DO you learn how to bake whole-wheat bread if you've never seen anyone do it?

The macrobiotics, who were dispensers of so much of the early advice on whole grains and vegetables, were not much help when it came to baking bread. George Ohsawa had declared yeast verboten because it fed off sugar—too yin—so macrobiotic breads tended to be blocks of compressed flour that one shaved off in the finest of slices.

Aveline Kushi's master recipe for whole-wheat bread, for example, called for three ingredients—flour, salt, and water—and insisted that nature would provide the yeast. "Place dough in a bowl lightly oiled with sesame oil and set aside in a cool spot for 8 to 12 hours to ferment. . . . The dough will naturally rise by attracting wild yeast in the air," she wrote. (Not in eight hours it wouldn't.)[45] Other hippie bread recipes flavored these dough quasars with sesame seeds, roasted soybeans, barley flour, rice gruel, even bone meal.[46]

In the late 1960s, then, the first counterculture bakers looked to respectable sources in the health-food movement for whole-wheat bread recipes—primarily Adelle Davis's *Let's Cook It Right* and Beatrice Trum Hunter's 1961 *Natural Foods Cookbook*.

Davis and Hunter took their cues from a Cornell University professor, Clive McCay. In the 1940s, when the great debates over enriching bleached flour with chemically manufactured vitamins were beginning, McCay developed an alternative to chemically fortified flour that he tested on rats. He added small amounts of soybean flour, powdered milk, and wheat germ or brewer's yeast to white flour to replace, in part, the lost protein and B vitamins, and the rats seemed to thrive. McCay called his mixture "Cornell flour," and though McCay convinced a number of bakeries and public schools to use it, "Cornell bread" never took off, because it would have required commercial bakeries to change their operations to use it.[47]

The two natural-foods icons didn't just include recipes for Cornell bread in their books. In fact, as both writers were accustomed to do, they improved on McCay's approach by doing a little extreme enriching.[48] The theory was: if you were already infusing your dough with extra vitality by baking with whole-wheat flour, you might as well double down by adding brewer's yeast by the half cup and as much soy flour as the bread could stand without turning into a sodden lump.

For both of these experts, taste was never as important as nutrition. Not a few of their recipes appear to have gone too far. Yet novice bakers who had never baked bread before might not have noticed. What they produced had to be healthy. And at least it wasn't poofy and bland.

IN THIS VACUUM of good taste and sound technical knowledge appeared a slim, poetic, practical cookbook with a brown kraft cover written by a young Zen student and put out in 1970 by an unseasoned Buddhist publisher in Berkeley.[49]

In the summer of 1966, while Emmett Grogan was passing out flyers and the Haight was collectively, permanently high, a San Franciscan named Edward Brown found himself washing dishes in a rambling resort and hot springs 150 miles to the south of San Francisco. Tassajara, as it was called, was situated in a valley so remote that you had—still have, in fact—to access it by driving down a twisty, steep fourteen-mile dirt road.

Brown had dropped out of Antioch College a year or two before, dissatisfied by the abstract intellectualism of his classes, and had joined his older brother in sitting zazen at the San Francisco Zen Center, led by a tiny Japanese monk named Shunryu Suzuki.[50] Suzuki and his head disciple had fallen in love with the idea of opening the United States' first Zen monastery in the area. While they scoped out Tassajara and surrounding properties, a couple of young students agreed to be the advance guard, finding jobs there to see how the operations worked.

Brown worked with a gay couple who had come to Tassajara from Esalen (another spiritual center) after working for a few years at the Ranch House Restaurant in Ojai, California, a legendary proto–California cuisine restaurant founded in 1949 by a professional baker named Alan Hooker. Hooker, a vegetarian in the tradition of Southern California's spiritual seekers and health foodists, had taught Ray Herslander and Jimmie Vaughan[51] to bake whole-wheat bread.

"The bread they were making was fabulous," Brown says. It had body and a flavor that was earthy and true, yet it was no wheaten brick. It was like nothing he could find on any grocery-store shelf. He asked the cooks if they could teach him.

"There was no recipe," he says. "You start with some water and you add about this much yeast and flour and this much sweetening and powdered milk. We let it rise as a sponge [a loose, wet, bubbly mass of dough]. Then we added oil, salt, and the rest of the flour. Pretty soon I was washing the dishes and baking the bread." When one member of the couple quit, Brown began making breakfast and lunch, too.

Brown returned to San Francisco at the end of the guest season, and the San Francisco Zen Center purchased Tassajara from its owners that winter. The next year Tassajara inaugurated a pattern it continues today: operating most of the year as a monastery, closed off to the world, and taking in paying guests during the warmer months. When Brown returned the next spring as a full-time monk, because he had worked in the kitchen before, he was named tenzo, or head monastery cook. Only somehow, the spacious old kitchen he had washed dishes in had been gutted and he was forced to cook for forty students and forty guests in a kitchen no bigger than his living room today.

The work was grueling and incessant—it was common for the cooks in those days to work four-days-on, one-day-off shifts cooking six meals a day before meditating all evening. The equipment was rudimentary, and the supplies could grow thin if money or transportation was short. A third of the monks at the time were macrobiotic. Brown says that he was always coming afoul of someone, even over a matter as insignificant as oatmeal: either it was too thick for people who thought they should start their day with easy-to-digest porridge, or too smooth and watery for monks embarking on a day of digging foundations, and if he added raisins, the macrobiotics would tell him he was poisoning them with yinness. For a time, Brown was infamous for his cook's temper.

Brown's bread, though, was great. He and the other cooks baked twenty-four to forty loaves a day, varying the grains and flavors with the cook's whim, and during periods of intense meditation, ravenous monks would bolt up to nine or ten full slices in a few minutes, spread with peanut butter or hummus. A third of the loaves were unyeasted, for the macrobiotic population, and he learned to vary the grains and even incorporate leftover brown rice from the night before to prevent it from going to waste.

During the summer guest season, guests would ask Brown if he could teach them to bake that amazing bread. He instructed dozens of them—free labor!—and began thinking about the fact that there were no detailed baking books on the market that could pass along the necessary knowledge: How to know what eggs or oil did to the bread if you added them. How to knead a lump of dough and know when it was done. How to judge whether loaves were ready to slide into a hot oven.

Encouraged by his teachers, in 1969 Brown wrote a recipe book, codifying the recipe he'd learned by feel into cups and tablespoons. The core of the book was the Tassajara bread method that descended from Alan Hooker. The two-part process—making a sponge from yeast, water, and flour and then mixing in the rest of the ingredients—proved easy for neophytes to master.

As with Cornell bread, the recipe incorporated a large amount of powdered milk—not only did it make the bread smoother and more nutritious, fresh milk was also hard to come by in a remote monastery. Brown also tested out dozens of variations incorporating grains like millet, rye, and oats, as well as sesame meal, cheese, and spices. Unlike for Adelle Davis, flavor came first, and suspect additions were kept to a minimum.

The Zen Center's head monk first sent Brown to Beat poet and publisher Lawrence Ferlinghetti, who wanted to reproduce the manuscript as is, with its sloping lines of handwriting; he thought the amateurish look of it would appeal to people in the communes.[52] Brown wanted something more, well, instructive. So he took the manuscript to Shambhala Publications, located in the basement of a Berkeley bookstore near the UC Berkeley campus. The publisher, Sam Bercholz, flipped through Brown's notes and said, "This is great. I'll give you a hundred-dollar advance and 10 percent royalties. OK?"

OK. Brown insisted on detailed, easy-to-interpret illustrations so people could study what he did with his hands. Bercholz wrapped the book in thick brown paper, with a calligraphic title, and printed the recipes in brown ink to make them more natural-looking. Aspiring bakers who opened the book were greeted with a seductive invitation infused with Zen spirit, not the way Brown's predecessors had begun, with treatises on nutrition or condemnations of commercially bleached white flour. He wrote:

> Bread makes itself, by your kindness, with your help, with imagination running through you, with dough under hand, you are breadmaking yourself, which is why breadmaking is so fulfilling and rewarding.[53]

The first edition was five thousand copies, Brown recalls. By the tenth printing, the runs were more like twenty-five thousand. At last count, *The Tassajara Bread Book* has gone through numerous anniversary editions and something like seven hundred fifty thousand copies. "Somehow the book captured the spirit of the time," he says.

The book and Brown's follow-up, *Tassajara Cooking*, put Shambhala Publications on solid financial footing. Brown continued as a monk, and the tens of thousands of dollars in royalties he donated back to the San Francisco Zen Center helped put it in the black as well. Even as an anonymous monk (his words) Brown says that he began to gain a sense of the book's impact when the letters began arriving. In that first edition, he'd invited people to write to him in care of the publisher, and hundreds of readers responded.

The letters were gushing, grateful, inspiring. "People said the most amazing things," he says: "'I feel like I've re-owned my life from corporate America because I can make bread at home.'"


JUST AS BREAD first became a symbol of freedom, then of a generation's discontent with an impersonal, chemically adulterated food supply, baking whole-wheat bread meant opting out of an economy that made a profit off nutritionally bankrupt foods. It required taking one's food supply back to its roots: whole, virgin foods. Anyone wanting to cut one additional link off the supply chain invested in a grain mill and clamped it to the kitchen counter, feeding wheat and rye berries into the hopper and leaning into the crank as they pushed it around and around.

Some longhair types saw baking as a way to contribute to an alternative economy, one that would support themselves as well as the rest of the community. Between 1970 and 1978, dozens of collective bakeries sprang up, in small college towns as well as major metropolises: In Minneapolis, People's Company. In Tucson, Small Planet Bakery. In Madison, Wisconsin, Nature's Bakery. In Washington, D.C., Women's Community Bakery. In Ann Arbor, Michigan, a bakery collective named Wildflour shared space with the local tofu collective. In Fayetteville, Arkansas, Summercorn Foods was both the bakery and the tofu collective. Many originated with a single recipe: the one they had read in Edward Brown's book.

In Buffalo, New York, in 1975, a couple of coordinators at the North Buffalo Food Co-op and members of the local Sufi community decided to fill the need for good bread. Bill Nowak, a guitarist in local rock bands who was working at the co-op, was living in a cooperative house with a bunch of cooks from a natural-foods restaurant named Greenfield Street. A cook there had displayed a rare talent for whole-grain baking, able to turn out sixty loaves a day while tripping his brains out every shift. But he'd moved on, and the closest bakery for a while was in Rochester, seventy miles away.

Buffalo needed good bread. The group asked themselves, Bill says, "Why not create some employment and some wealth?"

Wealth was desperately needed in Buffalo at the time. The 1970s were the worst decade the city had ever experienced. At the beginning of the twentieth century, heavy industry and Great Lakes shipping had made it a wealthy city of broad boulevards and massive, ornate public buildings. Seventy-five years in, though, the city was writhing and gasping. The steel mills were all closing down, and in the center city, the rates of unemployment and underemployment reached as high as 60 percent.[54] During the 1970s alone, a hundred thousand Buffalo residents moved away.[55]

Industry had turned sections of the city into a toxic wasteland. Lake Erie was so beset by sewage dumping, heavy metals, and algae blooms that entire fish populations had disappeared. The Buffalo River, which had last caught fire in 1968, was black and oily, and residents joked that if you fell in, the only part they'd be able to fish out was your teeth.

And yet Buffalo State, the University at Buffalo, and a smattering of small colleges had incubated a political culture that bubbled with activity—"the Berkeley of the East," one activist claimed.[56] A hip community had settled on the city's west side, and by 1976 it supported three food co-ops, a restaurant, and enough collective enterprises to merit a page of news and events in the local alternative newspaper. A saying circulated among the community: "You have to feed the revolution."

The fledgling bakers armed themselves with some seed funding from one of the co-ops and a copy of *The Tassajara Bread Book*. One of the big student houses allowed the crew into its basement kitchen at night, and they began baking the basic Tassajara whole-wheat bread recipe, selling it to the co-op where Nowak worked. They also spent long nights testing out recipes for other goods that might bring in cash: carob brownies, corn muffins, oat-sunflower cookies, all sweetened with honey or molasses instead of sugar.

"We were getting used to a lot of different foods that we hadn't seen before," Nowak says now. "Some of it had to do with the openness that we were all feeling to any alternative to what we had been fed, because so much of what we had been fed was plastic and military and oppressive and anti-quality. The flavors were good. They were fuller. You had this cultural bias toward anything that you had to struggle with a little bit—like whole-wheat bread versus white bread—but at the same time we were definitely willing to do that because it was proving to be fruitful in so many other areas."

Nowak and his friends found a pizza parlor on Buffalo's east side, scrounged enough money to put down a deposit on the rent and the baking equipment inside, and named the business "Fillmore Yeast," after the rock club in Manhattan. Then the landlord disappeared. So did their down payment. It took another four months to find a new space, a tiny corner spot barely big enough for six workers. To recoup the money stolen from them, Buffalo's co-ops organized a series of fund-raisers and the cash came in. Finally, mid-1976, Yeast West opened.

Like Edward Brown before them, collective bakeries like Yeast West advanced the cause of whole-wheat bread by embracing its flavor over its nutritional value. They incorporated tahini and dates in novel ways, sprouted every grain they came across, and played with the flavors of whole oats and rye until they came up with breads that would rise (if less than Wonder bread) and taste good (once you got accustomed to eating denser, earthier flavors). They resuscitated old American recipes and studied German and Eastern European baking books.

The Sufis eventually moved on, but Nowak stayed for a decade, joined by workers, primarily students and graduates from the local universities, many of them recruited off the bulletin boards at the nearby co-ops.

In that first, cramped space, Yeast West could fit basic ovens—nothing as fancy as the ones the Diggers had appropriated—but they couldn't afford a standing mixer. "You haven't lived until you've kneaded sixty pounds of dough by hand," says Josh Ingram, who joined the crew in 1978 after moving back to Buffalo to care for her mother and her daughter. Kneading could take an hour and a half. "I tried it once by feet," she says. "It felt so good and it took less time because you were putting your weight on it. Nobody wanted to eat it, though."

Yeast West supplied the food co-ops and the restaurant, later moving to a larger space down the block that could support a retail window. The co-op across the street soon dedicated an entire shelf to Yeast West products, and its staff would run across the street to reup if the stock emptied too early in the afternoon. On certain days of the week, cinnamon-raisin bread or sourdough loaves would appear there. Pizza came out once a week. Yeast West concocted apple cakes, cocoshoes (coconut cashew) cookies, familia (muesli), granola, savory vegetable spirals, and "anti-nukes" (carob-chip cookies). One day, Ingram baked up whole-wheat dildos as a joke, and Nowak stuck those onto the co-op shelves, too.

Like many of the 1970s collective bakeries, Yeast West did not generate much in the way of profits. The workers were practically nonprofit, too. After taxes, the full-timers received $40 a week (the equivalent of $157 in 2015 dollars). They invited volunteers to work shifts in exchange for bread.

It wasn't about the money, at least in those days—it was more important to keep the price of a loaf of whole-wheat bread at 79 cents, or 99 cents for the one made with organic flour. "Our impetus is to turn out the best possible products for people at the cheapest possible prices," worker Shari Ser told the *Buffalo Evening News*.[57]

The bakery worker-owners would meet every Tuesday afternoon for all-staff meetings to talk strategy and finances, not to mention what was going wrong and right. Conflicts could result in separate "feelings" meetings, where the aggrieved and the aggrievor would hash out their differences, tears flowing. They strived for gender equality—not to the extent that one bakery in Seattle did, by dressing everyone in skirts—but in terms of making sure everyone did the same hard work and could take on any role they wanted to play. One of the workers, a therapist, came up with a dirge that they'd sing at one another, mostly in jest, sometimes not: "Men are all pi-i-i-gs. Women are all won-der-ful."

What was most important to them was that they had taken charge. As Ser adds today, "If you could control your food, you controlled your body. And if you could control your body, you controlled your life."

Yeast West was providing some respite from the onslaught of chemicals that seemed to taint every can or box in the supermarket. They were making their own money, independent of the corporations that had set Buffalo afire and then left it poor and struggling. They were baking a new world in the ashes of the old, with new flavors, new textures, free of plastic and artifice.

# 4

# Tofu, the Political Dish

A SINGLE QUESTION DROVE FRANCES MOORE Lappé to UC Berkeley's Agricultural Economics Library in 1969: Was the world about to run out of food?

The only people who seemed to have dived into the issue of global hunger before Lappé resurfaced from their books spouting apocalyptic visions of famine on a scale never before seen in human history. The projections were so dire, so fantastical, that she questioned whether they could really be true. Even if global hunger was intractable, at least it might be quantifiable. She armed herself with notebooks, pencils, and a slide rule and descended into the stacks for days on end.

The vast basement library was often empty, its shelves of thick government reports populated by a librarian and perhaps a fellow scholar or two. Adding to the forlorn feeling was the sense that she was alone in this improbable quest for answers, a grad school dropout with no training in agriculture, economics, or global hunger. Almost fifty years on, Lappé admits a second question was propelling her into the stacks. It was the simpler of the two, perhaps, though just as hard to answer in the moment: What was she going to do with her life?

What "Frankie" Lappé discovered in that library—her life's work, as well as an answer that shocked her—and the book she wrote about it, *Diet for a Small Planet*, changed the way millions of Americans thought about how their country produced food. It hit the zeitgeist just as the counterculture was taking up the idea of eating as a political act and converted millions of people to vegetarianism, at least for a year or two.

The unintended impact of her book was almost as great: several of her readers, particularly a young couple in Tokyo and a hippie commune in rural Tennessee, zeroed in on a few short passages in the book and realized they could do something about hunger, too.

Soybeans, they decided, could save the world.

AT THE TIME eureka struck Lappé, a pixieish twenty-five-year-old with speech as fast and precise as her intellect, she had not given much thought to food or cooking. Raised in Fort Worth, Texas, and educated at Earlham College in Indiana, Lappé had moved to Philadelphia after graduation to join the local branch of the Welfare Rights Organization, a late-1960s movement to empower poor people to demonstrate and lobby for adequate income and justice.[1]

"The women I worked most closely with were all African American, all extraordinary, and I just loved them," she says now. "But the woman I felt most emotionally close to died of a heart attack at the age of forty. And I was convinced that Lily died of poverty, not of a heart attack. I was just struggling because I didn't see how the work I was doing was really getting to the root causes."

When her husband at the time, a toxicologist, took a postdoctoral position at UC Berkeley, Lappé enrolled in the School of Social Welfare. Her studies, however, left her rudderless. Poverty seemed like such an amorphous problem—if she couldn't even define it, how could she even work toward a solution? Newspaper headlines delivered the answer, declaring that the planet was no longer able to feed all its human inhabitants. "If I could just understand *why* people were hungry, then that would give me direction," she decided.

The hunger that became Lappé's intellectual polestar wasn't merely the kind that manifested itself in the empty cupboards and welfare-enrollment lines she saw in Philadelphia. This was much bigger. She had just read Paul Ehrlich's book *The Population Bomb*, which had come out in 1968. Its opening words:

> The battle to feed all of humanity is over. In the 1970s the world will undergo famines—hundreds of millions of people are going to starve to death in spite of any crash programs embarked on now. At this late date nothing can prevent a substantial increase in the world death rate.[2]

From that introduction, Ehrlich, a biology professor at Stanford, barreled into an argument that the earth's population was increasing at such a clip that, in 1965, the planet had already bypassed our collective ability to feed ourselves. (The press called Ehrlich a "neo-Malthusian" because he echoed the theories of Thomas Robert Malthus, an early-nineteenth-century British writer who argued that populations tended to grow faster than people's ability to feed themselves.) Famine was already endemic in India and Brazil, Ehrlich wrote, and only a handful of countries—notably the United States—would retain the ability to export food to the rest of the world without sacrificing their own populace. But even the United States was burning through its arable land through erosion and pesticide pollution, which meant the country couldn't stave off disaster through agricultural exports.

Delivering his terrifying conclusions in the manner of a fire-and-brimstone Puritan preacher, the biologist laid out a series of scenarios of what might happen as food shortages grew acute and Famine led the other three Horsemen of the Apocalypse in a berserker's rampage

across the planet. In just one of the scenarios, for example, Ehrlich predicted a war in Thailand, destabilized by the U.S.-Vietnam conflict,
flaring out of control; the Chinese massing at the borders; a panicked
and food-rationed United States dropping nuclear bombs on China;
and dirty-bomb retaliation from the Chinese that would kill 100 million
Americans. By 1974.[3]

That wasn't the only horrific news Lappé was reading. Ehrlich's
fellow members in the Legion of Doomsayers were William and Paul
Paddock, whose *Famine 1975!* was published in 1967. The year 1975 de-
served an exclamation mark, the Paddocks wrote, because it would be
the first time that the United States would no longer be able to supple-
ment the agriculture of countries such as India, Egypt, and Brazil to
keep them politically stable.

The United States, they argued, needed to do some quick-thinking
"triage" to dispassionately separate—in a horrifying exercise of pure
realpolitik—the nations that were already doomed, such as Haiti and
India, from those that were troubled but could be salvaged by mod-
erate food aid, like Tunisia and Pakistan. Influencing the decision,
of course, should be the need to privilege allies with benefits: ones
with natural resources the United States needed or those with military
value.

To anyone watching the news in 1968, everything the Paddocks and
Ehrlich were predicting appeared to be already taking place in Biafra,
a short-lived republic that split off from Nigeria from 1967 to 1970.
During the civil war that ensued, the Nigerians cut off food and other
supplies from the region. Airlifts and evacuations couldn't stop more
than a million people from dying during the conflict. Biafran children
with wrist-thin necks and swollen bellies stared out from *Life* magazine
and the front page of the *Washington Post*.

So with apocalyptic visions and a silent chorus of flat gazes goading
her forward, Lappé stole away to the basement library, reading political

tracts as well as agriculture reports. Slide rule in hand, she attempted to calculate how much food the available land could cultivate.

After running the calculations, a first truth struck: the answer wasn't how much food the earth could produce, it was what we did with it. Lappé linked together a chain of information to argue her case: Examining presidential committee investigations, reports from the U.S. Department of Agriculture and the United Nations, and scholarly journals, she compared the available farmland in the United States to the country's livestock production. From scholarly studies that analyzed the composition of various types of dietary protein, she gleaned an understanding of how animal protein compared to various forms of plant proteins. She consulted other reports to assemble a series of intricate tables on the amino acid composition of various foods.[4]

Lappé felt as if she'd wandered into the forest, stumbled off the path, and stubbed her toe on an abandoned elven treasure hoard. The numbers revealed to her that the neo-Malthusians were wrong. "There's more than enough food to feed everyone, but we're feeding such a huge portion of it to animals," she says now of her discovery, then puts it another way: "If we're creating hunger out of plenty, then we can reverse that. There's nothing inevitable about hunger."

Now, she wasn't the first person on record to come up with this thought. In the 1920s and early 1930s, a group of scientists at the Bureau of Agricultural Economics as well as a health-food-store operator in Los Angeles named Otto Carqué had both come to the conclusion that we would have more food for humans if we fed less of it to cows and chickens.[5] But these warnings were so esoteric only a few people of Lappé's parents' age might have come across them.

Lappé had to get the word out. At first, she figured she'd print it out on a one-page handout and hand it around Berkeley, just one of the many communiqués being argued about over cigarettes and burned coffee. But as her research continued, the handout became a seventy-five-page booklet that she planned to print herself, assuming Berkeley politicos would be her target audience.

As Lappé was arranging for a clean, typed copy to take to the printer in 1970, a friend offered to show it to Ian and Betty Ballantine of Ballantine Books, which had popularized the mass-market paperback. Betty Ballantine fell in love with the ideas in the book. In fact, they had recently had great success with *The Population Bomb;* now they were eager to publish Lappé's rebuttal. Ballantine came to Berkeley to meet Lappé. Lappé cooked a few dishes that she'd been playing with to show her that the diet she was proposing wasn't just a fantasy. In turn, the New York publisher reassured the young Berkeley activist her message would not get watered down or twisted; Ballantine would not alter a word without the author's consent.[6]

One thing, though: Ballantine wanted the book to include recipes. So Frankie Lappé recruited a friend named Ellen Buchman Ewald to help her come up with protein-filled recipes in just a few months. "I grew up in Fort Worth, Texas, with this meatloaf-and-mashed-potatoes diet, and it was so boring," she says. She had some exposure to the hippie alternative; she had baked whole-wheat bread to take to the activists camped out in People's Park, a vacant lot that had been turned into a communal garden and public space, and had tried brown rice and stir-fry at a spiritual vegetarian restaurant near campus. Ewald, however, was immersed in the Berkeley diet. "She was a very experimental cook—everything from soy grits and buckwheat oats, and all these different vegetables, to cooking barley," Lappé says.

There weren't many vegetarian cookbooks available, so the two scoured through cookbooks for recipes they could adapt and asked their friends for suggestions. Lappé's husband, Marc, brought a gram scale home from the lab. Frankie and Ewald consulted Lappé's charts to weigh and measure, cook and calculate, developing dozens of dishes that would let readers put all her theories into practice.

Ballantine published *Diet for a Small Planet* in August 1971, a paperback whose cover was illustrated with a Demeter's crown of grain stalks and bean plants.

"This book is about PROTEIN," it began.

In the United States, Lappé argued, the public and the experts alike assumed that the country's agricultural system was efficient, that farmers were feeding surplus grain and soybeans to animals to supply the market with meat protein. But in fact, animals were driving the agricultural economy, consuming 89 percent of the corn we grew, 87 percent of the oats, and 95 percent of the soybeans that we sold domestically. "Fully one-half of the harvested agricultural land in the U.S. is planted with feed crops," she wrote.

The benefit was *far* from efficient: animals, she noted, were essentially "protein factories in reverse." Americans fed a steer 21 pounds of protein over its life span for each pound of red, richly marbled flesh it would yield at its death. For pigs, the ratio was 8.3 to 1, for chickens 5.5. The grains and legumes that U.S. farmers were feeding to livestock instead of humans, she argued, could resolve 90 percent of the world's protein deficits.

Not only that, Lappé continued, but our idea of the nutritional superiority of meat was false. In the second half of the *Diet for a Small Planet* thesis, she introduced readers to the research she had been studying about the composition of animal and vegetable proteins, writing:

> The proteins our bodies use are made up of twenty-two amino acids, in varying combinations. Eight of these amino acids can't be synthesized by our bodies; they must be obtained from outside sources. These eight essential amino acids (which I will refer to as EAAs) are tryptophan, leucine, isoleucine, lysine, valine, threonine, the sulfur-containing amino acids, and the aromatic amino acids.

To make matters more difficult, our bodies need each of the EAAs *simultaneously* in order to carry out protein synthesis. If one EAA is missing, even temporarily, protein synthesis will fall to a very low level or stop altogether.[7]

To explain what she meant, Lappé came up with an illustration of an eight-pointed Christmas star, each point representing the proportion of amino acids our body's cells need to link together to form a complete protein chain. To illustrate how getting too little lysine, say, would affect the chain, she blacked out the tip of the lysine star at the halfway mark, then did the same to most of the other seven points.

You couldn't just look at the protein content of eggs or kidney beans or spinach and think you were getting the full amount, she informed readers. You had to study the ingredient's "net protein utilization," the amount that could be absorbed. Pork was pretty much a complete protein, which is why humans responded so well to it. So were eggs. In comparison, vegetable proteins—grains, seeds, nuts, legumes—were all missing one or two of the eight essential amino acids, so their profiles looked more like stars that your dog had batted around the house so much she had knocked all the tips off.

The recipes that followed all relied on another conclusion Lappé had come to from the research studies in the Berkeley Agricultural Economics Library: if you ate two imperfect foods together, and one (say, wheat) lacked lysine and the other (say, beans) had lysine up the wazoo, your cells could string together more protein chains than if you had eaten wheat alone. And since beans were short on sulfur-containing amino acids and wheat was long on those very same molecules, it's almost like the two ingredients were two souls separated at birth and only whole once Tinder brought them together.

This principle Lappé called "complementary proteins." At the time, she says, the research suggested you had to eat these complementary vegetable foods together at the same time to get the benefit. (Scientists soon debunked this theory, however, which was based on animal studies; they later discovered that the human body essentially retained excess reserves of amino acids, partially by recycling proteins from the body's own tissues and fluids through the digestive system. Nevertheless, the complementary-protein theory has endured to the present.)[8]

Lappé followed with dozens of tables allowing people to analyze the ingredients in their dinner, as well as general guidelines for classes of foods to be eaten together. If you had corn or rice for dinner, for example, you should complement it with legumes, or perhaps with peanuts and milk. Sesame seeds should be eaten with soybeans and wheat, or maybe milk.

Her tone was cheerful, encouraging, empowering. We can do this! We can use fewer resources, she was telling readers, plus feed the world, reduce our exposure to DDT by eating lower on the food chain, and spend less money at the same time.

Vegetarians since Sylvester Graham's day had put forward scores of arguments that a vegetarian diet would produce vigorous, athletic, fertile bodies, but no one had before made the case with figures that scientific researchers could confirm. More broadly than that, few nutrition writers up until that point had written about food in such overtly political terms. As Lappé telegraphed her intentions for the book in the introduction, her reasoning mirrored the same concerns of a generation rejecting plastic bread and embracing ecological concerns:

> Previously, when I went to a supermarket, I felt at the mercy of
> our advertising culture. My tastes were manipulated. And food,
> instead of being my most direct link with the nurturing earth,
> had become mere merchandise by which I fulfilled my role as
> a "good" consumer. But as I gained the understanding that I
> have tried to communicate to you in the book, I found that I

*was* making choices, choices based on real knowledge about food and about the effect on the earth of different types of food production.[9]

The message she was conveying was that as Americans, our personal consumer choices could have an impact on famine in India and Brazil. That same culinary empowerment squared, in many ways, with what Michio and Aveline Kushi were teaching counterculture kids: that what we physically consumed radiated out into our communities and the world at large. If the fear of pesticides, fertilizers, chemicals, and factory foods was driving us to reject the food that the capitalist-driven food system was selling us, *Diet for a Small Planet* pointed to a positive direction we could take.

And then, Lappé told us how to cook it.

Her recipes produced sturdy fare, packed with the same kinds of additives—soy flour, wheat germ—that health-food nutritionists like Adelle Davis had long trumpeted. Lappé and Ewald protein-boosted every dish. Confetti Rice flecked with vegetables and dried fruits was amped up with mixed nuts and sesame-seed meal. A casserole called Enchilada Bake, more or less a tortilla lasagna, supplemented corn with beans and cheeses. They concocted Peanut Butter Cookies with a Difference, the difference being whole-wheat flour and oats, as well as skim milk powder.

The queen of the protein add-ons, in the cookbook section of *Diet for a Small Planet,* was the soybean. Its superiority was apparent in all the charts: when you looked at the protein content of meats and plants by percentage, soybean flour soared above all the other ingredients, and plain old soybeans beat out turkey, lentils, oats, and milk. Lappé's net protein utilization scale—how "complete" a protein was in its natural state—put soybeans below eggs, cheese, and one or two grains, but well above every other legume or nut. It was not only high in protein, it was also high in all the right amino acids.

Lappé and Ewald added soybeans everywhere: They snuck soy grits into Indian pudding and slipped soy flour into Orange-Sesame Muffins and Cornmeal-Soy Waffles. They cooked whole soybeans with curry and peanuts, formed them into burgers and croquettes, and tossed them into a Mexican pilaf.

Lappé also introduced many readers to something she called "tofu (soybean curd)" in a leafy-green stir-fry. Left-leaning grad students in Berkeley had certainly encountered tofu before. The first shop to sell tofu in America, Wo Sing, opened in San Francisco's Chinatown in 1878, and several factories operated in Chinese and Japanese American neighborhoods around Northern California. Seventh-day Adventist food processors had introduced a sort of canned tofu, colored with pimentos, in 1928 under the brand name La Sierra Soya Cheese, which also inspired numerous imitators. A Los Angeles manufacturer named Matsuda Hinode had been distributing bags of tofu to California grocery stores since 1958, and the same company invented the water-filled plastic tofu tub that most tofu is sold in today in 1966.[10]

The macrobiotics talked up tofu. People who lived in California cities, or who grew up in and around Chinese and Japanese American enclaves, encountered it in markets. But to most Americans soybean curd would have been unfamiliar. "Tofu is truly an excellent protein source," Lappé wrote. "Lightly sauteed with a fresh vegetable accompaniment, one could easily eat 7 ounces of tofu and fulfill 25 to 30 percent of a day's need for protein—at the cost of only about 5 to 7 percent of a day's calorie allotment."[11]

What Lappé only touched on was that by 1970, the United States had become the largest producer of soybeans in the world. The country produced 1.27 billion bushels of soybeans in 1970, doubling soybean yields a decade before.[12] Yet only three groups of Americans were eating soy-beans as food: Asian Americans, Seventh-day Adventists, and health-food faddists. Fifty-six percent of the 1970 crop was crushed, turned into both oil and animal feed; more than 50 percent of vegetable oils in America at that time came from soybeans. In addition, the United States exported almost a third of its soybean crop to the rest of the world.

LAPPÉ SAYS NOW she awaited the publication of *Diet for a Small Planet* with dread, fearing that all it would take was one scientist to read through the book and go: *Lady, you got your facts wrong.* Yet, in the first two years after it was published, the book garnered zero mentions in the major newspapers and not one critical review, positive or negative, in a national magazine.

The book, in those first few years, was all but ignored by the general populace. Lappé, who had given birth to her first child the month before *Diet for a Small Planet* was published, ended up doing just a few speeches at universities and scattered presentations on television and radio.

Most of the producers who booked her misread her message, too, seeing this twenty-seven-year-old, soft-spoken woman as merely the author of a curious cookbook. "I became the queen of the soybean cir-cuit," she later wrote. Instead of quizzing her about eradicating global famine, TV stations asked her to talk to housewives about protein com-plementarity while stirring a pot of beans and rice, which she would have to bring to the studio herself. As she recounted in the 1981 edition of *Diet for a Small Planet,* the opportunities she was given presented her with a quandary:

> Did I refuse to be put in the women's slot on the talk shows, as
> the writer of a "cookbook," or did I seize the opportunity to
> reach out to people who would never pick up my book if they

knew it was about politics and economics? I chose the latter course. From Boston to San Francisco, from Houston to Minneapolis, I appeared on midday and midnight shows, on morning shows, and on the six o'clock news."[13]

The counterculture got the message, though.

"Finally, a response to the questions that have previously gone unanswered regarding the increasing starving multitudes, pesticide residues in foods, and all the latest food trips people have been turning to for whatever reasons," Jill Betts of the *Portland Scribe* wrote in 1972, a review republished in other alternative newspapers.[14]

*Diet for a Small Planet* sold five hundred thousand copies between 1971 and 1973, before the *San Francisco Chronicle*, the *Boston Globe*, and the *New York Review of Books* woke up to its existence, and another five hundred thousand copies by 1977.[15] With the exception of Rachel Carson's *Silent Spring*, no single book had a greater impact on the way her generation thought about food. The phrases "protein factory in reverse" and "complementary proteins" entered the lexicon. *Diet* offered a justification for vegetarianism to thousands of young Americans, something they could show their fretting parents, and converted more than a few of them to a meatless diet, at least for a spell.[16] It sent them, book in hand, to the co-ops and natural-foods stores looking for high-protein ingredients they'd never cooked before.

And in Tokyo, a Buddhist monk from California who was stranded in Japan read *Diet for a Small Planet* and realized his own life's purpose, too: to teach the world what soybeans could do.

WILLIAM SHURTLEFF HAD gone to Japan in 1971 as a sort of reverse missionary, with the intent of studying Zen and the Japanese language before setting up a retreat center for other young American Zen students who were buying plane tickets to Japan and knocking on the doors of tiny monasteries to ask if they could find enlightenment inside their walls. Six feet tall, with a shaved head and cut-glass features, Shurtleff had puckishly arched eyebrows that could have been drawn on by a cartoonist, so perfectly did they frame his intense curiosity.[17]

Born in 1941, he was raised on a two-and-a-half-acre estate in Lafayette, one of the more soigné suburbs east of San Francisco, and graduated from Stanford, where he had studied humanities, physics, and engineering.[18] One of the first to heed John F. Kennedy's call to public service, he joined the Peace Corps in 1963 and was sent to southern Nigeria—the area that would soon be known as Biafra—where he taught high school physics.

Shurtleff returned to Stanford for grad school, moved into a communal household, and plunged into both the political and the spiritual roil of the counterculture: he sent back his draft card and helped publish the much-circulated anti–Vietnam War manifesto *Six Statements for Peace in America*. He dropped acid, studied yoga and Zen meditation, became a vegetarian, and learned to bake (unyeasted) whole-wheat bread from a copy of Ohsawa's *Zen Macrobiotics* that one of his housemates picked up at a bookstore.

But his path away from traditional academia and toward tofu began when Shurtleff organized a series of workshops called Esalen at Stanford in 1968. Seeking to emulate the Big Sur spiritual community, he invited numerous spiritual teachers to give workshops on campus. One was Michio Kushi, who flew from Boston for a weekend of talks on the Unique Principle and the macrobiotic diet. Another guest was Shunryu Suzuki, founder of the San Francisco Zen Center and Tassajara Monastery in California. The latter so impressed the young Shurtleff that he left his studies and moved to Tassajara for a few years; in fact, he roomed with Edward Espe Brown for a spell.

By the time Shurtleff arrived in Japan, on Suzuki-roshi's suggestion, the former grad student and monk was practically destitute. He survived on brown rice, which he had to convince a rice miller to sell him; unmilled rice was so tainted in Japan with memories of wartime poverty that few Japanese ate it. He had been introduced to tofu at Tassajara and discovered that thirty cents' worth of fresh bean curd that he bought at the local tofu shop would supply the day's meals.

His plans were quickly ruptured. On December 4, 1971, Shunryu Suzuki died of stomach cancer in California, leaving the young monk adrift.

Less than four weeks later, the first lighthouse appeared when Shurtleff met Akiko Aoyagi, a fashion designer and spiritual seeker in her own right. If Shurtleff cut an eccentric figure, even among expats, so did Aoyagi among the Japanese. Aoyagi was working for a fashion house and was in the habit of lightening her hair with bleach and wearing tie-dyed maxi skirts. Nine years younger than him, Aoyagi had studied at a Quaker high school and then art school, her final thesis designing clothing for children with physical and mental deficits. She was harboring fantasies of becoming a Catholic nun or joining the Peace Corps in Africa. Her sister set the two up on a date, and despite their external differences—his pursuits ascetic, hers aesthetic—their pursuit of spirituality brought them together, as well as their desire to improve the world around them.

Instead of returning to Tassajara, Shurtleff stayed, for the language and for Aoyagi. She in turn sold all her clothes, quit the fashion company, and moved in with him. The two talked of traveling to India and making the ashram circuit. In the meantime, they began hitchhiking up and down the length of Japan, visiting temples to sit zazen for a spell and move on.

At some point in that year of destinationless pilgrimages, a copy of *Diet for a Small Planet* made its way to Japan and circulated among the expats. Shurtleff read the book with increasing excitement, particularly when he came across Lappé's figures showing that growing soybeans yielded the most protein from one acre of land. "I thought, Wow! That's going to be important in the future," he says now. "Because anything that gives the highest yield is going to be the lowest cost."

He looked at tofu, whose primary virtue was once its price, in a new light. The Biafran war and famine were still fresh in his mind. So was the bodhisattva vow he recited every day: "Beings are numberless; I vow to save them." If practicing the Buddhist ethic of "right livelihood" meant finding ways to relieve the suffering of humans, and if soybeans could relieve some of the hunger that had killed so many of his Biafran friends, then it struck him: he could teach the rich how and why to eat more sustainably, and teach the poor how they could feed themselves.

Frances Moore Lappé's book, he says, was the origin of forty years' work educating the world about all the foods we could make from soybeans.

LIKE LAPPÉ, SHURTLEFF and Aoyagi started modestly, with the idea of self-publishing a small booklet for Americans about tofu. They cooked tofu with more intention, Aoyagi dredging up memories of dishes that she had grown up eating or had read about, and they patronized a small tofu shop near their house with more frequency.

Then, in late 1972, they met with Nahum and Beverly Stiskin, who had started Autumn Press to publish books on macrobiotic cooking and the indigenous Japanese religion Shinto. As Shurtleff later recalled, the meeting was cursory: "[Nahum] quickly looked over the table of contents and a few pages I had written by hand on the subject, then pulled a publishing contract out of his desk drawer and said, 'Please sign here.' I didn't even read the contract. There was no discussion of terms or of an advance—I didn't even know what an advance was. I signed, he signed it, we each took a copy and that was it."[19]

Thus began two and a half years of research and cooking. "Traditional tofu masters," Shurtleff and Aoyagi later wrote in their book, "have a saying that there are two things they will not show another person: how to make babies and how to make tofu."[20] But when the American hesitantly approached Toshio Arai, the owner of San-gen-ya, the couple's local tofu shop, asking if he could apprentice with him in order to write his book, the tofu master agreed. "He would have the honor of being," they wrote, "like Bodhidharma transmitting Buddhism to the East, the transmitter of tofu to the West."[21]

Well before dawn, the American would arrive at the shop to light the fires under the water cauldrons and drain soaked soybeans, slowly pouring them into a stone grinder to produce a creamy white pulp. The apprentice would take notes—Aoyagi sometimes came along, too, to sketch the details—as his master cooked this *go,* or pulp, in water, stirring carefully, then transferred it to a draining sack set in a cedar barrel, pressing the sack to extract the maximum liquid. Then he'd stand at Arai's shoulder as the artisan would add *nigari,* a curdling agent, to the warm soy milk and stir it in with a wooden paddle in just the right way. Once white, amorphous curds formed, the master would pour them into molds, press and cut the resulting tofu, and begin taking it around the neighborhood. Shurtleff would stay through the end of the day, when the laborious process of washing the equipment with the reserved whey was over and a new batch of soybeans was put up to soak.

Between visits, the couple puzzled out how to reproduce this process in a home kitchen—something most Japanese never did—using a blender, small pots and vessels, and a small wooden mold. Aoyagi tested out one method, then another, and Shurtleff would critique the results. It took her more than one hundred times to get a reliable, reproducible method that he could describe in words and she could illustrate with ink-brush sketches.

Aoyagi then began testing recipes in the same way: She started by re-creating the recipes she would see in tofu shops, finding uses for soybeans at all points during the process—the beans, the leftover pulp, the soy milk, and the tofu in all its different varieties, from quivering kinogoshi (silken) tofu to pressed firm. She fried it, baked it, scrambled it, formed it into patties, creamed it, fermented it. She would document each recipe in a mix of English and Japanese, and they'd rate the recipe on a scale of 1 to 5, remaking certain promising recipes four or five times until each earned the highest marks.

As they continued on, Shurtleff pressed his girlfriend to find Western recipes, even though she had never visited the United States. So she pored over a copy of *The Joy of Cooking* and picked out dishes she thought she could remake with tofu, such as tofu spreads, tofu loaves, tofu-stuffed green peppers, cooked apples with fried tofu chunks, and whipped tofu cream. In the meantime, she was illustrating recipes as she went, up to ten drawings at a stretch, helping Shurtleff translate documents, and taking care of the house. The two of them worked fourteen hours a day.

Shurtleff's fascination with soybeans evolved into a collector's insatiable hunger for more information. The couple also undertook a second study of miso, a paste of cultured soybean and various other grains that the Japanese use to flavor soups and dressings, marinate meats and vegetables, and season sautés. During the warm months, they traveled farther and farther afield from Tokyo to chase down regional variations in tofu and miso. The former hippie assumed they could hitchhike, but no one would pick up a six-foot-tall bald white guy, so Aoyagi would stand cheerfully in the road, waving to passersby until a car stopped and her boyfriend would pop out of the underbrush.

Sometimes they would stay in Buddhist temples, sitting in meditation with the monks. Other times, they'd make arrangements with a tofu maker to come observe him, starting at three or four in the morning. Rather than disturb a monastic community, they'd roll out their sleeping bags and crash in the open fields—Aoyagi remembers waking up one cold, wet morning with their bags covered in snails—or sometimes in graveyards. They hiked up into the mountains to find women making country-style tofu, graced with the smoke of the open fire, and voyaged to an ashram on a tiny island at the southern tip of the country to observe the Japanese beatniks who lived there making tofu with seawater, another method almost lost to time.

As they traveled and studied, cooked and drew, the tofu book grew from a few recipes to five hundred. Shurtleff wrote a long, impassioned introduction whose gist was pulled straight from *Diet for a Small Planet*:

> In America, 95 percent of all non-exported soy protein ends up as feed for livestock, and of this, 77 to 95 percent is irretrievably lost in the process of animal metabolism. . . . These losses, creating the appearance of scarcity in the midst of actual plenty, are a direct result of our failure to understand and make use of the soybean's great potential as a food.[22]

The promise of tofu, he wrote, wasn't just that soybeans contained a complete protein, or that tofu was far more digestible and malleable than the unprocessed legume. It wasn't just that anyone in America could make or cook with this reliable, cheap food. Shurtleff saw an even bigger picture: the equipment needed to produce tofu commercially was low-tech and straightforward enough that anyone living in a population-stressed, famine-threatened region—Nigeria, Brazil, Bangladesh—had the means to keep their community alive.

As the book was coming together in 1974, Shurtleff began corresponding with Laurie Sythe Praskin, a twenty-one-year-old living on a commune in rural Tennessee. The six-hundred-some people who lived there, she wrote to him, had come to exactly the same conclusion as he had about how soybeans could prevent famine. While Shurtleff and Aoyagi were translating thousands of years of Japanese artisanship into recipes, Praskin's commune was eating soybeans in any form they could get. In fact, as Praskin explained to him, they were living off soybeans and little else.

LAURIE SYTHE PRASKIN—well, she was Laurie Sythe then—arrived at the Farm in Summertown, Tennessee, in 1973, at the age of nineteen, with nothing but her backpack. She hadn't planned to show up with so little. She'd carefully packed supplies into two giant bags and stored her belongings in the cargo container of the Greyhound bus she took across the country. Somewhere between the Rockies and the Plains, she loaned a Thomas Merton book to a fellow traveler, forgetting that she had left her luggage tags in the book to mark her place. When the passenger got off, long before the bus hit Nashville, he took the luggage tags and snuck off with all her belongings.

It was not an auspicious introduction to a place where she would live for most of the next decade. But it was in keeping, at least, with the life she would lead there.

Praskin had tracked the founding of the Farm through her brother, Dan Sythe, who joined the community back when it was just a group of heads attending lectures that Stephen Gaskin was giving to hippies in San Francisco.[23]

Gaskin—known throughout the counterculture as just "Stephen"— was much older than most of the commune members who followed his teachings. Born in 1935, he served in the Marines for three years and drifted out to the Bay Area after he was discharged. He earned an MFA in creative writing at San Francisco State, where he then taught freshman English in the mid-1960s. In his early thirties, the professor followed his students to the Haight-Ashbury when the neighborhood was a colorful, gently psychedelic community, before the Be-In and the Summer of Love made the scene famous and then destroyed it.

Gaskin's attempts to teach within the academic system faltered as he dropped more and more acid and traveled further into the astral spheres. However, in 1967, he signed up for a Monday-night slot at the free, volunteer Experimental College that had formed around the campus. The format of his class would be one part lecture to three parts discussion, turned-on kids rapping with Gaskin about the drugs, the sex, and the music they encountered in the Haight-Ashbury. Their leader would help them recast the psychedelic and the corporeal in terms of the spiritual. Together the group read the *Tao Te Ching*, Buddhist texts, and fairy tales.

Gaskin's Monday-night class swelled over the next three years until it took over an auditorium that seated fifteen hundred. Photos of the classes showed a telephone pole of a man, with wispy long hair and beard, bones pushing through his white turtleneck, sitting cross-legged onstage at the center of a human mandala made of concentric rings of hairy twenty-year-olds. Each class began with a giant OM, and then Stephen would invite the discussion to begin.

Gaskin wasn't just a compelling orator—the measured, low-voiced kind, not a rafter shaker—but a brilliant teacher as well. He'd face the mass of stoned bodies with a benevolent half smile, calm as can be, taunting them politely to ask him anything. He didn't just parry every question, he thrived on all the zigs and zags the conversation would take. Bible verses and stories of the Zen patriarchs peppered his responses, Gaskin interpreting them through the lens of a man who had rewired his circuits with LSD, returned to the day-to-day, and was trying to make sense of the profound and visceral lessons acid had taught him.

We monkeys, as Stephen called humans, live in great fields of energy, receiving and exchanging energy through the focus of our attention. "When they say that man does not live by bread alone they mean that we're kind of vibratory amphibians," he would explain to an audience in 1970, "and part of our amphibious body lives here in this medium, but part of us is electrical and vibratory, and that's a whole world there, and we live in that world, too."[24] And as anyone who had gotten really, really stoned had realized: we are telepathic.

Tripping was one way to show people how to bring ourselves to higher energetic states, but it was easy to lose those lessons in the colored lights and squiggles. We had to come down to soar higher. On the material and the astral plane, our goal as humans was to change the world for everyone.

Gaskin impressed a group of Christian pastors so much that, in 1970, they helped him set up a tour around the United States, talking to religious groups, universities, and community centers. When he told the class that he was going to shut it down for four months, some of the most faithful were so distraught they asked if they could travel with him. He agreed. Two hundred fifty of his students shed their belongings and bought sixty used buses with the money, organized themselves into carloads, and met on October 12, 1970, to set out across the United States. The Caravan, as they called it, would visit forty cities in four months, attracting considerable attention as it snaked across the country.

Ten days after returning to San Francisco, the Caravan decided they'd drive back to Tennessee, where land was cheap and the people had seemed friendly, to see if they could form some kind of permanent community. After a few weeks in Nashville, one of the members walked into a guitar shop to sell his old electric guitar for food money, and he charmed the woman who owned the shop so much she offered them a spot on her land in Summertown, sixty-five miles southwest of Nashville in Lewis County, while they hunted for property.

In August 1971, a thousand-acre parcel next door to their temporary home came on the market, and they scraped together savings and a few inheritances and bought it. From this moment on, the group would practice total communal living, sharing every penny in what they called "voluntary poverty." They considered the commune, in fact, a family monastery. They called themselves the Technicolor Amish.

Lewis County was, and still is, one of the poorest communities in Tennessee. The center of Summertown at the time was a decrepit general store, where the locals would sit around the potbellied stove, greeting visitors with wary stares. They spoke in vowels that rolled around their palates like pinballs. In those first few weeks after the Caravan arrived, the roads would clog up with local sightseers, some of them with shotguns; rumors of drugs, Commies, and freaky orgies abounded. The plot of land the Farm had purchased was made of wide, fallow fields interspersed with blackjack oak, with a large stream running through the community. Near the entrance stood an old house; they installed a gate and a gatekeeper in the house, and parked their buses beyond.

So here is the situation that some two hundred fifty young college grads, plus their slightly older teacher and a clutch of small children, found themselves in—on a plot of untested farmland, with their seed money gone, living in school buses and tents. Add to that another complicating factor: they had all become vegan.

"PURE VEGETARIANS," THEY called themselves. No meat, no dairy or eggs, no honey. Avoiding animal products squared with their ethos of clearing the vibes by living free of violence. As Stephen put it, "I'm as telepathic with animals as I am with people and it's weird to eat them."[25] *Diet for a Small Planet*, which circulated around the community, also influenced their decision; they wanted to eat low on the food chain, and Farm books often repeated Frances Moore Lappé's truism that land planted with soybeans could feed ten times as many people as land used to raise cattle.[26]

The Farm members set to work changing the world through their own example and would not stop for the next twelve years. They planted the fields, growing acres of sweet potatoes and canning vegetables to feed themselves through the winter. Neither kept them from some brutal bouts of hunger. One year, a truckload of wheat berries that someone had managed to secure kept them alive until spring. Another year they lived off chewy textured vegetable protein "steaks."[27] A few people got scurvy; others collapsed from lack of salt.[28]

During that time, Stephen acted, in one member's words, as both their pastor and their CEO. At the beginning his authority was absolute— today, some members wonder whether they were a cult or not—but unlike many cult leaders, Stephen and his family lived everything they preached from the first day to the last.

By the time the Farm community arrived, Lewis County had been shedding children for decades, moving to the cities to find work, and there was a dearth of young, able bodies to do hard labor. The Farm sent work crews to circulate around the county, not just to bring in enough cash to buy what the community couldn't grow but to serve as emissaries. A couple of local farmers hired them on jobs—at a fourth of the going rate, no less—and reported to other farmers that the Farm kids were pleasant and hardworking, and never showed up late or too hungover to bale hay. Another crew, led by a couple of trained builders, did construction and renovation work.

Two of Gaskin's edicts would shape the community in untold ways. The first was "If you were sleeping with someone, you were engaged, and if you were pregnant, you were married," which was enforced with dozens of legal marriages. The other was to ban birth control and abortion. Babies became one of the most prolific crops the Farm produced. Margaret, Stephen's wife at the time, and Ina May, who became his legal wife a few years later, led the efforts to oversee all these births safely and to feed both adults and children, given their exotic, largely understudied diet.

Margaret's research, which included correspondence with UNICEF and study of USDA reports and scholarly journals, led her to establish a diet centered on soybeans and nutritional yeast.

Soybeans were everywhere in Tennessee, sold as cheap animal feed. In the early days, people on the Farm could boil them up, grind them into grits, and bake crude soufflés with soy flour. There were just two critical problems with soybeans: Uncooked beans contain a trypsin inhibitor, which slows the body's absorption of a specific amino acid, a problem that was easily solved by cooking them long enough. If you didn't cook them until, as the Farm members would repeat to newcomers, "you can squish one between your tongue and the roof of your mouth,"[29] they were barely palatable as well and rumbled all the way through the digestive tract. Cooking soybeans to that point, though, could take eight hours in a regular pot. A few groups coordinated overnight cooking shifts, but within a few months, households had scrounged up pressure cookers, which shortened the cooking time to forty-five minutes.

Margaret also learned from the nutritional charts that a vegan diet would leave them deficient in vitamin $B_{12}$. In the beginning, Farm folk believed that they could get this crucial element from nutritional yeast.[30] By the time they learned that yeast organisms generate other B vitamins and that most nutritional yeast was actually fortified with $B_{12}$, they'd cottoned to another of the ingredient's key characteristics: it contained loads of free glutamic acid, an amino acid with huge umami-bestowing powers. The more you added to a dish, the more savory it tasted.

Health-food pundits like Gaylord Hauser or Adelle Davis used yeast by the tablespoon. The Farm members used it by the cup to make fake cheese and yeast gravy, which sounds like the most disgusting sludge on Earth until someone who knows how to toast it just so makes it for you, and then you realize the stuff can actually be delicious.[31]

The dish that quickly came to define Farm cuisine was soybean tortillas. They emerged during the time when two hundred fifty people were living out of buses, tents, and lean-tos, cooking over campfires, with a few outhouses and a water capacity so paltry that the lucky would only wait an hour for a shower. Vegetables would come and go, but larders were always stocked with soybeans, whole-wheat flour, and margarine. Cook up a stack of tortillas, spoon on some squishy soybeans, and top it with a few tablespoons of nutritional yeast for flavor, and there you were. By the second summer, when the fields were producing tomatoes, soybean tortillas could be garnished with canned salsa as well.

So you can understand, perhaps, what a godsend it was when Laurie Praskin learned how to make big batches of tofu.

PRASKIN MOVED ONTO the Farm from Los Altos, California, just south of San Francisco, with her older brother's blessing and her father's fury. Her parents wanted her to be a nurse, and in fact, she had studied nutrition and worked as a nurse's aide during her freshman year of college. But that first year of college was a bit of a disaster. She dropped out, went to visit her brother on the Farm, and fell in love with the spirit of the community. "I liked what they were trying to do, and the fact that there was this group of people really trying to do something with a purpose," she says. "I really wanted a sense of purpose. I think that is pretty normal for nineteen. They were trying to do something that would maybe serve humanity."

She returned to California, packed her bags, and got on the bus, thinking that instead of studying nursing she'd work in one of the clinics that Ina May Gaskin and a couple of the doctors in the community had founded. However, when she arrived, penniless, she moved into a tent with a group of other unmarried singles and volunteered to work at the Soy Dairy.

The Soy Dairy was the work of a Farm resident named Alexander Lyon, who had a doctorate in microbiology. Margaret Gaskin had encouraged Lyon to travel to Nashville to conduct research on soy foods. He found himself corresponding with Seventh-day Adventists in Loma Linda, California, as well as scientists at Cornell University and the USDA Northern Utilization Research and Development Division in Peoria, Illinois. Both research institutes had been studying traditional Asian methods of preparing soybeans since the 1950s, examining how to prepare them commercially in the United States.

From their work, Lyon first learned the principles of making soy milk. The Farm members had become expert scavengers, scouring scrap yards and abandoned farmsteads for anything they could cobble together into housing and equipment. Lyon's first soy-milk-making setup involved a peanut grinder, a fifteen-gallon coffeepot, and a washing machine that they ran on the spin cycle to use as a de facto centrifuge. It was replaced by salvaged equipment from a defunct goat dairy.

The nineteen-year-old Praskin figured she would channel her nutrition studies into helping the community, in part because the food was so sparse. "We were living on pressure-cooked soybeans and soy flour soufflés," she says, the latter dull gritty cakes, "and when I lived in the Park Tent, we loved [a resident named] Robert Levi because his mother sent us care packages of ketchup or garlic powder." It was the only seasoning they'd see for months.

So she learned, from Lyon, how to make soy milk safely, guided by the same principles that Lyon had learned in his microbiology lab. Praskin woke up at 3:30 each morning to make her way in the pitch black down the dirt paths to the Soy Dairy. There, a crew of four or five would fire up the boilers, heat giant kettles of water, and painstakingly grind soybeans they had soaked overnight. With their rudimentary equipment, it would take hours to heat the water and press the soy milk, and even more to scrub all the equipment spotless. They'd fortify the milk with vitamins A and $B_{12}$, pour it into ten-gallon dairy jugs, and finally drag it up to the road to wait for a tractor to trundle by and give

them a ride to the Farm store, which was the central distribution center
for the community.

She was working well into the evenings, and in the humid summers
the heat in the dairy was brutal. But there was something she loved
about it—the meditative quality of those hours, the camaraderie among
the crew, the sense of purpose she had been craving.

The soy milk was a hit with the families. Households would come
down to the store to fetch their allotment of food and wander home
with buckets of soy milk, which they would either serve to their families for breakfast or cook if it soured—few of the tents or shacks had
refrigeration—into a tart soy cheese. The Soy Dairy also learned to
make yogurt and frozen "Ice Bean," though they reserved the dessert
for sickly children and adults too ill to keep much nutritious food down.

Lyon learned of another curiosity that would come to define the
Farm's culinary legacy. The scientists he corresponded with described
an Indonesian food that was almost impossible to find in America: cakes
of cooked soybeans cultured with the *Rhizopus oligosporus* mold. After
forty-eight hours in a warm room or incubator, the mycelium of the
mold forms a thick white coating that binds the cake together, gives it
a nutty flavor, and renders the soybeans more digestible. The scientists
called it tempeh.[32] Lyon helped a Soy Dairy worker named Cynthia
Bates piece together a lab for culturing spores and tempeh production
equipment out of discarded lab equipment and other machinery the motor pool helped them construct out of spare parts.

By 1975, Praskin's life wasn't quite as deprived as it had been. Sure,
she was still working fourteen-hour days, but everyone was, playing
music with one another in the rare empty hours and, increasingly,
shepherding small children around the property. While the majority
of newcomers were still bunking in army tents, Praskin had found her
way into a group house cobbled together out of reclaimed wood and
scrap metal, which would eventually house forty people. She was also

scheming up a way to move a handsome farmer named Alan Praskin, whom she'd met at one of the Farm's satellite communities in Florida, into her household.

Lyon had left operations of the Soy Dairy to her, its most devoted crewmember, the one who showed up every morning without fail and taught newcomers how to help out. Her CB radio handle was now "Bean Queen," and the dairy was working with a couple of Farm engineers to bring the production of soy milk up to eight hundred gallons a week.

That may seem like a lot of soy milk, but it could barely keep up with the growth of the community. The Farm's two hundred fifty inaugural members had swelled to six hundred by 1974, and they were growing eighty-seven acres of soybeans for food, when Gaskin encouraged the community to publish a book all about the place. *Hey Beatnik! This Is the Farm Book*, filled with folksy essays and Gaskin's philosophizing, illustrated with hundreds of photos of beautiful longhairs in their pastoral setting, was one of the first salvos in the community's efforts to teach the outside world about its ethos of voluntary poverty and communal living.

At the time, many of the members considered Gaskin's portrayal of their lives "airbrushed." There was certainly little mention of the muddy roads, the chiggers and ticks, the ice-crusted tents, the fatigue of dawn-to-dusk shifts in the field. But *Hey Beatnik!* did lay out specific details on the practical matters of surviving, making soy milk, farming for six hundred, and home birth. It also issued an invitation: "Hey, ladies! Don't have an abortion, come to the Farm and we'll deliver your baby and take care of it, and if you ever decide you want it back, you can have it."[33] The Farm's antiabortion stance set them at odds with many other liberals their age, given the recent Supreme Court decision to legalize abortion in *Roe v. Wade*, but it helped endear the community to their conservative Tennessee neighbors.

After the book came out—followed in 1975 by the self-published *The Farm Vegetarian Cookbook*, compiling recipes coaxed out of the best cooks in the community, and a pamphlet titled *Yay Soybeans! How You Can Eat Better for Less and Help Feed the World*—the flow of aspiring members increased. Single mothers did indeed make their way to Summertown, though few actually left their children to be fostered. By 1975, the commune had seven hundred fifty residents; by 1977, eleven hundred, half of them minors. Six thousand visitors spent at least a night there over the life of the commune, and it was common to have two hundred visitors staying on the Farm at once.[34]

Somehow, Bill Shurtleff heard about the Farm in Japan, most likely from the scientists he and Alexander Lyon both corresponded with. He sent a letter to the Farm, and Laurie Praskin answered it. Their correspondence grew more frequent, as they wrote to each other about what they were doing, sharing their hopes that soy protein would one day help solve global hunger.

When Shurtleff sent Praskin prepublication pages from *The Book of Tofu*, she was thrilled. The Northern Californian had encountered Japanese American tofu in grocery stores before moving to Tennessee, and some of the households were experimenting with a Seventh-day Adventist recipe for bean curd made by boiling soy flour, a method akin to making polenta. Praskin was enraptured by the peaceful, Zen-inflected picture that Shurtleff and Aoyagi painted of the tofu maker's craft and was eager to add tofu to the Farm's diet.

She practiced stirring coagulant into larger and larger batches of warm soy milk and convinced a few machinists to build large molds and a press to turn the curd into cakes. The Farm store added tofu to the tempeh and soy yogurt that they were distributing—the communards still subsisted on soybean tortillas, sweet potatoes, and greens in the summer, but once or twice a week, they were given a reprieve with tofu for stir-frying or scrambling.

Praskin sent Shurtleff in turn a copy of *The Farm Vegetarian Cookbook* with a note directing him to its two-page description of tempeh.

*Tempeh? What was tempeh?* Shurtleff's collector brain stomped on the accelerator.

The book mentioned that tempeh was Indonesian, Shurtleff says, so he phoned the Indonesian embassy and asked, "Do you have anybody in Tokyo who makes tempeh?" Within five minutes of receiving Praskin's package, Shurtleff had secured an invitation to a tempeh-making demonstration, and he delayed the publication of *The Book of Tofu* in order to shoehorn in a few pages of information about tempeh.[35]

OVER THE NEXT three years, Shurtleff and Aoyagi and the Farm would become the soybean's biggest missionaries. The world travelers spread the gospel while the family monastery attracted converts.

Autumn Press published Bill Shurtleff and Akiko Aoyagi's book in December 1975, and the couple immediately turned their attention to finishing a follow-up book about miso, which would come out in September 1976. To publicize their book in the United States, the Shurtleffs took an epic road trip.

Their publisher secured huge, multi-issue features about the book in counterculture publications like *Mother Earth News* and the macrobiotic *East West Journal*. Shurtleff in turn placed small announcements in the backs of magazines like *Prevention*. It may be hard to remember or believe, depending on your age, but before the Internet arrived people actually pored over the classifieds and announcements, seeking books, foods, housing, love, spiritual enlightenment, and entertainment. Shurtleff's announcement read:

> For the past four years, I have been living in Japan, studying and writing books about tofu and miso. This summer, the Japanese cook and artist with whom I have been working, Akiko Aoyagi, and I will be visiting communities and natural food

centers around the United States teaching about these fine, traditional soybean foods so high in protein and low in cost. Anyone interested in learning to cook with or prepare tofu or miso
on a family, community, or commercial scale, please write . . . [36]

More than a hundred people responded. Shurtleff offered them a deal:
if you put us up, pay for the venue, and publicize the event, promising
not to charge more than a dollar per person, then we'll send you promotional materials that you can staple onto telephone poles and co-op
bulletin boards. An itinerary of sixty-four stops emerged, looping all the
way around the country.

Shurtleff and Aoyagi flew to California that fall and bought a white
Dodge Tradesman van with forty thousand miles on it, stacking copies
of *The Book of Tofu* and the just-published *Book of Miso* to the roof. A
Berkeley woodworker named Ganesha designed a perforated pinewood
tofu box sized just right to mold one-pound blocks of soybean curd. The
couple assembled tofu kits with Ganesha's boxes, bags of soybeans, and
small bags of nigari tofu coagulant to sell on the side. Their cargo was
so heavy the van blew a tire.

On September 29, 1976, Shurtleff and Aoyagi embarked on a four-
month, fifteen-thousand-mile journey. It took them north to Seattle,
east through Minnesota, meandering through the Midwest and out to
New York. They headed south as far as Florida, then slowly worked
their way back to California through Louisiana, the Kansas plains, and
the high desert of the Southwest. The couple stayed in private houses,
mobile homes, Quaker communes, dormitories, houseboats, and Zen
centers. They conducted interviews with counterculture magazines and
television stations at the stops. Sometimes three hundred people showed
up, sometimes five or six. The couple would drive, unload, meet, speak,
work on another manuscript in every free moment, get up, drive again.

At each stop, Shurtleff would begin the presentation by talking about world hunger and the vast waste of resources that meat production entailed. He would show a series of slides demonstrating how tofu and miso are made. At the intermission, Aoyagi would serve a simple creamy tofu dip with potato chips and cut vegetables. Then Shurtleff would field the flood of questions, and Aoyagi would sell the books and tofu kits.

Their audiences, Shurtleff recalls, were almost overwhelmingly young and counterculture. Many had never heard of soybean curd before, let alone tasted the Americanized dip that Aoyagi was making for them. Older meat eaters tended to screw up their mouths after downing a few bites, saying they still preferred sour cream. Vegetarians and vegans, however, were ecstatic, and not just at the prospect of finding a new food source.

"On the tour, I had the feeling, we're onto something here," Shurtleff says now. "We're on the right track. This is what young people in America want. I was one of them, and so I thought like they did. I knew that they wanted to start their own businesses, and I knew that they wanted to eat vegetarian and I knew that they were hungry for information." One more way that the counterculture could take control of their lives.

Aoyagi in turn remembers how grueling it was to make sixty-four stops in four months. And not just because of the work itself. Shortly after their stop in Minnesota, Shurtleff's mother died of colon cancer, but they were unable to break their schedule, giving presentations that night and the next. In the final month of the trip, Aoyagi developed a cold that turned into bronchitis so acute that she broke a rib coughing. Still, they forged through it all, earning $8,000 in the process—a year's salary back then.

The midpoint of their tour brought Shurtleff and Aoyagi to the Farm, where they spent two weeks.[37] Praskin found them a spot in her house, and so they bedded down in a nook off the main room, separated by a hanging blanket. The visit wasn't easy—Aoyagi found the community friendly but *way* too crowded for her, and Shurtleff encountered the

Farm's famous radical honesty when a couple of members confronted him on his prickly personality—but he was able to study tempeh making with Cynthia Bates and look over Praskin's nascent tofu operation. Despite the discomfort of the stay, it forged Shurtleff and Praskin's bond of common purpose.

The tour was successful beyond even Shurtleff and Aoyagi's imagination. They had judged the country's mood correctly. The book sold thirty thousand copies in the first year alone, and after Ballantine Books, publishers of *Diet for a Small Planet,* came out with a pocket paperback, sales jumped into the hundreds of thousands. The couple considered themselves tofu's Johnny Appleseeds, and indeed, Shurtleff claims that at almost every one of their sixty-four stops, a small tofu shop sprang up within the succeeding year.

In the decade after *The Book of Tofu* was first published, Shurtleff counted the publication of fifty tofu cookbooks.[38] Recipes like the 1979 *Tofu Cookbook*'s tofu ravioli, tofu-stuffed zucchini, tarragon tofu dressing, and eggless Eggnog Mousse would reframe soybean curd for mainstream American palates. Many more vegetarian cookbooks incorporated tofu as a banal, everyday ingredient.

The 1975 edition of *The Book of Tofu* included a directory to fifty-four tofu shops in the United States, all owned by Japanese Americans or Chinese Americans, most on the coasts and in Hawaii. Just seven years later, Shurtleff counted more than 170.[39] Hinode, the plastic tofu tub pioneer from Los Angeles, was the largest manufacturer in the country at that time, but companies like White Wave in Boulder, Wildwood in the San Francisco Bay Area, and Nasoya in rural Massachusetts would overtake it in sales.[40]

The Shurtleffs would go on to publish technical books on tofu and tempeh production to help all these fledgling producers out, and in 1978 they organized a group of these counterculture businesses in Ann Arbor, Michigan, who collectively founded the Soycrafters Association.

The couple settled in the suburbs of San Francisco where Shurtleff had grown up, and Shurtleff's collection of data grew into one of the world's most comprehensive archives.

As Bill Shurtleff and Akiko Aoyagi were to tofu, the Farm was to tempeh: the incubator, both literally and figuratively. The first counterculture articles about tempeh told readers they could request *Rhizopus oligosporus* spores from the USDA. The scientists soon told the Farm they were overwhelmed with requests and passed the task on to the commune. Cynthia Bates and Alexander Lyon built a new lab to incubate and freeze-dry mold spores and started selling tempeh-making kits through mail order, bringing the Farm thousands of dollars it desperately needed. The Farm's Book Publishing Company followed up on *Hey Beatnik!* and *The Farm Vegetarian Cookbook* with recipe books for tofu and tempeh, all of which sold well.

Praskin left the Soy Dairy with her husband in 1979 to join Plenty, the Farm's nonprofit relief wing, in Guatemala for several years. The Farm was sending workers down to remote villages there to rebuild after a disastrous earthquake, and the volunteers asked Praskin to set up a tofu shop there to help the Mayan-speaking villagers make tofu and Ice Bean.[41]

In 1983, stressed to the breaking point by bad investments and overpopulation, the Farm would give up radical communal living. It voted to end communal spending and asked every resident to pay his or her own way. The painful decision sent a thousand members out across the country, leaving a skeleton population of several hundred in Tennessee. (Two of them, in fact, took over the Soy Dairy and ran it for the next few decades before passing it on to the next generation.)

But before the "Changeover," as the Farm community calls the breakup, it would train a number of new-generation tofu and tempeh makers—including Jeremiah Ridenour, who went on to run Wildwood, and Michael Cohen, founder of Lightlife Foods—as guests or short-term residents, learning at the elbow of Laurie Praskin, Cynthia Bates, Alexander Lyon, and the Soy Dairy crew.

ONE OF THE best-known meat substitutes in America owes its existence to Frances Moore Lappé, the Shurtleffs, and the Farm.

Seth Tibbott was a Wittenberg University student who became a vegetarian in the early 1970s after reading *Diet for a Small Planet*. Shortly afterward, he came across Gaskin's writings, and the teacher's synthesis of spiritual traditions and psychedelic lessons spoke to him. It was the guru era, he says, and Gaskin was his. In that spirit, he went vegan, despite the fact that it meant he was mostly surviving on soybeans and Nilla wafers. There were no vegetable burgers in stores, and the only fake meats he could heat and cook were Adventist substitutes that came in cans.

When he spent a summer working as an environmental educator for the Youth Conservation Corps in eastern Tennessee in 1977, he took a weekend off to visit the Farm with the thought that he might move there permanently, returning for a week a year or two later.

Those stays killed that fantasy. Like most visitors, he was assigned to one of the twenty-person army tents. The experience was excruciating. "They would work really hard all day, and then at night they'd sit around this table and critique each other because they were all about telling the truth," he says now. "They'd smoke up all this reefer and start telling everybody where it's at. It was uncomfortable."

Food was scarce and basic. However, at the Farm someone told him about tempeh, and when he returned to his Youth Conservation Corps station he sent for a packet of spores and directions. He mixed up a batch and let it culture for a day—it was easy, given the humid heat of a Tennessee summer—and cooked the resulting tempeh cake with fresh corn and okra. "It was like this revelation," he says. "Up to that point, the main way I'd been getting protein was cooking soy grits and making these soy burgers. It was laborious and they were okay, but not real digestible or delicious. You make this stuff, though, and throw it in a pan, and it tastes delicious and feels good." In short, tempeh, like tofu, was one of the first vegetarian convenience foods.

After Tibbott moved to Oregon to work as an environmental educator in the mid-1970s, making tempeh became a hobby, a way to make some food for himself that didn't scour itself through his intestines the way soy grits did. Funding for environmental education was drying up, and he decided to make tempeh to support his activism, one more way to help humans live more lightly on the earth. His first incubator was an out-of-service refrigerator that he lined with Christmas lights to heat the interior up to the perfect temperature. In 1980, Tibbott settled in the Hood River Valley, a ninety-minute drive east of Portland, where he built a treehouse to live in. He rented an abandoned elementary school for $150 a month to transform into Turtle Island Foods' tempeh factory, and Alexander Lyon moved to Oregon to work with him. Tibbott called Bill Shurtleff on the phone one night to ask for advice, and the two began a telephone correspondence that lasted for decades.

The income was barely enough to survive on, Tibbott says, but it was just lucrative enough to keep him from quitting. Then, one Thanksgiving in the 1990s, Turtle Island Foods played with a recipe for a seitan-tofu meat analogue that was circulating in vegetarian circles and sold it as a frozen roast he called "Tofurky."[42] Within a few years his fortune changed.

IN SOME WAYS, the spread of mass-market tofu was an ironic legacy for *Diet for a Small Planet:* a book written to unleash great societal shifts inspired the creation of new ingredients for Americans to buy. For all the book's success, per capita meat consumption in the United States did not drop.[43] At the same time, neither Ehrlich's nor the Paddocks' doomsday scenarios came true, thanks in large part to the green revolution in Asia and South America. Even as the Cassandras wailed, agronomists were introducing new varietals of grains like rice and wheat that required more chemical fertilizers and machinery to cultivate but produced yields big enough by the early 1970s to relieve the population pressures.

Soybeans did not save the planet, or at least they haven't yet. But they helped a small cadre of tofu and tempeh makers give the U.S. public tools—in the form of nutritious, digestible, reasonably appealing foods—that made it easier for them to go meatless or eat less meat, eventually growing into a 4.5-billion-dollar industry in the United States.[44]

As the 1970s progressed, Frances Moore Lappé moved further away from teaching Americans about complementary proteins and closer to her life's work of understanding the root of hunger and poverty. In 1975, she teamed up with public policy expert Joseph Collins to found the Institute for Food and Development Policy and write *Food First*, which examined how capitalism, global markets, and technology affected hunger around the world. Each new edition of *Diet for a Small Planet*—the second in 1975, the third in 1981—would elaborate more forcefully her core argument that humans were creating hunger out of plenty and that famine was solvable. Even then, half of each edition would contain new recipes for high-protein vegetarian food. Shopping and cooking, *Diet* would continue to convince its readers, were political acts, hopeful acts, whose cumulative impact would be felt around the world.

# 5

# Back-to-the-Landers and Organic Farming

SAMUEL KAYMEN WAS AS UNLIKELY A prophet of organic agriculture as you might imagine, though he did share a trait or two with the prophets of biblical times: The wild black beard that spilled from his cheeks like a cataract gushing down a cliffside. A gaze that lasered out from beneath thick black brows, its intensity softened by eyes that crinkled with impishness and warmth. Kaymen spoke with a forcefulness propelled by passion, and words sometimes surged out of his mouth faster than his breath.

But then there was that thick Brooklyn accent. And the fact that, for all the searching brilliance with which he would speak about compost and soil amendments, he had never farmed a plot of land until 1969.

That didn't matter to the 135 people who came to meet Kaymen in June 1971 on a hillside field in Westminster West, Vermont. Weeks before, he had posted flyers in feed stores and farm bureau offices all over Vermont and New Hampshire, informing the world he was founding the Natural Organic Farming Association (whose name was changed to the Northeast Organic Farming Association in 1993), and anyone interested in joining should just show up.

Eight or nine older gardeners were in the crowd, Kaymen recalls, as well as a stolid, middle-aged New Hampshire dairyman who had given up farming with chemicals years ago but had kept it a secret from his neighbors until that day. The majority of the people seated around him, though, were hirsute, homespun, and under the age of thirty. Like Kaymen, they had fled the cities just a few years before, back-to-the-landers who had settled in homesteads and communes, and were teaching themselves to grow their own food.

NOFA, the organization that emerged out of Kaymen's call to action, was the first regional organic farming association of its kind. It harnessed the energy of hundreds of young back-to-the-landers who were bringing their ideas about food, politics, and community to rural New England.

Members of the counterculture didn't just form the backbone of the fledgling organic movement. Their values shaped it. Their tastes shaped it. Their fear of the damage that chemicals were wreaking on the environment drove them to find new ways to grow food. Their mistrust of capitalism and big business dictated the form the organization would take. Their aptitude for community organizing, forged in the protest years, gave them the patience to talk NOFA into existence and build an infrastructure for the organic movement. And their numbers were big enough—so many young middle-class people moving to rural America, all fantasizing about returning to preindustrial ways of life—to make a difference.

IN 1969, THIRTY-THREE-YEAR-OLD Samuel Kaymen, his wife, Louise, and their children talked their way into a position as caretakers for a summer cabin near Unity, New Hampshire, their last big move after six years of counterculture surfing. Just a few years before, Kaymen was an engineer whose business building inflatable clean rooms for the space industry had prospered enough to set him up in a *Playboy* magazine pad—his words—with a shag rug and a thousand-dollar stereo.

But an encounter with the *Tao Te Ching*, Laozi's ancient Taoist masterpiece, in 1963 grabbed him by the lapels and shook him so hard that he rattled. "I realized that I was doing my life all wrong," he says. "It was like this giant hand appeared in the sky with a finger pointing somewhere else, telling me, 'You got to do something else.'" The giant hand, though, couldn't signal exactly what that should be.

The search for a direction took Kaymen and Louise on an epic tour of the counterculture. They stopped in California, New Mexico, Texas, and the Florida Keys. They lived in beach shacks and geodesic domes. They protested the war. They studied Indian spirituality and macrobiotics.[1]

Louise gave birth to daughter after daughter, six children in less than a decade, and the money ran out. The engineer turned to manual labor. Their last big move, in 1969, took them east to be closer to Louise's family, which is how they ended up in New Hampshire. The house there looked out over a half-acre field, and Kaymen asked for permission to plant a garden there. Then he had to figure out how to get food out of the ground. "I thought food was assembled in the back of a grocery store," he later said. "I was starting from scratch."[2]

It was winter at the time, so while he waited for the ground to thaw, Kaymen checked out every book about gardening that he could from the nearest public library. One, in particular, changed Kaymen's thinking: Edward Hyams's 1952 book, *Soil and Civilization*.

Hyams, a novelist, biographer, and ardent gardener, examined the history of agriculture in ancient civilizations and came to a conclusion that startled the Brooklyn-born autodidact. "Man, over a very great part of the surface of the earth, has become a disease of soil communities," Hyams argued. "A few men can live parasitically upon a soil, without destroying it, but should they become too many they inevitably and in-

variably destroy it unless they find means to enhance its annual incre-
ment of fertility. For, as fleas suck men's blood, so men suck the fertility
of soils."[3] Rome, Inca, Indus Valley: each of these great civilizations collapsed after the society had neglected the fertility of its soils and could
no longer support its population.

*Soil and Civilization* had a similar effect on Samuel Kaymen that Paul
Ehrlich's *Population Bomb* did on Frances Moore Lappé. In fact, it struck
the same note of Malthusian panic. "It became my touchstone for everything," Kaymen says of the book. "The future for me was to think about
how soil education could affect people's thinking so perhaps we won't
collapse."

He gleaned enough practical education from the library that the
garden they planted in the spring—somewhat willy-nilly, he admits—
produced five times more than the family could eat. "It was thrilling," he
said. "We both came from knowing nothing about what nature could do
when it's treated right. We had barrels of carrots and beets and turnips
and potatoes."[4]

Samuel Kaymen didn't just become a gardener. He became a farmer.
And he didn't just become a farmer. He became an organic one.


BY 1970, WHEN Kaymen was marveling over his bumper beet crop, the
phrase *organic farming* was certainly circulating, but few knew what it
meant, let alone how to do it professionally. As Kaymen ripped through
the books at the library, hunting for farming practices that would pre-
serve the health of the soil, he came across the works of British writers
who had first used the term: Sir Albert Howard, Lady Eve Balfour, and
Walter James, Lord Northbourne.

Howard was a mycologist who was posted to a research station in
India in 1905 to breed better varieties of wheat.[5] As his research progressed, though, he became more and more convinced that modern

farming was moving in the wrong direction. The more industrial the economy, the more farmers planted large plots of a single crop on fields that they fed with chemical fertilizers to boost the soil's nitrogen, phosphorus, and potassium levels. As Howard worked with large farms, his conviction grew that this approach depleted the land of its natural fertility and exposed both crops and livestock to more disease.

Contributing to the problem, Howard reasoned, was his own field of agricultural science: it divvied up infinitely complex systems into separate, independent disciplines like mycology, plant breeding, and soil health, and demanded that researchers in each pursue small, verifiable facts and ignore the whole.

Over the next twenty-six years, until he retired in 1931, Howard set up a series of field studies to test a theory that if he treated the soil as a living organism in itself and studied what made it healthy, he could grow healthier plants. His overarching idea—that sickness was a symptom of a more dangerous imbalance in nature, not the primary problem—echoed the argument that naturopathic doctors and health-food faddists in America were making about human bodies. After studying traditional farming practices in both India and China, the mycologist developed what he called the "Indore method," a method for creating compost in quantities large enough to apply on a commercial scale.[6]

After his retirement, Howard published his findings and a series of lectures about the Indore method in scientific circles. He modeled the method, he wrote, after the slow, patient soil-building processes that took place on the prairies and in the forests. Farmers could mimic nature by collecting their animals' manure, combining it with wood shavings and plant trimmings, and piling this mixture in wide compost beds. By keeping the heaps wet enough to foster the growth of bacteria and fungi, and by aerating the pile by punching holes in the mixture and turning it over at regular intervals, the compost would eventually transmute into rich, black, living soil itself: humus.

Howard recapped his philosophy for the public in *An Agricultural Testament* in 1940 and *The Soil and Health* in 1947. His ideas meshed with those of two other British scientists and authors: Walter James, Lord Northbourne, who coined the term *organic farming* in his 1940 *Look to the Land*, and Lady Eve Balfour, who summarized her own experiences on her experimental farm in 1943's *The Living Soil* and founded the Soil Association, an organization devoted to this ancient-new farming method, in 1946.

Kaymen devoured these books as quickly as he could acquire them, as well as other early agricultural testaments, such as Louis Bromfield's *Malabar Farm* and *The Wealth of the Soil*, and F. H. King's *Farmers of Forty Centuries: Permanent Agriculture in China, Korea, and Japan*.[7]

He also read the magazine that had brought Howard's ideas to North America: *Organic Gardening and Farming*.

Its publisher, J. I. Rodale, was born Jerome Irving Cohen on Manhattan's Lower East Side and worked for the Internal Revenue Service as an accountant before going into business with his older brother manufacturing small parts for electrical appliances. (Cohen legally changed his name to Rodale in 1921.) After the stock market crash of 1929, the brothers moved the factory to Emmaus, Pennsylvania, a small town outside the industrial hub of Allentown. The move saved the business, which ended up earning Rodale a good amount of money. He poured his new wealth into his growing hobby: publishing.[8]

The Rodale Press started by putting out humor magazines such as *The American Humorist* and *The Clown*. Rodale bought printing equipment to limit his losses and tested out titles like *You Can't Eat That*, *Health Guide*, and *Modern Tempo*, most of them cheap-to-produce digests of previously published work. Some were flops; others, like *Fact Digest*, had print runs as large as one hundred thousand copies.[9]

Rodale sold off all his other titles after he came across an article written by Sir Albert Howard and secured a copy of *An Agricultural Testa-*

*ment.* The publisher later wrote of the thunderclap that struck him when he read Howard's theory that modern, chemical-dependent farming depleted the organic matter in the soil and might eventually affect the health of the people who ate what the soil produced.

Rodale and his wife, Anna, bought a dilapidated farm in Emmaus to test Howard's theories and decided to turn America on to the British scientist's ideas by putting out a new magazine, *Organic Farming,* in 1942, introducing the word *organic* to the States. The publisher mailed out advertising flyers to ten thousand people and received eleven subscriptions. That number didn't pick up after a year, so he renamed it *Organic Gardening* in 1943 and retooled the magazine toward Victory gardeners growing vegetable plots to enhance rationing-constricted diets. (The magazine went through a few more incarnations before it took the name *Organic Gardening and Farming* in 1954.) For the first few years, Sir Howard was listed as an assistant editor, and Rodale Press published U.S. editions of Balfour's and Howard's books. Rodale also wrote and published a few practical guides of his own, including *Pay Dirt* (1945), which was reprinted fourteen times by 1970, describing how to garden according to the British scientists' methods.

Rodale's organic approach to farming was also influenced by a mystical German named Rudolf Steiner, an intellectual and Theosophist who called the school of esoteric thought he developed at the turn of the twentieth century "anthroposophy."[10] Shortly before he died, Steiner gave a series of eight lectures in 1924 to a group of his followers in what is now Poland. An anthroposophical approach to farming, Steiner taught, treated the land—the complex systems within each farmstead, incorporating the soil bacteria, the animals, the humans, and the spirit of them all—as a living entity. He intuited, pretty much psychically, a series of six "preparations" that would simultaneously harness the spiritual forces and nourish the soil's physical needs. The preparations involved manure, compost, herbs, and pre-Christian rituals such as burying cow horns stuffed with manure or powdered quartz in the field at certain times of the year, then making a tea with the substance and spraying it over the plants.[11]

The people who attended the course circulated Steiner's lectures among the true believers, but resolved to publicly test his theories and his preparations. A protégé named Ehrenfried Pfeiffer translated Steiner's agricultural philosophy for a broader public, removing the references to astral-aetherial forces and calling the system "biodynamics." Pfeiffer moved to the United States in the 1930s, after which he joined forces with the existing anthroposophical community, which by then was based at Threefold Farm in Spring Valley, New York.

J. I. Rodale frequently referred to biodynamic thought in *Organic Gardening and Farming*, though with his aim of bringing organic agriculture to the American middle class he ignored or avoided any mention of mysticism. He digested research studies by the thousands, reporting in *Organic Gardening and Farming* on the ones that backed his principles, even if they were taken out of their original context. He sold the organic philosophy with a pragmatic, boosterish approach that grew more *aw-shucks* with every year. Even more significant, perhaps, his magazine grew into a connecting point for similar-minded advertisers, enthusiasts, letter writers, organizations, and publications.

*Organic Gardening and Farming* lost money for the first sixteen years, and public awareness about its ideas spread slowly, until Rodale launched another title in 1950 called *Prevention*, focusing on health. J. I.'s son, Robert, who took over operations in 1954 at the age of twenty, later claimed his father had started a second publication because *Organic Gardening* readers kept complaining that he devoted too many pages to general health topics. Where *Organic Gardening* sputtered to life, *Prevention* shot off: the prepublication campaign drew more than forty thousand subscribers, and circulation soon doubled the gardening publication.

The *Prevention* magazine of the 1950s was a home for many of

Rodale's pet theories: that bone meal could prevent cavities and fluoridated water could poison people; that excess sugar made us violent; and that pesticides and food additives were harmful to our health. The critical component of J. I. Rodale's "prevention system" was the belief that whole, fresh foods were more nutritious than processed ones and that the vitamins in natural supplements were better for human health than chemical vitamins. He believed that organic vegetables better absorbed nourishment from compost, and that humans would similarly benefit from concentrated doses of bone meal, halibut liver oil, rose hips, desiccated liver, vitamin E pearls, and dolomite, a source of magnesium. Rodale told one newspaper reporter he took seventy of these pills—pretty much a measuring cup's worth—a day.[12]

Rodale's writings on health put him squarely in the camp of the nutritional-supplement-taking, wheat-germ-swilling health nuts. Rodale both enjoyed being on the fringe and railed against it, especially after being called on the carpet during a 1950 congressional hearing on chemicals in agriculture, when other experts dismissed him as a know-nothing kook and put him in the crosshairs of the Federal Trade Commission and the American Medical Association. In the mid-1960s, Rodale Press spent years fighting an FTC complaint over the health claims in a few of its advertisements.[13] Harvard nutritionist Frederick Stare, who spent his career jousting against health-food faddists and the organic movement, called Rodale Press "leading purveyors of nutritional nonsense."[14]

Nevertheless, through the 1950s and 1960s, the two flagship Rodale Press magazines—not to mention the company's prolific output of health guides, gardening books, and polemics—brought organic produce into health-food stores and connected the small number of professional organic farms to people wanting to buy their goods. *Prevention* routinely ran ads for organic vegetables, and numerous issues included a back-page directory to organic food sources.[15] In turn, most of the major health-food writers—Adelle Davis, Paul Bragg, Beatrice Trum Hunter, even television fitness star Jack LaLanne—took up the cause of organic food in their books and lectures. By the late 1950s, that tight connection between health and organic food was in evidence all over Los Angeles, but particularly in Gypsy Boots's Health Hut and Jim and Elaine Baker's Aware Inn.

The organic idea tended to attract home gardeners in greater numbers than it did large-scale enterprises, but scattered farmers across the country switched (or switched back to) antichemical methods, their work trumpeted in Rodale Press magazines and directories. *Organic Gardening and Farming* directly inspired farming enterprises like Paul and Betty Keene's Walnut Acres in Penns Creek, Pennsylvania, whose natural-foods mail-order business boomed in the 1950s and whose catalogs became another source of popular information about the dangers and deficits of conventional farming.

The organic cause took on new urgency in 1962 with the publication of Rachel Carson's *Silent Spring*. Carson was a conservation-minded marine biologist who ran the editing division at the U.S. Fish and Wildlife Service for many years and wrote books and magazine features on the side. Her books *The Sea Around Us* and *The Edge of the Sea* were bestselling literary masterpieces—praised by critics and scientists alike—that clothed scientific rigor in poetry and introduced readers to the oceans and their inhabitants.[16]

Even as she studied the oceans, Carson clipped and filed away articles and research studies about DDT for more than fifteen years. After World War II, the pesticide, which one advocate called "the atomic bomb of the insect world,"[17] was so good at its job that American farmers and government agencies used it as their go-to cure for major infestations of fire ants and gypsy moths; it was sprayed gleefully over huge swaths of land, much of it populated by humans. With each new insect-eradication campaign, more and more bystanders raised a cry over how the pesticide killed off beneficial insects and birds as well, their complaints refuted by government agencies and university scientists at every turn. Carson tracked all these incidents, as well as reports that exposure to DDT and other pesticides could cause cancer.

*Organic Gardening and Farming,* as well as a number of chemical-food muckrakers, had warned of the dangers of DDT for years. But none of them had the authority or the audience as the bestselling, National Book Award–winning author. Carson gathered all the evidence she had collected into a greater narrative about pollution—how pesticides spread through the soils and waters, how they traveled up the food chain, how they poisoned the environment long after they were applied—that was as devastating as it was well written. The *New Yorker* devoted most of an issue to Carson's argument in June 1962, and the book *Silent Spring* came out soon after.

The industry and the academy attacked her, yet they weren't able to disprove her findings. In 1963 the President's Science Advisory Committee investigated her allegations and came out with a series of recommendations that supported her work. In the next few years, legislators introduced dozens of bills in states around the country limiting or regulating pesticides.

It would take another decade for the federal government to ban DDT use—Carson died of cancer long before that—but *Silent Spring* had a massive impact on young Americans in the 1960s. It is often credited as the predecessor to the U.S. ecology movement, which burst into the zeitgeist on April 22, 1970, with the first Earth Day. The fall before, a U.S. senator from Wisconsin named Gaylord Nelson had called for a day of activities and education about the environment. The idea swelled into a nationwide event. More than twelve thousand "teach-ins"—at ten thousand schools and fifteen hundred colleges, plus churches and public parks—drew in more than a million participants. The day wasn't just devoted to panels and film screenings. Schoolkids in Wisconsin collected aluminum cans. Others mounted protests such as wearing gas masks or dumping dead fish on power plants. Newspapers all over the country covered the local actions as well as the national discussion of ecology that came out of Earth Day.[18]

*Silent Spring* certainly validated the spirit, if not the specific claims, of the organic movement. But the movement was still so fringe that Carson refused to endorse it. So much so that she backed out of a panel after hearing that J. I. Rodale was invited to join her onstage.

Even if J. I. Rodale grumbled that he had gotten to DDT first, the reach of his magazines gave him no reason to complain. By 1968, *Organic Gardening and Farming* had a respectable circulation of four hundred thousand. Between 1968 and 1971, that number increased to seven hundred thousand, jumping 40 percent between 1970 and 1971 alone. It was clearly reaching a new, and younger, audience.

Robert Rodale, the magazine's editor by that time, tended to address the readers of *Organic Gardening and Farming* as if they were a separate bloc from the long-haired rebels who were taking an interest in organic farming. But it was clear that a generation of back-to-the-landers like Samuel Kaymen—who had very different political and social views than the socially middle-of-the-road, politics-averse Rodale family— took to the magazine's philosophy in a new spirit: as a form of salvation, perhaps. Or at least a way forward when so many other things in the country were going so wrong.


NOBODY ALIVE, NOT even Samuel Kaymen himself, can remember quite how, but after a year of house-sitting, he met up with a man named Kim Hubbard, who asked the Kaymens to farm on the property Hubbard had bought in Vermont, thirty miles southwest of their house-sitting gig. It just happened, Kaymen says, in the half-conscious manner of a charismatic charmer who doesn't fully understand his appeal. "I got a reputation as a loudmouth," he guesses.

There was an old hunter's cabin on the property, which two adults and a clutch of small children moved into that winter while they built a house for themselves. But Kaymen was too extroverted to be an isolated homesteader. He says he thought he'd learn more about organic farming if he began teaching it, so he named the land Nature Farms and called it a farm school. The man who barely knew where vegetables came from five years before advertised that he was taking students.

Twenty-some people came that summer to work on the land. Kaymen would wake his charges up at 5:30 A.M. by banging on a big Chinese gong every morning, until the neighbors complained. The students would climb out of their tents or tipis (eventually, as the months passed, they would graduate up to shacks) and make their way to the main house, where their teacher would pass out mugs of hot mint tea or watered-down apple cider vinegar and honey. The farm students would first spend an hour reading a chapter in one of the books Kaymen had amassed. Then they would head out into the fields, breaking for a lunch of salads and gathering again in the evenings to brew up big pots of brown rice and stir-fried vegetables picked from the fields. They had no chickens, so eggs were scarce, and they occasionally scored enough milk from a neighbor to ferment up a batch of yogurt.

Kaymen set up contracts with macrobiotic restaurants in Boston, grocery chains in Massachusetts, and even pickle factories in New York's Chinatown to buy the vegetables they were growing. In the winter, the students would take off to warmer cities and reassemble when the snow melted into mud.

In his orgy of reading about soil, Kaymen had come across biodynamics, too, and he took a truckload of his students to a conference of the Biodynamic Association in Spring Valley, New York. Young and scruffy, the newbie farmers seemed the opposite of the older German, Austrian, and English anthroposophists. But the two groups soon found common ground. Not only were they both interested in farming without chemicals, the youngsters were open to esoteric spiritual theories that the older generation had hidden from the public for decades, and the anthroposophists began sharing with the hippie kids the full extent of Steiner's philosophy. Along with the Howard-inspired compost piles that it cultivated, Nature Farms buried horns filled with manure and applied biodynamic preparations to the land.

IN 1970, IT wasn't hard to find young people willing to camp out on a farmstead and teach themselves how to grow vegetables organically. In the late 1960s, Vermont emerged as one of the major destinations for counterculture types escaping the cities and moving back to the land.[19]

The state, a close network of small townships whose largest city, Burlington, barely topped thirty-five thousand residents, was largely poor and agricultural. At the beginning of the 1960s its population was stalling and, at the same time, growing older. As the older farmers retired or died, their children left for the cities; by 1969, the number of farmers dropped over two decades from 19,000 to 4,850.[20] Upper New England's short growing seasons, combined with the decreasing prices of produce shipped in from the West Coast, had made it less profitable for Vermont farmers to grow vegetables commercially, so most of the remaining farms raised dairy cows. There was a common saying among the old-timers: "Getting by is doing good in Vermont." By the late 1960s, it was becoming unclear whether even that was possible.

Ever since the Depression, however, cheap land had drawn urbanites to Vermont to reinvent themselves in the manner of nineteenth-century peasants. Among them, for instance, were Helen and Scott Nearing, respectively a Theosophist musician and Communist firebrand who moved to the state in 1932 to eke out a self-sufficient lifestyle. They chronicled their stone-house building, maple sugaring, and organic gardening in a 1954 book titled *Living the Good Life*, which was republished in 1970, just in time to capture the attention of young readers.

Cheap land, the appeal of the Nearings' books, plus the arrival of the interstate highways connecting southern Vermont to the big northeastern cities made the state attractive to a generation that was fed up with the war, Nixon, and the revolutionary struggle. They had no interest in taking their college educations and grand ideas and squishing them into a forty-hour office job with two weeks' vacation and maybe a future in middle management.

In the late 1960s, hundreds of thousands of counterculture types all over North America took up "back to the land" as a rallying cry. The *San Francisco Oracle* proclaimed in 1967, just as the Summer of Love was turning ugly, "Land is being made available at a time when many of us in the Haight-Ashbury and elsewhere are voicing our need to return to the soil, to straighten our heads in a natural environment, to straighten our bodies with healthier foods and Pan's work, toe to toe with the physical world, just doing what must be done."[21]

A few pioneering communes in the mid-1960s captured the counterculture's imagination—Tolstoy Farm in Washington, Drop City and New Buffalo in New Mexico, Morningstar and Wheeler's Ranch in Northern California—first as curiosities, and then the template for a new society that they could build.

Previous generations might have lived at home until marriage or sequestered themselves in single-sex boardinghouses. But the baby boom kids disregarded the old notions of sex-segregated propriety, as well as their parents' hard-won bungalows with their fresh-mowed lawns. Education and, more important, birth control kept them from being thrust into marriages at eighteen or even twenty-one. So where were they going to live? Together, of course.

Contemporary academics estimate that somewhere around ten thousand rural communes formed between 1965 and 1975 and that as many as a million young adults moved into communes of some sort, whether in major cities or small towns. There were a few open-land communes where anyone who showed up could camp out. There were Vedantic ashrams, leftist filmmaking collectives, radical feminist households, gay male tribes, heterosexual group marriages, and highly structured social experiments. There were groups of friends from college who simply wanted to buy a house together. The commune dwellers may have come from middle-class homes or working-class families, but they were more likely to be educated than not and they were overwhelmingly, almost exclusively, white.[22]

Many of the people moving into communes saw themselves as continuing the revolution, or giving the city revolutionaries a place to escape when the fighting got too fierce. The Tick Creek Tribe in North Carolina, for instance, wrote in 1972:

> Living outside the pig economy, gaining intimate, sure control over the mode & quality of our lives—these are revolutionary actions. They extend the outlaw area which supports and serves and—when necessary—hides us. Farming collectives, media collectives, transportation, food, organizing, and spiritual collectives of all kinds: All of these help to create a truly liberated zone, on the land and in our own minds, from which we can work to transform this oppressive society.[23]

Or, as Mark Kramer wrote wryly in *Mother Walter & the Pig Tragedy*, his 1972 memoir of forming a back-to-the-land commune in western Massachusetts:

> The move to the country is a doomsday decision. It almost always starts out as a retreat, after other alternatives become too unpalatable. It would be nicer to change the world and make it

a decent place. But after having a good whack at it, perhaps the best decision for some is to make the best of a bad lot. It turns out that a farm with friends is a very pleasant street corner to hang out on while waiting for the bomb to fall. Once you look for it, the sense of doom on New England communes seems pervasive.[24]

They had no idea of what exactly they were going to do when they got back to the land, only that they needed to go. Robert Houriet, a journalist from Camden, New Jersey, quit his job at the Camden *Courier-Post* in 1968 and spent two years traveling around the country, visiting more than fifty of these "tribes, nests, affinity groups, collectives, intentional communities or simply families." He wrote in the introduction to his 1971 book, *Getting Back Together,* "Only afterward was it called a movement. At the outset it was the gut reaction of a generation."[25]

Between 1966 and 1967, when the first tentative communes appeared in Vermont, and the early 1970s, when they were at their peak, between seventy-five and two hundred counterculture communes operated in the state.[26] And those were the ones with formal names, like Red Clover, Pie in the Sky, Tree Frog Farm, and the most famous, Packer Corners, founded by movement journalist Ray Mungo, poet Verandah Porche, and a cluster of intellectual activists who chronicled their agrarian immigration in books such as *Total Loss Farm, Home Comfort,* and *Burnt Toast.* Many other communes were simply groups who'd rented a big house and were sharing rooms and expenses. The existence of households flickered on and off with the speed of a busted fluorescent bulb, and some members hopped from one disintegrating commune to the next newly forming one.

Starting a few years later, a separate but spiritually connected wave of homesteaders—young couples, perhaps not so radical in their views, many with families—quit their middle-class jobs, looked for cheap tracts of land far from the cities, and took off with the fantasy of building a cabin, living without electricity or modern conveniences, and making a living off what they could grow.

It is impossible to measure just how many homesteaders followed the communards back to the land, or how many people altogether made the urban-rural migration.[27] The U.S. Census registered the movement, however. The rural population of the United States had decreased slightly during the 1960s, but between 1970 and 1980, it increased 11.1 percent, growth rates not seen since 1900.[28]

The back-to-the-land movement was particularly strong in Northern California and the Pacific Northwest, the northeastern states, a few clumps in the Southwest, and the Ozarks. The movement could be sensed in rural counties all over the country, as well as seen in every Vanagon that headed down some country road, laden with boxes of clothes and tools, and every small child named Blackberry or Liberty who appeared in a rural kindergarten class.

In Vermont, one of the first states to attract young counterculture types, the population increased 14 percent between 1960 and 1970 and 15 percent in the next decade. Enough people moved into the state with the intention to farm that the number of reported farmers, which had been falling so precipitously, increased 9.4 percent in the 1970s.[29]

The natives were by no means quietly observing this influx. In the spring of 1971, a series of articles in the *Rutland Herald* and *Newport Daily Express* projected that fifty thousand hippies were going to invade Vermont in the summer; some stories even added Governor Deane Davis had invited them and promised them jobs. Rumors circulated around the state that hitchhikers in California were cadging rides with placards that read "Go to Vermont and Get on Welfare at Once."[30] So many complaints reached Governor Davis's office that spring that he was forced to hold a press conference in May 1971 to deny the charges. However, there was nothing he could do to prevent these "tourists," as he called them in a moment of misplaced hope, except to enforce state laws. "The bulk of the young transients go about their business in a self-sufficient, peaceful manner," he reassured the intimidated masses, "although their habits and appearance may not be to our taste."[31]

Homesteaders and communards alike didn't just bring their fears of what the country was descending to or their hope for a revolution to Vermont. They brought their copies of Thoreau's *Walden*, their history-class ideas of the Jeffersonian ideal of America as an agrarian democracy. They brought their urbane fantasies about how the natural world operated, as well as their memories of all the times they sat in front of the television watching westerns like *The Adventures of Kit Carson* and *Bonanza*, which could be seen in their hand-sewed gingham aprons and their hayseed overalls.[32] They were determined to strip away all the flaws of modern American life—to hit the reset button and build a more humane, more holistic society outside the one they were leaving behind. An unexamined nostalgia for the nineteenth century, and the fantasy of self-sufficiency, blinded them to the hardships of pretechnological life. But they were young and strong-bodied and excited and not a little arrogant. They didn't care. They'd figure it out.

As Robert Houriet, the commune traveler, wrote in the conclusion to *Getting Back Together*, when he was settled back on the communal farm he'd established in Hardwick, Vermont:

> We talk of moving away into the last reaches of the wilderness, far off the hardtop. Our friends in the city, still fighting the good fight within the system, regard us as escapists. . . . Instead of starting with war, exploitation and imperialism, we begin at the center—ourselves—and work outward. A matter of interlocked priorities: The self needs a community; a community needs a culture; and a culture—here's the rub—needs spirit. Without it, a society falls flat like bread without yeast.

Somewhere the spirit lives; through the woods, over the hills there lies some unknown pond in the lap of mountains reflecting the infinite sky.[33]

WHAT THE HOMESTEADERS and communards didn't bring, as Samuel Kaymen recognized in 1971, was any practical knowledge. They were educated enough to create their own resources, such as the *Whole Earth Catalog*, whose listings described "Tools for the New Society," including books about composting, rototillers, geodesic domes, and cheesemaking. Back-to-the-landers subscribed to *Organic Gardening and Farming* and *Mother Earth News*, a magazine founded in 1970 to serve the movement. *Mother Earth News* ran intellectual fodder (interviews with Allen Ginsberg or anarchist Murray Bookchin) alongside practical advice (how to build a cold frame, how to can for the winter) and encouraging testimonials from people who'd already landed in backwoods Maine or northern Wisconsin.[34]

Fleeing the cities, following their own path, telling the Man to go fuck himself and the $16,000 a year he was paying for their souls was one thing. But what were these urban dropouts supposed to do after they'd built their yurts on twelve acres of wilderness, dug their outhouses, and carved paths to the streams from which they could haul water? After they'd settled in to commune with nature and follow their passion?

Why, they had to feed themselves.

By 1971, Samuel Kaymen wasn't content to merely educate a handful of youngsters how to grow their own food. "It was apparent to me," he said later, "that what was needed was a way to bring people together to share information, to learn from each other and from experts—which were very few—and to learn from people who were growing food who would know anything about the land."

So he magicked an organization out of the ether, coming up with the name Natural Organic Farming Association almost on a whim. He set the date for his first meeting and printed up a flyer, which listed nine points that NOFA would tackle: How do you make compost? How do you build soil fertility? How do you manage seeds? How do you deal with pests? How do you mulch?

At that inaugural meeting in the farm school's field, Kaymen announced that NOFA wouldn't just meet to discuss the how-tos of organic farming and gardening. The organization would offer an apprenticeship program, in the manner of Nature Farms, to teach young people how to farm without chemicals. Kaymen would also circulate a mimeographed newsletter, which he would call *The Natural Farmer,* and start a seed exchange—not just for vegetables but cover crops and forage.[35] The group would also arrange for large deliveries of soil amendments like rock phosphate, a Rodale-approved natural fertilizer, and granite dust, which would add potassium to the soil. Kaymen passed around a hat and collected $35: the extent of NOFA's seed money.

Kaymen's students were at the meeting, of course, and a number of the people who would become Vermont's first organic farmers. They included Howie Prussack, a nineteen-year-old Brooklynite who had left art school to spend the summer in Vermont and ended up moving onto Nature Farms to live in a tipi and apprentice under Kaymen. Also present were some of the members of Erewhon Farm, a macrobiotic commune in New Hampshire that was founded in part to supply vegetables to Erewhon and Boston's macrobiotic community. A fiction writer named Peter Gould who was living in a nearby commune called Packer Corners[36] showed up; Gould had no intention of becoming a commercial farmer, but Packer Corners was growing all its food organically and he was learning to press cider, make cheese, and raise hogs all the same. And some of the communards in attendance, like Jake Guest, who had left the revolution for life in a New Hampshire anarchist commune called Wooden Shoe, were discovering that they were good at growing food and might want to do it to build a livelihood.[37]

Organic agriculture appealed to countercultural types like them for some of the same reasons it made sense to NOFA's founder. First of all, it rejected the prevailing scientific-industrial view of farming as a series of inputs and outputs, the same view that was resulting in DDT poisoning and soil erosion. Farming organically meant looking to nature to discover what the land wanted—re-creating the decomposition of the forest floor in the compost pile, or planting horns to focus its spiritual energies. The farmer was merely one point in the great whirling mandala of nature, not lord of his or her dominion.

At the same time, the return to nature represented a return to self-sufficiency. Farming required no boss but yourself and your comrades in arms. You might pay a little money for seeds and organic soil amendments—some farmers in those days even dispensed with tractors and mechanical equipment in favor of horses and plows—but the rest of your investment was locked in the sinew and skin that wrapped around your bones.

The back-to-the-landers also saw, in small-scale organic farming, a reflection of their own desires to depopulate the cities, disassemble the great machineries of state and corporation, and return to a more authentic existence. If leaving the cities was a negative movement, building up a new form of agriculture was a positive one.

"The political implications of organic farming are immense," Jeff Cox wrote in 1972:

> It will mean a transfer of power from the large conglomerates back into the hands of the people. It will mean land for people and people on the land. Instead of fewer, larger farms and more crowding in the cities, it means that the traditional way

of making a living, the stewardship of a piece of dirt, will be given to the disenfranchised and poor. Blacks are forming organic growing cooperatives in the South now and the trend will continue.

It will mean local growers supplying local folks. An end to plastic supermarkets. It will mean building up the fertility of the soil as a national policy instead of subsidizing those who can rip off the most land. It will mean, in other words, a complete breakdown in the way we now do things.[38]

KAYMEN LIKES TO say that the nine questions on his original flyer advertising the NOFA meeting were one short. The question he forgot to ask turned out to be the most critical one: How are we going to sell organic food?

The counterculture thinking on that front tilted toward the anticapitalist. "Agriculture must be viewed in social terms and not as a business," Martin Jezer, one of the Packer Corners residents, wrote in *Mother Earth News* in 1970. Agriculture could support subsistence farms like the homesteaders and communes and interrupt the great supply chains that were funneling cheaply grown California produce to Vermont in conditions no gardener would condone. Communes, Jezer thought, could play a critical role in changing agriculture:

The communes can do this by getting involved in organic farming and marketing their produce in ways that educate the public and create a demand for organically grown food. (For instance, distribute literature with the produce, "compete" by comparing the poison-free vegetables with the crap that passes for food in supermarkets; supply urban communes and food-buying cooperatives with low-priced healthy foods.)[39]

The first solution that NOFA came up with, in the summer of 1971, was to tap into the counterculture network remaining in the big cities to sell the farms' organic produce. Kaymen says he made contact with the Bowery Co-op on the Lower East Side and a group of day-care centers in Harlem, agreeing to grow collard greens, sweet corn, and other vegetables hard to find, fresh, in Manhattan.

A few of the NOFA farmers made weekly trips to New York, convening early in the morning at Kaymen's farm in Vermont to deliver everything they had picked. Kaymen says he would load up the truck with sweet corn at midnight, to keep it cold, and drive six hours to the city before it warmed up. "It was a long trip and very inefficient and crazy and we didn't make any money," he says. "But it was a great experience dealing with markets." The macrobiotic folks arranged to supply the Erewhon produce store in Boston and the macrobiotic restaurants with rarities like daikon and Chinese cabbage, peddling the excess to Chinese groceries, who would take the radishes and dismiss their wan greens.

In 1973, Robert Houriet, the commune chronicler behind *Getting Back Together,* traveled to New Hampshire to meet with Kaymen. He had left Frog Run Farm, his first commune, and was looking to join the effort. Tall and lanky, his lantern jaw ringed in an airy beard, Houriet was almost as fast a talker as the organization's founder, as capable of filling the room with his voice and backing every opinion with an equal amount of passion. Nevertheless, Houriet saw Kaymen as a prophet, one who had galvanized a loose, bumbling, inspired following. "I had been an investigative reporter and an editor," he says. "I was pretty hip on community organizing because I had reported on it. I knew what a prophet needs is a Paul."[40]

Houriet made Kaymen an offer. The mimeographed NOFA newsletter that Kaymen had been producing was sloppily written and assembled, and Houriet wanted to take it over and turn it into a vehicle for organizing. Kaymen, in turn, was deep in toddlers and a new farm and eagerly handed the duties over. Under Houriet's aegis, *The Natural Farmer* evolved into a proper newspaper, printed at Dartmouth College by students and workers who believed in the cause.

Besides, Kaymen had to step back from running the show for a while. He had disbanded Nature Farms and moved to Cornish, New Hampshire, where yet another person enthralled with his ideas bought him a farm to live on. Kaymen handed off the growing of vegetables to former protégé Prussack, who at the age of twenty-one was then ensconced in a love affair with the neighbor's daughter and smitten with the idea of becoming a "real" farmer.

While editing the newspaper, Houriet ended up helping organize the farm deliveries. By 1973, NOFA had acquired two trucks and a full-time driver and had convinced a number of communes and small farms to grow specific vegetables to supply a network of eighteen food co-ops in New York. It took the work of many farmers and volunteers to take orders and travel up and down the Connecticut River Valley.

The deliveries were exhausting: fourteen-hour days, collecting truckloads of vegetables and driving them to the Bowery Co-op, their delivery point, by midnight. If they arrived too late in the morning, they could be forced to pull up on the corner, open up the back of the truck, and haul their crates of broccoli onto the sidewalk to hawk. But deliveries that went well could make a rural farmer feel like a hero. Houriet remembers one night when a hundred people showed up to offload his truck. "They'd give us the power salute, as if we had done something revolutionary delivering this organic stuff to the city," he says.

The problem was that the farmers weren't nearly as reliable. He could place an order for four hundred pounds of carrots with a commune that managed a vast garden, call over and over as the date approached to arrange pickup, and discover that they'd only managed to grow one hundred pounds worthy of a sale. Another time, Houriet remembers driving out to a homestead to pick up a massive order of tomatoes, only to find the geodesic dome empty and hundreds of unstaked tomato plants sprawled across a field overtaken by switchgrass. When he tracked down one of the would-be farmers, he explained that he and his girlfriend had broken up, his ex had moved into a women's commune, and he'd abandoned tomato farming. NOFA once called one of the co-ops it supplied to tell them, "Sorry, but all your food is dead."[41]

It became clear in 1974 that NOFA was at a crossroads. Wholesale vegetable distribution was bringing together dozens of growers but consuming all the volunteers' time and the organization's resources. The start-up grant that helped fund its operations was about to run out. Given the shrug-if-it'll-work nature of the supply chain, no one was sure NOFA could make enough money to sustain the operation.

Houriet says he felt that the operation was taking them in a direction antithetical to everything the communal-living movement stood for. "If you're trucking wholesale produce, you have to be centrally organized," he says. "The organizers become the directors of the organization. We said we're going to turn into a corporation and lose our funky, decentralized way of operating."

At a 1974 meeting at a Grange Hall in Corinth, New Hampshire, Houriet says, he stepped up from being a newsletter editor and ardent volunteer to an organizer. In just three years, NOFA had already morphed from an information-sharing network to a wholesale distributor. He proposed that NOFA make another radical shift: abandon New York, abandon the matter of sales and marketing, and become a grassroots community.

"NOFA should be an organizer of other small, locally based cooperatives," he proposed. "Food should not be centrally distributed but locally grown and locally distributed." The organic movement wasn't supposed to be about building giant companies or supply chains to rival industrial agriculture. It was supposed to be human scale. NOFA should be a collective, decentralized enterprise, a collective of collectives of collectives, a series of interlocking knots in a great postcapitalist web.

The mechanism Houriet proposed for establishing tiny NOFA collectives in every town and burg in the two states and building local food systems: farmers' markets.

The proposal was accepted.

BRATTLEBORO'S FIRST FARMERS' market—at least, the first market the town of twelve thousand had seen in many decades—took place in July 1974.

The winter before, Robert Houriet had written a how-to manual on starting a farmers' market cooperative and called established farmers up and down the state to recruit them. NOFA had even shelled out $15 to place an ad in the Brattleboro paper to invite farmers to attend a planning meeting at St. Michael's Church. More critically, Houriet had applied to the state for a grant that would pay a couple of organizers to establish market cooperatives in cities all over Vermont.

The notion of a farmers' market, in 1974, had been dying away since the early part of the nineteenth century. Large public markets, housed in permanent structures, existed in many large cities in the eastern half of the country, and you could still find "courthouse markets" in small towns throughout the Midwest. However, by 1970, one survey counted only 340 farmers' markets in the country, most of them populated by vendors who had not grown the food they were selling.[42]

Those numbers began reversing in the early 1970s. Santa Fe, New Mexico; Madison, Wisconsin; and the college towns of Athens, Ohio; Olympia, Washington; and Ithaca, New York, all established weekly open-air farmers' markets, most of them organized by students and back-to-the-landers.

None of those areas saw anything like what happened in Vermont.

Over the course of just a few years, NOFA seeded farmers' markets in Norwich, Rutland, Burlington, Middlebury, St. Johnsbury, and Randolph, followed by Ludlow, Springfield, Bellows Falls, Morrisville, Charlotte, Pownal, and Northfield.[43]

Brattleboro was one of the first cities to respond, though the local merchants put up a fuss at the thought that people could just appear in the center of town and make money without paying the same downtown rents. Five or six farmers, including a few people who had attended the first organizational meeting of NOFA in 1971, set up tables in a vacant lot. A few were communards like Peter Gould, who sold some of the excess fruits and vegetables that the Packer Corners commune was producing and later switched to pies baked in its wood-fired oven.

Another was Howard Prussack, the compact, sleepy-eyed, and dimpled Brooklynite who had stayed on at Nature Farms after Samuel Kaymen left, and turned the communal school into a one-man operation he called High Meadows Farm. Farming in Vermont gave Prussack a life he would never have anticipated for himself just five years before—an alternate universe from his New York City upbringing, a perpetual adventure. "I really like pulling weeds," he says he had discovered. "I like working outside. I like working on a tractor. I like doing physical work with my hands and also having to think about it." In the first post-Kaymen years, he survived by working for the dairy farmer across the road and collecting maple sap for a neighbor with a sugaring outfit.

By the mid-1970s, Prussack was growing vegetables on eight to nine acres of land, renting large farming equipment, and grossing $40,000 a year—practically crazy money. ("Cash went a lot further in those days," he says. "I had no idea how good I had it.") The work was sixteen hours a day during the peak season, despite the fact that he was now taking on apprentices of his own.

Prussack, like many of the communards and homesteaders in Vermont, also found that the longer he stayed in Vermont, the more the older

Vermonters took him in. Their initial fears of drugs and VD abated once they realized the newcomers wanted to learn from them. Here was a young generation enthusiastic to do all the things their own children had moved to the cities to avoid. Even more quixotically, the kids were eager to farm like their elder neighbors' parents and grandparents—the hard way. Back-to-the-landers would gather up outdated farm equipment to restore, then ask their elder neighbors how to use it. Old farmers would wander over to the nearby commune to peek at the nude gardening and find themselves answering questions about how to build a fence or when to sow potatoes. *Mother Earth News* ran articles like "The Gentle Art of Hunkering," giving urban readers tips on how to make friends with their new rural neighbors.

This was hardly unique to Vermont, though modern-day Vermonters like to talk up the independent Vermonter spirit that brought longhair kids and rock-ribbed Republicans together. As the Technicolor Amish at the Farm were simultaneously discovering in rural Tennessee, aging farmers in Vermont came to rely on their young neighbors' strong backs when it was time to hay fields and muck out barns in springtime.

Prussack's organic farming methods may have been a source of snickering for his older neighbors, but he discovered that the conventional sweet corn and winter squash farmers in the area had a lot to teach him about planting, reaping, working with tools, and preparing vegetables after harvest for the market. He accrued ice machines and coolers and vowed not to have some kind of "funky hippie operation," as he calls it, though he was forced to make small deliveries to New York in a VW bug with the passenger seat torn out. He cut his hair short and shaved the beard. He tried harder to fit in with the locals.

Prussack's professional farming sense rubbed off on the other farmers' market vendors, the homesteaders he thought of as "playing farm." In the early days of organics, a certain ugly-is-beautiful aesthetic reigned. As the *San Francisco Chronicle* wrote in 1972, "The oranges are dark and spotty because they haven't been dyed, the apples have been attacked by bugs because they weren't sprayed, the carrots are dirty because the grower wants you to see what kind of soil they came from and the potatoes are puny because their growth wasn't boosted by chemical fertilizers. . . . The defects reassure the buyer that, as one put it, 'This is God's own food, bitten by God's own bugs.'"[44] In Brattleboro, Prussack says, amateur farmers would pull their carrots out of the garden, throw them into the baskets, and bring them to the market, more black than orange, until they realized that they had to compete with commercial farmers like him.

Most of the customers couldn't have cared less, in fact, that the produce was organic. It was enough that it was fresh. Vermont had been at the end of a long supply chain that stretched from California to the rural Northeast for so long that its own supply of fresh vegetables had withered and shrunk to the dregs of what was commercially available— the red mealy apples, the yellowing broccoli, the hard pink tomatoes, and iceberg lettuce with brown-spotted exterior leaves. The people who bought from Prussack were locals, many of whom had given up gardening but remembered how good their own food had once tasted.

Though he attended the farmers' market faithfully, Prussack says, where he could make $200 a day ($900 in 2016 dollars), most of his produce was going to wholesalers and the fledgling food co-ops that were appearing in Brattleboro and other small cities. He was taking vegetables around to restaurants, too, convincing the chefs of even high-end places that they should cook the weirdly frilly lettuces he was presenting them and peas packaged in their pods rather than a freezer bag.

Yet it took effort for Prussack, a natural charmer if there ever was one, to sell his freshly grown Vermont produce to restaurants and grocery stores. The quality would eventually hook them, he says. What wouldn't, outside the food co-ops and counterculture: the "organic" label. Even though Prussack was hewing close to the organic and biodynamic ideas he had learned from Kaymen, marketing his farming practices was another thing. "Some places I don't tell them it's organic until many weeks have passed and they see that it sells," he told one Rodale Press writer in 1977.[45]

THE RODALES MAY have brought the word *organic* to the attention of the mainstream, but they couldn't make the mainstream respect it.

*Vogue* magazine considered organics fashionable enough in 1971 to ask a Hamptons caterer to develop a special "organic" dinner party of hard-cooked fertile eggs, poached pike with yogurt sauce, soy bread, and macrobiotic mu tea. The magazine drawled, "The newest and most delicious party foods are real ones—no sprays, chemicals, additives, preservatives, stiffeners, or laboratory dyes used or needed." Yet it warned, "Don't count on organically grown fruits or vegetables for a centerpiece. The skins of natural fruits and vegetables may be splotchy, often can't compete esthetically with their chemical-sprayed counterparts, which may even be 'color perfected'—dyed."[46]

What did catch newspapers and magazines' attention was money. "What are all these health nuts doing in stores like Safeway, Montgomery Ward, Walgreens, Rich's, and Lord & Taylor?" asked *Business Week* in 1971. "Well, for one thing, the nuts these days include a growing group of otherwise conventional shoppers who are concerned about the possible hazards of pesticides, chemical fertilizers, additives, hormones, and food processing that may destroy nutrients. The result is that 'organic' or 'natural' foods and cosmetics, long confined to small specialty shops, are moving into supermarkets and the other large retail outlets."[47]

The National Nutritional Foods Association estimated in 1971 that there were two hundred fifty organic-food manufacturers and distributors and two thousand retail stores that specialized in organic products.[48]

In the same year, the Rodales printed a directory of approximately fifteen hundred organic food suppliers: tiny health-food stores, apiarists,
bakers, grain suppliers, fruit and vegetable farmers, ranchers, dairies,
even one Vermont farmer who raised snapping turtles (to eat? It wasn't
clear).[49]

In 1972, the *San Francisco Chronicle* estimated the organic industry
generated $400 million in sales a year, four times that of just two years
before.[50] Newspapers and business magazines noted, with a blend of disdain and admiration, that the markup on organic products could be 35
to 50 percent.[51]

But the newspapers, as well as farm groups, academic nutritionists,
and agronomists, just as quickly trumpeted their qualms about organic
food. "Fads come and fads go," Victor Herbert, a Columbia University
professor of pathology, told the *New York Times* in 1970, typical of the
most benign criticism. "There is no convincing scientific evidence that
so-called organically grown foods contain any extra nutritional value
as compared with the same food grown in a conventional way."[52] (The
same article pointed out, however, that no one thought eating DDT-free
food would hurt.)

Scientists attacked J. I. Rodale's longtime claims that chemical fertilizers harmed the microbial life in the soil, reducing fertility, and that
the vitamins and minerals in produce grown on organic soil were better
for people. An FDA scientist warned *Science Digest* that organic foods
could be contaminated with parasites from human and animal manures.
Secretary of Agriculture Earl Butz frequently argued that the United
States could convert to organic farming if we wanted fifty million Americans to starve.[53]

The most caustic critic, perhaps, who took it as his personal mission
to attack the natural-foods industry was Frederick Stare, head of the nutrition department of Harvard's School of Public Health. In fact, Stare
was a reactionary advocate of industrially produced food. In the 1975

book *Panic in the Pantry*, for example, Stare and coauthor Elizabeth
Whelan wrote, "Food additives are like friends. We need and depend on
them but often take them for granted." He defended artificial colors and
flavors, preservatives, artificial sweeteners, and pesticides—even DDT.
Typical of his rhetoric was a quote he gave *Harper's Bazaar* in 1972:

> It's a sort of Christian Science attitude you attach to your or-
> ganically grown carrots, availing little in the way of real nutri-
> tional benefits. *All* foods are composed of chemicals. You and I
> are composed of chemicals. And strictly speaking, *all* foods are
> organic—containing protein, fat, carbohydrate and vitamins.[54]

As the 1970s progressed, the critics of organic food added another
concern: that no one could tell whether a food was organic anyway, citing incident after incident where merchants chasing dollars were found
to have adulterated or flat out faked organic food.

That, at least, was a criticism the organic food industry shared.

WHEN GRACE GERSHUNY, a homesteader in the northern Vermont city
of West Charleston, answered an ad in the *Natural Farmer* to help
NOFA draft organic certification standards, she was already plagued
by the same question: What would it take to guarantee that food was
organic?[55]

Gershuny, or Grace Jensen, as she was in 1977, was a native New
Yorker who had moved to Vermont in 1973, a blond, bespectacled
woman with an acre-wide smile and a deep, measured contralto. She
joined NOFA two years later after Robert Houriet, who lived near her,
noticed that the half-acre garden she had planted outside her farmhouse
was fecund. He recruited her to organize a farmers' market in the town
of Newport. She began attending the annual NOFA conferences that

Samuel Kaymen was organizing, drawing hundreds of people to hear the likes of farmer-poet Wendell Berry and attend demonstrations on drying food or milking cows. She joined up with a group of female NOFA members who were pushing against the organization's boys' club atmosphere and talked directly about issues unique to women who farmed.

In 1974, Gershuny signed on to grow beets and green beans for a community cannery. A church group had funded a commercial kitchen for low-income families to can the vegetables and fruits they had grown in their own gardens. The cooperative would pay for its antipoverty work by selling organic pickled beets, apple–rose hip butter, and dilly beans, and Gershuny, who was then reading everything she could about soil and organic farming methods, took charge of growing the raw materials.

Even though she oversaw the garden plot from seed to harvest, when she saw the cans of pickles with the word *organic* printed on the label, it seemed to her such a flimsy and fallible way to delineate clean from chemical addled, small scale from industrial. As she would later write:

> If ["organic"] only meant that no chemical pesticides or herbicides and no synthetic fertilizers were used, we clearly met that standard. But to me this wasn't enough. I thought that organic should be defined by positive values—what it is that's good, not what it isn't that's bad. And I also understood that "organic by neglect" was not acceptable—just because the apples and rosehips were not being sprayed or fertilized doesn't mean they were any better than orchard-grown fruit, and could actually be of poorer quality.[56]

Gershuny's concerns weren't idle speculation. At the Brattleboro farmers' market, Howie Prussack would notice amateur farmers looking at the lines that formed in front of his own stand, which advertised organic food, and start telling people they were growing organically, too. "We felt you can't just be organic if you say you're organic, so what does organic mean?" he says.

When NOFA advertised the part-time certification job in 1977, Gershuny was the only applicant. She proved so apt for the task that the subject of organic certification would frame the next twenty years of her career.

At the time, NOFA was still a casual affair, she says, not the high-profile alliance of seven state NOFA chapters and five thousand members that it is today. It may have been the first organic farming association, but it was no longer the only one. The Maine Organic Farmers and Gardeners Association had started within months of the founding meeting at Samuel Kaymen's farm. A group of fifty-four California farmers—including the Lundberg family who had first grown rice organically—formed the California Certified Organic Farmers in 1973. Soon after, farmers in Oregon and Washington formed a loose association they called Tilth, and the Organic Growers of Michigan formed in the same year. By the late 1970s, most of these associations were discussing the topic of organic certification.[57]

The Rodales first tackled the issue in 1971 by inviting farmers to submit soil samples for testing by an independent lab, which the publisher would pay for. If the soil contained 3 percent organic matter, the Rodales judged it proof that the farmer was amending his or her soil with the right materials and would award the farm a seal. In January 1972, Rodale Press reported that 942 farms had earned the mark, but the company soon decided that it did not want to be a regulatory agency.[58] So the publisher's nonprofit Rodale Institute helped California Certified Organic Farmers lay out its own standards, which were cursory enough to fit on one page, and then aided Tilth in drafting its own.[59]

Around the same time, a representative from the U.S. Food and Drug Administration told the *San Francisco Chronicle* that the government wasn't interested in developing organic standards. "We're not thinking about moving into this area because there's no way to inspect the end product," the representative said. "I know of no laboratory test that indicates what kind of fertilizer has gone into something. In fact, nobody has actually proved there's any real difference between organic and nonorganic food."[60] Which was fine with the counterculture farmers of NOFA, who had no great trust in the feds.

Working on the smallest of stipends, Gershuny drew up a one-page list of certification standards for growing produce organically. Farmers could be certified as organic or in transition, and the guidelines specified farmers had to show that 5 percent of their soil was organic matter; the guidelines made no mention of milk or meat. The program was run by and for farmers, whom Gershuny asked to approve the standards, as did the board of NOFA. They agreed to meet every year to reassess what the requirements would be and would pay their $15 a year for the right to use NOFA's logo as a seal.[61]

Howie Prussack, Samuel Kaymen's apprentice and a witness to the organization's founding, was the first to sign up.

Gershuny could only recruit a dozen farmers in 1978. That number would stay low, she says, until a spike in 1984, when a large Maryland wholesaler began buying organic produce from Vermont farmers on the condition they got certified—it wanted some way to verify to its retail customers that the farmers were doing what they claimed—and another surge in 1989 after a scandal over Alar pesticide residues on apples brought organics out of the fringe and into the public eye.

It wouldn't be until the 1990s that the federal government took up the charge of regulating organic agriculture, passing the Organic Foods Production Act of 1990 (a bill introduced by Senator Patrick Leahy of Vermont) and adopting national organic standards, overseen by the USDA, in 2000.

Some of the back-to-the-landers would see the standards—with their lists of approved soil amendments and controversial food additives, the copious paperwork and fees they required, their exposure to the influence of large corporations—as a betrayal of their original agrarian vision. Robert Houriet's vision of a web of small rural farms, working cooperatively, endured only in the form of farmers' markets.

By 2000, though, Samuel Kaymen was able to take advantage of the new federal organic standards. In 1982, he had established his third teaching farm on a rocky plot of land in Wilton, New Hampshire, where he raised a herd of Jersey cows. The farm school didn't survive. The cattle herds were soon sold off. But the business Kaymen started in his kitchen, Stonyfield Farm, became the largest organic yogurt producer in the United States.

# 6

# Vegetarians on the Curry Trail

THE FOUNDERS OF THE NEW RIVERSIDE Cafe in Minneapolis say the decision to go vegetarian was almost arbitrary, made in 1971 at one of the collective's first Monday-night meetings, which could be interminable or enjoyable depending on whether the pot smoke or the rancor was thickest.

Whether or not to serve meat was, some say, the group's first big argument, and the meeting stretched on for hours. A few of the members were vegetarian, fewer devotedly so, but the problem was more practical than ideological: since there were no other vegetarian restaurants in town, they had no idea whether anyone would patronize the place. Finally, one of the cooks broke down and told the group she couldn't think of working at a restaurant that served meat. She would have to quit if they didn't lay down the braunschweiger. It was the defining dissent, the one that everyone lined up behind.

Once the New Riverside Cafe—"the Riv," as they'd call it—made the decision, they faced the same challenges as millions of people in their generation: figuring out what to cook.

Not only were they giving up meat, they were also giving up soup cans and frozen entrées and white flour and sugar. They were, in many ways, stripping down the standard American diet of the late 1960s, as monotonous and prepackaged as it could be. They were taking their diets back to the preindustrial era and rebuilding them anew, with whole grains, legumes, and fresh vegetables.

The chefs of this utopian cuisine were masses of twenty-year-olds, living in communes, thirdhand buses, and rambling houses. A generation of cooks instilled with the virtues of voluntary poverty and anti-imperialism, stirred by Marcuse or dope or the need to remake the world in their own image, whatever that might be. A generation willing to pluck any idea out of the fringe and test it out, whether it came from occult bookstores, Chinatown acupuncturists, or health-food stores.

They willed this new cuisine into existence. Then came the real struggle of making it delicious.

Vegetarian food—which was not quite synonymous with hippie food, but rather was its aesthetic vanguard—underwent a radical transformation between the late 1960s and late 1970s: from the wan to the polychrome, from austere to bold and playful, even, at times, extravagant. The transformation happened in millions of communes and homesteads, aided by restaurants like the New Riverside Cafe and a small cadre of vegetarian cookbook authors. These professional cooks didn't just make vegetarian food taste better. They helped shoppers at natural-foods stores and co-ops figure out what to do with all the new natural foods they decided they should be eating, and in the process, broadened the American palate.

THE NEW RIVERSIDE Cafe was located in the heart of a gently decaying neighborhood called the West Bank. As the working-class Scandinavians who occupied its warren of houses died or moved to the suburbs, they were replaced by University of Minnesota students, activists, and hippies, who opened shops and community centers to serve their new clientele.[1]

Father Bill Teska, a twenty-eight-year-old, big-boned Episcopalian priest with a bulldog grin and a laugh so sharp and loud it could crack pavement, called the café into being as a way to reach out to the hippie kids. Teska wasn't far from one himself. He had frequented the West Bank during his summer breaks from divinity school at Yale. Upon graduation, the priest-to-be presented the Twin Cities bishop with a proposal that he should attend to the counterculture—in the spirit of what the church was calling "ministries of presence," finding ways to be present in marginal communities without proselytizing.[2]

In his official title as assistant Episcopalian chaplain at the University of Minnesota, Teska was out most nights engaging with the freaks, wearing his clerical collar under a blue-jean jacket, showing them at minimum that living a spiritual life didn't preclude being a two-fisted drinker and a swearer of some repute.

He also became a bridge between hippies and the Establishment. "One of the things that I could contribute," Teska says now, "was the illusion of respectability. Even though I had long hair and a beard, I had a collar on, I was Ivy League educated, and I could talk." Teska set up a storefront church in a neighborhood that also housed a Free Store inspired by the Diggers. He established a free clinic as well. Then he persuaded an ecumenical group of mainstream Christian chaplains that they should give him the seed money to open a gathering spot, bringing the community together with coffee, music, and food.

When the neighborhood residents discovered that their enclave was in danger of being obliterated, the café took on a new role: a space to organize the opposition. For a decade or so, a local corporation named Heller Segal had been buying huge tracts of houses in the West Bank and renting them, at low rates, to students and artists. The property owner, then, was ideally poised to profit from the Minneapolis Housing and Redevelopment Authority's 1968 plan to redevelop the West Bank. The agency gave the private developer permission to raze a hundred acres of slumping houses and decaying retail buildings and to replace them with high-rise, low-rent apartments. Heller Segal hadn't reckoned with the fact that all the young, itinerant students and artists depending on the neighborhood's cheap rents didn't want the West Bank to become a forest of high-rise towers.[3]

Teska pitched his idea of a café and social-organizing spot to his friends in West Bank activist circles. It would be set up along the lines of a European café, complete with strong coffee, croissants, and newspapers clipped onto wooden rods. One of the friends who bought in was Ralph Wittcoff, a graduate of the New School for Social Research in New York who had recently come back to Minneapolis after motorcycling around Europe and spending seven months on a kibbutz in Israel.

Another West Bank connection, Carolyn Brown Zniewski, signed on to work in the kitchen, and recruited friends to help her cook. Brown Zniewski was working in a bookstore at the time and had just helped a couple of friends set up a buying club for natural foods on their enclosed back porch. They wanted to bypass the local health-food store in downtown Minneapolis. "It was all very expensive and kind of for weirdos from Hollywood," she says. The friends bought hundred-pound sacks of brown rice and giant tubs of peanut butter and honey, setting out a scale and a money box for people to pay for what they took.[4]

In September 1970, the New Riverside Cafe opened on the corner of Nineteenth and Riverside with a small front room, a tiny kitchen stocked only with a hot plate, and a back room expansive enough to fit a stage and a bunch of tables. The menu wasn't much more extensive than egg salad, tuna salad, and braunschweiger sandwiches, as well as coffee and fresh apple cider. The cooks would make pots of soup and batches of granola in their home kitchens, wheeling them to the Riv in a child's wagon and praying that they wouldn't encounter a health inspector on their route.

Within a few weeks of opening, Wittcoff realized that he had hired too many of his friends and the café was already going to go under. He had to fire some of them. "I sat down with the rest of the staff," Wittcoff says, "and told them, 'I'm going to do it, but that's it. I'm also firing myself as the manager because obviously I'm not a very good manager.'"

Wittcoff proposed to the remaining five or six staff that, in order to make the economics work, they operate on a kibbutz model. Many of them were already living together. Instead of receiving wages, the café would pay their rent and a few people's car payments. They could eat at the café and use its wholesalers to stock their home pantries. In return, they'd have to work at least three shifts. Since Wittcoff had fired himself as manager, all decisions had to be settled through consensus.

When the rest of the Riv staff backed Wittcoff's proposal, they became a tribe as much as an anarchist collective or an activist cell. They soon called themselves the "Dire Wolf Gang," after a song by their favorite band, the Grateful Dead.


THE NEW RIVERSIDE Cafe's decision to go vegetarian was one that millions of young Americans were making in the early 1970s. Some of them had tapped into the oneness of all existence through LSD and realized they couldn't eat their fellow beings, just as Stephen Gaskin and his followers had.[5] Some had come across George Ohsawa's *Zen Macrobiotics* and had become convinced that meat was way too yang for their systems. Others committed themselves so deeply to the peace movement that their abhorrence of violence extended to their diets as well. Frankie Lappé's bestselling *Diet for a Small Planet* convinced many more to bring their diet in line with their politics, swapping out pork chops for complementary proteins.

Lucy Horton, who hitched around the country for a year collecting recipes for her 1971 cookbook, *Country Commune Cooking,* found West Coast freaks to be predominantly vegetarian, while the communards she interviewed in New Mexico and the Northeast raised all manner of livestock for food. She couldn't decide whether the split was due to the weather or the spiritual climate. ("Commune people in California and Oregon seemed more religious and idealistic, less intellectual, political, and profane than their counterparts elsewhere," she wrote.) The vegetarian communards she quizzed told her that they were most concerned over the hormones in commercial meat, felt that it put a drag on their energetic resonance, or were convinced that evolution had intended humans to eat only fruits and nuts. Some simply couldn't afford it.[6]

Mainstream newspapers of the early 1970s reported incessantly on the vegetarian "fad." "The Age of Vegetarius has dawned," one *Chicago Tribune* reporter wrote in July 1971. "No longer confined to beansprout-thin mystics of the Far East (who, I was taught, could not afford meat anyhow), vegetarianism has become the passionately endorsed routine for a growing number of Counter-Culture people."[7]

"Some youngsters say it's because they're against killing; others cite ecological concerns and a few point to religion," commented the *New York Times* in a 1972 article about teenage vegetarians. "But whatever their reasons, clearly more young people are turning to vegetarianism."[8] The *Los Angeles Times* chronicled the demand for vegetarian food at college cafeterias.[9] Newspapers cautioned the parents of young vegetarians on how to help their children get the right amounts of protein and vitamins.

ANOTHER OF THE New Riverside's key cooks, Ruth Ann Torstenson (now LeMasters), says now that she had always wanted to be a vegetarian but never knew how until college, when one of her friends fed her a bowl of brown rice and vegetables and she said to herself, "'Oh, yeah, you could eat this and you don't have to eat meat.' It was just natural to me."

She learned about macrobiotics from the Jook Savages, an inhumanly cool jug band who lived together on a commune in northern Minnesota and kept to the Ohsawa diet. Torstenson tried Ohsawa's ten-day brown-rice fast.[10] "You really don't need drugs after that," she says. "You're pretty much walking around in a higher state. But I eventually realized that it wasn't the right diet for me. I'm too much of a midwesterner. I need cheese."

Her commitment to vegetarianism escalated as she studied with a University of Minnesota lecturer named Usharbudh Arya, who also taught yoga and meditation in the attic of his house. Dr. Arya taught the students about mantras and pranayama (yogic breathing) but also about ethics. He would screen films of slaughterhouses and exhort his pupils to back away from the suffering they were causing. Torstenson would iron Arya's dhotis for him as a devotional practice and, in turn, stay for vegetarian dinners cooked by his wife.

Food became her cause. When University of Minnesota students went on strike in May 1970, protesting the Kent State shootings and the Vietnam War, she brought wagonfuls of natural-foods dishes to the strikers. She would try, as she says, "to raise consciousness about food at the same time." Just after graduating, she was wandering Riverside Avenue, in search of a job, and came across a storefront with a sign reading LOOKING FOR WORKERS. Inside were Carolyn Brown Zniewski, Ralph Wittcoff, and a few others, plotting the opening of the New Riv. "I just fell in with them," she says, and stayed for the rest of the decade, recruiting her sister Linnea to join the crew.

When the New Riverside Cafe collective went vegetarian (aside from Gracie's Amazing Special, a tuna salad sandwich with lettuce, tomato, and sprouts on whole-wheat bread[11]), they had to work out what would bring in customers and how to feed themselves, since the café was their dining room.

"Our aim was just to make vegetarian food so delicious that you didn't really want meat with it," Brown Zniewski says. It took them a few years to get there.

FOR MORE THAN a century, the standard bearers for the vegetarian cause in America had been the Seventh-day Adventists. In June 1863, Ellen G. White, the prophetess and spiritual leader of the sect, had the first of a series of visions that she wrote about in her 1864 book, *Spiritual Gifts*. The visions guided her followers to give up meat, milk, and eggs, as well as tobacco, stimulating drinks like coffee and tea, and drugs, whether physician prescribed or otherwise; the Adventists had joined the temperance movement before that, so alcohol was out as well.[12] White's spiritual guides must have been attending Sylvester Graham's lectures, because the new proscriptions echoed Graham's crusade against refined flour, his suspicion of spices, and his advice to eat only two meals a day.

Diet was only one aspect of Sister White's visions. Two years later, the Adventists founded a health sanitarium in Battle Creek, Michigan. Within a few decades it would be nationally known, as would its head physician and the Adventists' most renowned dietary emissary, John Harvey Kellogg, who would lead the "San" from 1876 until his death in 1943.

Kellogg was an ardent advocate of drugless treatments like the water cure, vibrating belts, enema machines, and electrotherapy. He was also a staunch vegetarian—meat would putrefy in the intestines and poison the blood, he preached to his patients—who invented a score of convenience foods for meatless eaters and general gut health. Kellogg, his wife, and his brother, Will, created a breakfast cereal they called Granola (see page 235) and had an even greater success with cornflakes.

He also concocted Protose and Nuttose, amalgams of wheat gluten and ground tree nuts or peanuts. They were two of the first meat analogues that vegetarian Adventist families would survive on through the mid-twentieth century. Later generations of Adventists learned from Chinese artisans how to make soy milk and soybean curd, and by the 1920s, Adventist-founded companies like Loma Linda and Worthington Foods were producing canned soy cutlets and sausages that they sold through Adventist groceries and health-food stores located around the country.

By the early twentieth century, Adventist cookbooks spelled out a repertoire of vegetarian dishes that relied heavily on meat substitutes— Frizzled Protose in Eggs, Nut Fricassee with Browned Sweet Potatoes, Lentil Fritters, Baked Eggplant à la Creme.[13] Graham himself would have been pleased with Adventist food, which rarely had more than eight ingredients in a dish. Spices and dried herbs were seen almost as rarely as giant squid in the Pacific Ocean.[14]

The Adventist diet did not evolve all that radically until 1968, when Frank and Rosalie Hurd, a middle-aged couple from rural Minnesota, published *Ten Talents*. Their cookbook merged Adventist vegetarian cuisine with the Southern California health food of Paul Bragg and Gayelord Hauser. Frank Hurd was a chiropractic doctor, Rosalie a researcher by temperament. The couple, who ran a small health-food store and homeschooled their five children, also lectured on nutrition and sold a breakfast cereal called Get Up and Go around the health-food circuit.

The Hurds disdained the canned Swiss Stakes and FriChik that Adventist companies would sell. Instead, they took their inspiration from the Bible, particularly the books of Genesis and Daniel. "*Ten Talents* focuses on fresh grains, fresh fruits, fresh vegetables, seeds, nuts, all of the foods that God gave us in the beginning," Rosalie Hurd now says. "This book goes back to God's original diet. That's what he gave Adam and Eve in the beginning. He told them, 'I give you every herb that bears seed and every tree in which there was the fruit with the seed in it. To you it shall be for meat or for food.' And to the cattle he gave every green herb and the grasses. So we have in the original diet that God gave us all the elements of nutrition that we need. Nothing is missing."

In *Ten Talents,* the Hurds published some of the first recipes for modern granola and "familia" (untoasted granola, which some people would call muesli) to appear in print.[15] Forty-five years before cashew and coconut creams became staples in vegan kitchens, the Hurds concocted methods to make these nondairy milks. They also used nutritional yeast and soy sauce as flavor builders rather than vitamin power-ups, concocted soy ice cream, and incorporated sprouted grains and pulses into a plethora of recipes.

With the exception of chop suey and a short list of respectable Italian dishes—Rosalie came from a family of Italy-born vegetarians—the Hurds' palate was as British American as that of their predecessors: loaf after loaf (millet barley, carrot rice), seconded by fritters and patties (peanuts with cornmeal, sprouted garbanzos, soybeans with millet and peanut butter). An eighth teaspoon of celery seed might sneak its way into a dish here, a half teaspoon of cumin there, but the dishes tended to be seasoned with onion powder, soy sauce, and the sparing use of dried herbs—not altogether different from what you'd find in the Betty Crocker cookbook of the time.

Frank and Rosalie Hurd's *Ten Talents* would sell hundreds of thousands of copies, inspire the vegan cooking at the Farm in Tennessee, and make its way onto the shelves of the New Riverside Cafe, one of the collective's very first cookbooks.

BY 1972, BILL Teska's vision of a café where he could stop in before work
for an espresso, a croissant, and a bottle of Perrier was so obfuscated
that you would never have guessed the New Riverside's European inspiration.

For one, the café had been forced out of its first location, after Heller
Segal announced they were razing the block, a sort of teaser for their ar-
chitectural clear-cutting plans. The Riv had moved two blocks away to
a prime location on the corner of Cedar and Riverside Avenues, gaining
a full kitchen and losing a piano, which had taken one bump too many
when the collective rolled it down the block.

Now it had a long, triangular counter with a steam table and pastry
case, walls paneled in reclaimed barn wood, stained-glass panels and
plants hanging around the room, and a small stage where live bands
played almost every night. The collective installed a darkroom and
printing press in the basement of the building, where members would
design elaborate calendars for the upcoming performances. Most of the
West Bank found out about shows and neighborhood demonstrations,
however, just by passing by the café's bank of windows, on which the
workers would write in drippy white shoe polish.

Inspired by Wittcoff's kibbutz experience, the Riv was even more of
an anarchist collective than ever. The Dire Wolf Gang's membership
had swelled to twenty, and to bring in cash the tribe had started a catering operation, a car repair collective, and a moving service (Macho Mov-
ers, Uninc.), all run out of a pay phone in the café (it took years to get
everyone to agree to pay for a business phone). Some friends had bought
a farm in Wisconsin, and the tribe would make regular runs down there
to help with chores, hosting back-to-the-landers who wanted a break
from the country in return.

The no-paycheck system worked for at least a few years. The households would order food from the café's suppliers—the tiny backroom
buying club Brown Zniewski's friends had started, which had evolved

into the North Country Food Co-op, and a co-op wholesaler called the People's Warehouse. If someone needed cash for cigarettes or a beer, she'd pull it out of the till and write a note in the logbook next to the cash register.

Not only had the Riv abolished wages, it had gotten rid of prices as well. "We decided not to have any," early member Gracie Schwartz says. "Teska wanted to charge what the market would bear and everybody else would say no." Instead, a portrait of a furry, benevolent Karl Marx hung next to the register, presiding over one of his most famous sayings: "FROM EACH ACCORDING TO HIS ABILITY, TO EACH ACCORDING TO HIS NEED." The policy delighted some customers and befuddled others, and when pressed, the staff provided hints about what most people would pay. "It made some people very uncomfortable," Schwartz says. "So it was really kind of fun."[16]

The new kitchen allowed the Riv to become a full-service vegetarian restaurant, too, its food overseen by a cadre of women, including Carolyn Brown Zniewski, Gracie Schwartz, and Ruth Ann and Linnea Torstenson.

At the collective's Monday-night meetings, where they'd discuss anti–Heller Segal actions and choose their shifts, the food coordinator chosen for the week would set the menu, create the shopping lists, and direct the action, as much as anyone could direct an anarchist counterculture crew.

Grilled cheese sandwiches with vegetables were always on the menu, as well as a few salads, Yogi Yogurt banana milk shakes, and the day's soup—split pea, miso dill, creamy pumpkin. Tofu was a rarity then, but the cooks concocted a soyburger with vegetables that went down with the university students who frequented the place. The Riv's most famous staple was a holdout from the cooks' early experiments in macrobiotics: Rice and Vegetables (or "RNV"), fried brown rice with whatever produce the crew had on hand, seasoned with tamari and the chef's choice of herbs. They'd sell it in sizes from cup to bowl and give it away to homeless neighbors or students too poor to eat.

The crux of the kitchen's creativity could always be found at the steam table: the main dish of the day, which would feed the masses from lunch until the bands began to play.

The cooks, who had begun grinding their own wheat berries into flour, plucked the café's whole-wheat bread recipe from Beatrice Trum Hunter's *Natural Foods Cookbook* and baked loaves once a week, along with whole-grain pies, muffins, and cheesecakes sweetened with honey, reminiscent of Jim Baker's famous dessert at the Aware Inn a decade and a half before.[17]

Baking with whole grains was an ever-evolving challenge, the Riv's early cooks say. So was finding substitutes for meat. Brown Zniewski remembers consulting *Ten Talents* for recipe ideas and Adelle Davis for nutritional advice.

Even the most pedestrian ingredient—the fresh produce they bought through the co-op warehouse—represented terra incognita for cooks raised with pantries stocked with colored boxes and silvery cylinders. "Vegetables were just a wonder," Gracie Schwartz says. "When I was growing up, we had canned vegetables and they tasted terrible. The difference between canned and fresh was mind-blowing."

Like so many counterculture cooks, especially in the early 1970s, most of the main dishes the Riv cooks invented were casseroles: grains and pulses layered with vegetables and almost always topped with cheese. They'd give the dishes names like "Bengali Boogie" or "Guerrilla Garbanzos." It was bulk over bang, homestyle food, designed to feed a campground's worth of customers, not fancy but always wholesome. A later collective member characterized those early mains as "brown and grayish food" and said some days she dubbed the Riv, in fond exasperation, the "House of Beans."[18] Ruth Ann Torstenson says that so many of the dishes were seasoned with soy sauce, the great macrobiotic gift to hippies, that she used to tell her coworkers that when she had children she would name them Tamari and Tahini. (She didn't.)

Just as quickly, the collective identified ways to make their food less leaden and more interesting. They'd do "Oriental night" on Mondays, with chop suey and egg rolls, or stir-fried noodles from the Chinese food producer across the street. Italian day would be some familiar pasta dish, often lasagna, which they reenvisioned without meat. Mexican night usually featured tamale pie or enchiladas. They learned to make falafel and hummus. Greek moussaka became a hit.

In the absence of a strong culinary heritage, many people in the counterculture—particularly vegetarians—raided other traditions for dishes and flavors. It was a matter of survival as much as it was romanticizing the Other: if American vegetarian cookbooks couldn't teach them how to make this new natural-foods cuisine delicious, then perhaps the rest of the world could.


IN 1970, THE United States was predominantly white and non-Hispanic, but the country was on the brink of a demographic shift that would soon be sensed in every elementary school and every small town in the country. When President Johnson signed the 1965 Immigration and Naturalization Act, it eradicated quotas that concurrently made it easy to move from the United Kingdom, Ireland, and Germany and strangled legal immigration from Asia, Africa, Mexico, and Central America. From 1965 on, the act decreed, the United States immigration policy would now give preference to family members of American residents and to skilled workers. Immigration from Asia and Mexico immediately outpaced European arrivals as immigrants settled in the States and then brought over their families.[19]

Mexican Americans and Asian immigrants had long influenced American cuisine, particularly on the West Coast and in the Southwest and Hawaii. Even before macaroni and pizza went native, early-twentieth-century cookbooks already included dishes like tamale pie, chop suey, and sukiyaki. Calling a dish a "curry" usually meant a small spoonful of Madras curry powder, a spice blend that traveled with British colonists from South Asia to Europe, North America, Hong Kong, and Japan.

You could find Lebanese markets, Russian delis, and Indian restaurants in the major U.S. cities by the 1960s, but in gastronomic terms, American food was still largely beholden to Western Europe. It would be decades before the full effect of these waves of post-1965 immigration was sensed in restaurant listings, on grocery-store shelves, at farmers' markets, and in work potlucks. Most native-born Americans had lost their family culinary traditions, unless they lived in an urban Italian or Hungarian Jewish enclave. Traditional dishes had been filtered through the tastes of succeeding generations, original flavors gutted in the era of canned soups and frozen peas.

The key that opened the American palate up to the flavors of Asia and Central America may have been not immigration but romance. Baby boomers, raised in a time of European peace and educated about Asia in a time of television cameras and war, grew up with a visceral awareness of faraway countries. They were citizens of the world in a way few generations before them had been.

Young Americans developed a serious case of wanderlust, which the democratization of air travel helped satisfy. Between 1965 and 1975, airlines spent some $14 billion on new and bigger planes, like the Boeing 747 and the DC-10. Airlines were shuttling seven times more people in 1966 than they did in 1950,[20] and airports were building new runways at a furious clip. There were so many seats on the new jumbo jets that airlines were forced to begin offering discount rates to keep them filled.[21]

The price wars of the early 1970s were ferocious. Charter airlines would sell transatlantic fares for as low as $120; you could get from San

Francisco to Brussels for $99. Mainstream airlines began offering youth fares to compete. Pan Am even scheduled one flight a week with rock music piped in from the speakers and flight attendants who dispensed beer and sangria with their peanuts.[22]

According to *Newsweek,* in the summer of 1970, seven hundred thousand Americans traveled to Europe—the magazine, in fact, used the word *swarmed.* The twenty-one-year-olds who would jet from New York to Luxembourg on Icelandic Air were not carrying enough traveler's checks to stay in two-star pensions and dine at country inns they had looked up in the Michelin Guide. "There's this fetish, a sort of self-imposed cultural modesty about American kids spending money here," Garry Cok, who ran a student hotel in Holland, told *Newsweek* in 1970.[23]

Young travelers were buying the new Eurailpasses that allowed them to travel anywhere in a thirteen-country zone, sleeping like sardines on the trains' pull-out couches.[24] Or they would take a bus from the station to the nearest highway and hold up a sign and an outstretched thumb.

"Costs you nothing to flake out in farm fields or barns, in toolsheds, doorways, buildings under construction, on beaches, in parks, especially in London, in Amsterdam's big open hippie-splattered Dam Square, in the tunnels of undergrounds," advised the *Los Angeles Times*'s "Vagabond Youth" columnist.[25] In Greece, they stayed in Cretan caves. In Norway, they camped in the Oslo parklands surrounding King Olav's palace. Like Ralph Wittcoff, they caught a boat from Cyprus to Israel and joined the kibbutzim.

Legions of young Americans dispensed with the initial plane trip and drove their tents and campers south to Mexico, some fleeing the draft, others in search of cheap food and abundant sun. The tiny town of San Miguel de Allende, home to a small artist colony of northerners, became a hippie mecca; so did Acapulco and the state of Oaxaca.

So many ambled south with no clear plans to return to their home country that, by 1969, American newspapers were warning that Mexican border guards were refusing to issue tourist visas to kids whose hair was too long or who needed a bath. Other stories reported, with a smirk obvious from the first paragraph to the last, that Mexican police were rounding up nudist camps and jailing hundreds of young Americans on drug charges.[26]

Some hippies headed east.

In the late 1960s and all through the 1970s, India—both the geopolitical entity and the India of orientalist fantasies—infiltrated American pop culture in ways it had never before.

Indian spiritual teachers had been traveling through North America, drawing followers to them like static-charged balloons, since the late nineteenth century.[27] A. C. Bhaktivedanta arrived in Boston in 1965, and members of his International Society for Krishna Consciousness, also known as "Hare Krishnas," were soon dancing in public parks and serving free vegetarian meals in their temples.

Though Swamis Satchidananda and Muktananda, Meher Baba, Sri Chinmoy, and Maharaj Ji all accumulated followers in the 1960s, a quartet of four British seekers may have done the most to ignite the American counterculture's curiosity about Indian spirituality. In 1967, Beatles guitarist George Harrison brought his bandmates to a lecture in London by Maharishi Mahesh Yogi, who was teaching transcendental meditation, or TM. In February 1968, all four Beatles flew to the maharishi's ashram in Rishikesh, north of Delhi, to study for two months in the company of Donovan, one of the Beach Boys, and Mia Farrow, then known as much for being Frank Sinatra's estranged wife as the star of *Rosemary's Baby*.[28] The trip made international news.

Before the two months were up, George and John fell out with the maharishi, but the band was at the peak of its influence on American pop culture at the time, and TM took off. Millions of young Americans, freaks and squares alike, showed up for the basic four-day training in

TM with six fresh flowers, two pieces of fruit, a white handkerchief, and $35. The outpouring of interest was so great *Life* magazine called 1968 the "Year of the Guru."[29]

The impact of the spiritual onslaught on pop culture was undeniable: guru jackets, sitar-infused psychedelic rock, Ravi Shankar's international stardom, Indian-print sheets, and the Hippie Trail.

The Hippie Trail brought aspiring sadhus (spiritual renunciates), as well as adventurers who had no idea which limbs to fold to form the basic yoga poses, overland from Europe to India from 1965 until the 1979 Islamic Revolution in Iran, when the country closed its doors.

The first regular London-to-Calcutta bus service, known as "The Indiaman," started up in 1957, succeeded by budget tours, Land Rovers, 4WD trucks, independent operators, and an Amsterdam-based service called the Magic Bus, which legendarily smuggled kilos of Afghan hash as it traveled back west.[30] The Indian government estimated in 1966 that forty-seven thousand Americans a year were touring around India and Nepal. In 1971, that number rose to fifty-five thousand—and ninety thousand annual visitors besieged Nepal alone by 1974.[31]

The thing about traveling on the cheap, among the poor, was that there was little buffering between travelers and host countries. Westerners clung to Westerners and frequented the businesses whose proprietors learned English, French, or German. But they ate whatever they could get their hands on, not coddled by the cosmopolitan mediocrity of higher-priced hotels. Hippie trekkers would eat gristly mutton kebabs scoured by cumin and smoke, banana leaves colorfully spotted with rice, sambar, and avial. They dredged flatbreads through thick pools of minted yogurt and gorged on silky eggplant stuffed with rice. The lucky ones came home, burdened by the weight of all the stories they had accumulated, and fed the curiosity of their friends who never left North America.

THE EFFECTS OF this new cultural porousness and openness to innovation could be seen in U.S. cookbooks of the 1970s. Some of the greatest
English-language experts on foreign cuisines published their first books
during this decade, including Richard Olney (*The French Menu Cookbook*, 1970, and *Simple French Food*, 1974), Claudia Roden (*A Book of
Middle Eastern Food*, 1968), Diana Kennedy (*The Cuisines of Mexico*,
1972), Irene Kuo (*The Key to Chinese Cooking*, 1977), Madhur Jaffrey
(*An Invitation to Indian Cooking*, 1973), and Paula Wolfert (*Couscous and
Other Good Food from Morocco*, 1973, and *Mediterranean Cooking*, 1977).

Just as significant, perhaps, was the rollout of the Time Life "Foods of
the World" series, which began publication in 1968. Households would
sign up to begin receiving installments, each containing a hardbound,
full-color cookbook describing a different region's culinary traditions,
accompanied by a smaller spiral-bound booklet of recipes. Big names in
the food world like M. F. K. Fisher and Craig Claiborne authored volumes, the funding was lavish, and the cookbooks gave the same weight
to Southeast Asian, West African, and Creole food as they did to Austrian or French provincial cooking. It's hard to find a cook who came of
age between 1970 and 1990 who hadn't spent hours poring over them.

All those cuisines influenced vegetarian cooks, and simultaneously.
Given that vegetarian food up until the 1970s was either beige—literally
and figuratively—or heavy on the raw and the juiced, the macrobiotic
cookbooks that the fledgling hippies circulated in the mid-1960s came
across as rampantly exotic. Despite their esoteric yin-yang polarities and
the fact that the strongest flavors came from soy sauce, toasted sesame,
and miso, they provided young cooks with a new template for vegetarian
dishes made with whole grains. There was just one problem with most
macrobiotic recipes: in the hands of American kids, who didn't have the
exposure to subtler Japanese cooking techniques, the food could come
out as flavorful as a bath towel.

As Lucy Horton's 1972 *Country Commune Cooking* documented, hippies in the remotest of farms were already pulling ideas out of other cuisines. In her travels among back-to-the-land enclaves, Horton took down recipes for the Atlantis commune's West African ground nut stew; a few simple curries, one seasoned with tamari (she called the soy sauce "the sine qua non of commune cooking"); an herbed vegetable stew served over bulgur, which one Vermont commune wishfully dubbed "couscous"; something called Mexican-Italian Goulash; and falafel, which a resident of Goat Farm in Oregon learned how to make on a kibbutz in Israel.

Two of the cookbooks that set the tone for the New Riverside Cafe's food in those early years were Frances Moore Lappé's first edition of *Diet for a Small Planet* and the 1973 *Recipes for a Small Planet,* written by Ellen Buchman Ewald, who had contributed recipes to Lappé's first book. Their approach: protein first.

The more Lappé looked into the key ingredient pairings that she considered "complementary proteins," such as grains with dairy, or grains with beans or lentils, the more she recognized that the ancients had long ago intuited these lessons, serving tortillas with pintos, or rice and dal. She and Ewald included a few non-American combinations in her first version, like a Brazilian black-bean feijoada made without pig tails and ears, and an attempt at South Indian masala dosa (rice-and-mung-bean crepes).

*Diet for a Small Planet* changed the way many Americans thought about vegetarian food. It did not, however, result in *amazing* vegetarian food. Lappé and Ewald started their recipe development with the premise "How can we get enough protein in our diets?" and then used gram scales to measure out ingredients in the right combinations. For every appetizing-looking tabouli there were three dishes with names like Nutty Noodle Casserole and Herbed Soybean Bulgur Casserole.

So much of vegetarian food in the early 1970s continued in the noble tradition of function over form. It would take a twenty-two-year-old film student named Anna Thomas at the University of California, Los Angeles to teach Americans how to make delicious food that, incidentally, didn't include meat.

When Thomas began cooking for herself, she found that she wasn't so much an ethical vegetarian as someone who didn't like meat all that much. She had that semiconscious gift for deliciousness that descends on some people or takes hold of cooks who have grown up enveloped in good food. In her earliest years, her Polish-speaking parents would throw massive dinner parties for their Detroit emigré circle and spend days preparing holiday feasts, painstakingly stuffing mushroom dumplings to float in beet-tinted barscz, cooking a dozen vegetables separately to combine into a jewel-toned salad, and filling a sideboard with cakes and confections.

In college, Thomas worked as a server in one of Los Angeles's health-food stores, but the food there didn't inspire her as much as her trips to Italian or Greek neighborhoods where she would root around the markets, examining their contents. She subscribed to *Gourmet*. Even more inspirational was Julia Child, Simone Beck, and Louisette Bertholle's magnum opus, *Mastering the Art of French Cooking*. The first volume, published in 1961, had already changed the nature of dinner parties among the middle class. But where anxious hosts attempted to master Coq au Vin or Blanquette de Veau to impress their guests, Thomas zeroed in on recipes for Épinards Gratinés (gratinéed spinach) and crepes filled with cheese and mushrooms.[32]

She studied books from the established gastronomes James Beard and the British chef Robert Carrier and pored over Italian and Middle Eastern cookbooks, in which vegetables were integrated in ways meat-and-potato Americans never imagined. She would go out to dinner at yogic restaurants in Los Angeles like the Yogi Bhajan–influenced Golden Temple, which became popular among meat eaters and vegetarians alike. "I was learning how somebody approached cooking, what they thought about, and what flavors they put together," she says. "Even in a cookbook that's meat-centric, there are a lot of things that aren't meat. Because there's a lot of food that everybody eats."

The more skilled she became, the more she enjoyed cooking, the more dinner parties she would throw. "My friends, who were also poverty-stricken students trying to make their student films, would come over and we'd eat together," she says. "They'd say, 'Oh, Anna, your cooking is so good, you should really make a cookbook.' This makes you feel like you're a genius." (Only when she had college-age children, she says, did she realize that everything tastes good when you're young and broke.) She documented the dishes she was cooking for her friends and eventually had enough recipes to fit into a book proposal.

The legendary Judith Jones at Knopf—Julia Child's editor!—thought Thomas's recipes were fresh and timely, and all of a sudden Thomas's lark resulted in an advance that kept her alive for a year. Knopf published *The Vegetarian Epicure* in 1972, and it became an immediate success.

Where the Seventh-day Adventists had focused on meat substitutes, and Frankie Lappé and Ellen Ewald on complementary proteins, Thomas waved off nutrition as if it were a pesky gnat and barreled into flavor. *The Vegetarian Epicure* was unabashedly, almost lasciviously rich: Cheese and Scallion Quiche. Trenette Pasta with Pesto. Polish classics peppered the book, as did French, Italian, Greek, and Indian—and not just a few vegetables doctored up with curry powder, but full spice blends.

Just as critically, Thomas gave instructions on how to put together a dinner party without meat at the center. She pooh-poohed the idea of one main course flanked by a few limp sides. "There is no one-dish meal," she wrote. Look, she added, at how Swedish smorgasbords or Thai dinners were arranged: "It is the possibility of endless variety that helps create a whole new style of eating—a new set of nonconventions." You might segue from almond soup to Camembert à la Vierge, potato salad, and cherry tomatoes, ending with chilled fresh fruit compote. Or you could start with creamed artichoke soup, put out a platter of mushroom pierogi, and knock 'em out with asparagus soufflé and dill sauce.

The book captured the imagination of vegetarians in the counterculture as well as the urban intelligentsia who wanted the most epicurean of earthly pleasures. Royalty checks began arriving in the mail, shocking Thomas. It wasn't until she headed to a theater one night with friends and passed Pickwick Book Shop, spying an entire window tiled with her cookbooks, that she realized that *The Vegetarian Epicure* had become a cultural event in itself.

Anna Thomas's 1978 bestselling sequel, *Vegetarian Epicure, Book Two,* was even more international in its scope than her first. Thomas took advantage of the royalties and her more sizable book advance, traveling to Portugal, Spain, Italy, France, Greece, Austria, Hungary, Poland, Mexico, Great Britain, and the Middle East. (She spent the considerable advance on making a feature-length film for her master's thesis.)

"Nearly everywhere I went," she wrote in the introduction to book two, "I discovered that the emphasis on meat was much less overwhelming than it is here in the United States, for economic reasons as well as from long-standing tradition. Most restaurant menus commonly include some enticing dishes made of fresh vegetables and fruits, eggs, cheese, or grains. In the *tavernas, trattorias, kellars,* cafés and ristorantes I visited, the choices offered me ranged from adequate to exciting."

From Spain came asparagus tortilla and white bean salad. From Poland, cabbage stuffed with mushrooms and barley. A host of vegetarian pastas followed her home from Italy, rajas con queso (roast peppers with cream cheese) and avocado tacos from Mexico, and from London's Indian restaurants, almost two dozen dishes, including Uppama (farina with spices and vegetables), Cachumber (tomato-cucumber salad), and Curried Cabbage and Peas. The food was so stimulating it would have made Sylvester Graham apoplectic.

THE MID-1970S BROUGHT the same culture-inhaling approach to cooking
to the New Riverside Cafe, too, even as the Dire Wolf Gang split up and
the restaurant started paying wages and charging fixed prices.

Ralph Wittcoff left when the pay-what-you-can era ended—he was
more interested in the social experiment than the restaurant business,
he says—and some of the early members joined a Marxist cult that de-
camped to Chicago.[33] Others had children and left for better-paying jobs.
The grand Riverside communes emptied, though many of the members
bought houses close by. Though Heller Segal built one shoddy-looking
high-rise, the West Bank's hippie resistance helped drive the developer
bankrupt and secure the café's future.

The nature of successful collectives—as the New Riverside was for
more than twenty years—is that they replenish themselves, each new
person who joins adding his or her experience and ideas to the group.
Ruth Ann Torstenson and her sister stayed on, as well as Eve MacLeish,
who had joined the collective in 1971 after high school and remained on
staff until she was twenty-eight. Every year, it seemed, the New Riverside's food would improve incrementally, usually at the same time its
recipes got more and more diverse.

A number of the cooks, including Torstenson and MacLeish, took
off in the winter and drove down to Mexico or Brazil for a few months,
returning to the embrace of the Riv when the season changed. They
brought back recipes for red and green sauces that required proper
chiles and tomatillos, and their cheese enchiladas became legendary. Mexican American quesadillas appeared on the menus regularly,
as did tostadas and something they called "Mexican Lasagna." The
cooks weren't doctrinaire.

One café poster from the late 1970s lists the week's specials: on Tuesday it was lasagna and minestrone, on Wednesday "sukiyaki" with egg
rolls and miso egg-drop soup. On Thursday they served the famous enchiladas, with barley-veggie soup, and on Friday, a whole-wheat pizza

that former cooks say would lure in as many customers as the night's entertainment did.

The first crew of chefs trained a crop of newcomers to the café collective who cared about food as food, not an economic experiment or a way to see a lot of good music. A new generation of bakers augmented the honey cheesecake and chocolate mousse with scones and fruit crumbles. Starting in the mid- to late 1970s, quiche made a strong showing. Jeff Garetz, who had worked in mainstream restaurants before joining the collective, introduced the concept of the French mother sauces, concocting wine-inflected cream sauces for morning crepes and tofu balls; he was known for his three-alarm, two-day chili that would burn the frost right off you in January. Chrycinda Bourdon arrived in 1979 and stayed for more than a decade, her name appearing on recipe after recipe in the New Riverside's binder, their origins Turkish, Polish, Armenian.

It would be a few more years before the collective would install a bank of woks and churn out tofu and tempeh stir-fries and before Hippie Trail veterans would add curries to the menu, but the New Riverside's millet-lentil-cheese casserole days were over.

DESPITE ITS GLOBAL inspiration, the vegetarian food that was emerging in the 1970s did not—could not—replicate the flavors of the cuisines it was appropriating. Dishes were stripped down, adapted, bastardized, often denuded of spice.

A few dishes that became iconic in the 1970s may, perhaps, have benefited from this waving off of tradition: both crepes and quiche—soigné in the 1960s, ubiquitous in vegetarian restaurants in the 1970s—were liberated from their classic forms to become containers for thousands of variations. Other dishes didn't fare as well. Sometimes taking out the meat meant removing the one ingredient that gave a particular dish any flavor. Some of the world's culinary glories were reduced to puddles of melted cheese.

Often, vegetarian cooks' ideals altered a classic dish beyond recognition—dispensing with sweeteners, substituting ingredients with earthier flavors, and loading up on complementary-protein seeds, wheat germ, or other inexcusable additions. So you find, say, a dosa—fermented rice-and-lentil crepes—in *Laurel's Kitchen* made from brown-rice flour and soy flour. The Tibetan Buddhist *Odiyan Country Cookbook* (1977) amplified Rich Nut Tabouleh with chopped cashews, tamari, and dry sherry. *The Organic Yenta* (1976) stuffed green peppers with brown rice, mushrooms, wheat-germ oil, and sunflower seeds.

Whether or not young cooks had made a pilgrimage across Asia or had driven their truck around the Yucatan Peninsula, they would pluck ideas from cookbooks or travelers' tales and reverse-engineer them with the ingredients they were able to find in suburban American grocery stores—a much more limited selection than cooks would find forty years later.

And yet, to read these recipes, for all their counterintuitive adaptations and culinary betrayals, is exciting, too: witnessing vegetarian American cuisine become a glorious mishmash, united only by its reliance on whole foods and by its eclecticism. Nonvegetarian, noncounterculture eaters at the time may only have seen hippie food, vegetarian food, as brown or lacking. They were missing out on how it was transforming kitchens across the country.

Cooking from the vegetarian cookbooks of the mid- to late 1970s would fill home cooks' cabinets with jars of new spices, make tahini and soy sauce refrigerator essentials, lead the American-born to tiny markets that catered to new immigrants, and stuff their canvas totes with produce their parents may never have cooked, or even seen.

For a short period, vegetarians were the culinary avant-garde, evidence that Americans—particularly white Americans—were emerging from an era of dominant-culture assimilation into a multicultural one. However halfhearted, naive, or imperialist, American vegetarians were bringing once-foreign flavors into their homes, transforming the alien into the quotidian, making these tastes their own.

THE APOGEE OF this transition would be a cookbook that came out of another collective restaurant, this one in Ithaca, New York.

The cookbook's author, Mollie Katzen, grew up in upstate New York, in a kosher household where meat was at the center of the plate and vegetables were rarely fresh, unless you counted the iceberg lettuce or cabbage in the salad bowl.[34]

As a college freshman at Cornell, Katzen went to work for a macrobiotic café at the Ithaca Seed Company, learning the ins and outs of yin and yang and overdosing, she says, on soy sauce. But when she transferred to the San Francisco Art Institute, she came across vegetarian food of a very different character. A radio advertisement for the Shandygaff, on the corner of Polk and Washington, caught her attention and she went to check it out.

The Shandygaff brought to vegetarian cuisine the profligate freshness of California's produce farms as well as San Francisco's urbane culinary sensibility. It was as if the cooks had combined Jim Baker's two restaurants, the classic European-inspired Aware Inn and the beatific raw-food Source. "I'd never seen anything like it," Katzen says. "It was beautiful plant food with gorgeous vegetable preparations." Omelettes, pastas, and sandwiches on house-baked bread were staples. She tasted North African stews and Indian curries, salads with avocados, basil pesto made with fresh herbs and real pine nuts.

She worked at the Shandygaff as a cook from 1970 to 1972, at the height of its hipness. "We had become the food of the pretty people," she says. (In fact, in August 1972, the *San Francisco Chronicle* devoted a photo essay to organic waitresses at places like the Shandygaff, defining their style as "free-flowing long dresses, sexy jeans with bare halter tops, tie-dyed T-shirts, all worn over freely bouncing bosoms and hirsute armpits.") Decorated with colorful screen prints and a primeval forest of ferns, the restaurant drew rock bands, professional tennis players, and actors, despite the fact that you had to leave the main dining room to smoke.

In 1972, Katzen's brother asked her if she wanted to come back to Ithaca to join him, his girlfriend, and four of their friends in establishing a business, which they thought should be a restaurant. They rented a room in an old gymnasium, pooled their money to decorate it, and opened Moosewood in January 1973. That first night, they made a moussaka that Katzen had learned from some of her friends in folk-dancing circles, a French onion soup with a lot of butter, a couple of salads, and a macrobiotic-esque stir-fry of vegetables over brown rice. They opened at 6:00 P.M., though the moussaka wouldn't be ready until 8:00 and they had forgotten to get change for the cash register.

By March 1974, *Cornell Daily Sun* reviewer Bill Stevenson called Moosewood "one of the most pleasant additions to the town's dining scene in some time," praising its "interesting vegetable concoctions served in sizeable heaps" such as a Dill-More-on-Casserole, Cream Cheese Yogurt Pie, Mulligatawny Soup, and Cheese-Louis Beans containing "some of the freshest slices of squash to be found this side of the ag school's gardens."[35]

Like the New Riverside Cafe, the restaurant changed its menu every day and swapped out the menu coordinator every week. The cooks pulled ideas from the *Vegetarian Epicure, Ten Talents, The Tassajara Bread Book,* and *Diet for a Small Planet.* They cooked dishes from their childhoods as well as ones they'd encountered in their travels. They went to the library and pored over the cookbooks on the shelves. In the summers, they brought produce from local gardens; one local communard, David Hirsch, brought in an oversupply of basil and ended up cooking at Moosewood for forty years.

"Miraculously, the food was pretty darn good," Katzen said. What it wasn't was consistent. No one bothered to write down recipes. Customers would come in requesting something they'd eaten on a previous visit, and no one would remember how to make it. Or a dish would come out beautifully, but they knew they wouldn't be able to re-create it. Katzen documented the dishes, working from taste, and then scaled down the amounts from the industrial to the generous dinner party. Eventually, the former art student wrote her recipes out neatly, illustrated them, and printed up spiral-bound copies in 1974 to sell. A few newspapers wrote about the book, and a small publisher in Berkeley called Ten Speed Press asked Katzen to draft a bigger copy in 1977.[36]

The *Moosewood Cookbook* appealed to a broader audience because so many of its recipes worked and because its tone was so approachable. Every stop on the Hippie Trail was represented in its pages: Balkan Cucumber Salad, Stuffed Zucchini Turkish Style, Vegetarian Shish Kebabs, Satyamma's Famous Cauliflower Curry. Indonesian Gado-Gado followed Bulgarian Pepper and Cheese Delight; Russian Cabbage Borscht and Brazilian Black Bean Sauce were presented on facing pages. There was no way to predict what you might find when you flipped through the book.

The book itself looked like a gift assembled by a friend. Katzen's text was rife with puns (a dish called "Soy Gevult") and quips ("If you need two hands to eat [a tostada], find a trusted friend to hold up your plate for you"). It didn't shy from unusual ingredients like achiote or masa, but most of the recipes could be assembled from a grocery-store trip, no matter where you lived. Pages were decorated with sketches of frilly herbs and ringed with ornate patterns. They encouraged the book's owners to add their own notes and doodles.

"If there is a 'new' American cooking, you will find it in the *Moose-*

wood Cookbook," a reviewer from the *Washington Post* wrote in 1978. "Mollie Katzen, the author who also illustrated and hand-lettered the book, describes this as 'an eclectic cuisine, with vegetarian, international emphases, using the freshest ingredients available.'"

"Missing from most vegetarian cookbooks is a spirit of joy and indulgence in cooking for cooking's sake," the *Detroit Free Press* wrote. "So hurray for the *Moosewood Cookbook*."[37] Katzen's recipes appeared in newspapers in Florida, South Carolina, and Pennsylvania. Oftentimes, the articles in which they appeared weren't even about vegetarianism.

Slowly, quietly, the *Moosewood Cookbook* went on to sell three million copies over the next few decades, teaching millions of twenty-year-olds and their parents how to cook without meat. Not only did it become the bestselling vegetarian cookbook of all time, it is also one of the biggest cookbook releases, ever. By the early 1980s, says one New Riverside cook, the Minneapolis café was scaling up *Moosewood Cookbook* recipes to feed two hundred.

### Granola

Brown rice, wheat germ, alfalfa sprouts, and whole-wheat bread may have all earned permanent places in the longhair culinary repertoire, but only one food became a shorthand for psychedelic culture long after the Summer of Love: granola. Which is curious, considering granola was invented one hundred and fifty years ago.

In 1863, a Grahamite health reformer named James Caleb Jackson searched for a ready-to-eat alternative to the meaty breakfasts that clogged Americans' intestines every morning. (At the time, oatmeal had just been introduced to the United States and wouldn't go into mass production until the 1870s.) Jackson stirred up a paste of coarse graham flour and water, spread it on a tray,

baked it hard, then broke it into chunks and roasted it again, calling the coarse, inedible pebbles Granula. Granula resembled oversized Grape-Nuts. It was convenient in the sense that you only had
to soak the bran rocks in milk overnight in order to eat them the
next morning.[38]

John Harvey Kellogg, director of a Seventh-day Adventist sanitarium in Battle Creek, Michigan, espouser of fiber, and inventor
of vegetarian foods, stole Jackson's idea and released a multigrain
cereal called Granula in 1878. He changed its name to Granola after Jackson sued him for trademark infringement. (Granola was
soon eclipsed by another Kellogg breakfast cereal after the inventor developed a process to turn cooked corn into crisp flakes.)

Granola lingered in Adventist homes and cookbooks for eighty
years, long after both Granula and Granola disappeared from store
shelves. At some point, Adventist cooks elaborated on the recipe,
toasting a variety of nuts and seeds along with rolled oats, wheat
bran, and sometimes soy flour. They may have been playing off the
rising popularity of oatmeal, or perhaps adapting a Swiss cereal
called Bio-Birchermuesli ("muesli") that arrived in U.S. health-food
stores in 1960.[39]

In 1965, an Adventist baker in Nashville named Layton Gentry
sold one of these recipes—whether he invented it himself no one
knows—to a health-food company in Tennessee, which produced
a cereal the company called Crunchy Granola. The company allowed Gentry to buy back the right to sell his formula in other regions, and so he did: in California, Hawaii, Canada, Australia, and
Missouri. By 1972, *Time* called Gentry "Johnny Granola-Seed,"
and newspapers estimated that granola had become a five-
million-dollar-a-year business.[40] Adelle Davis signed her name to
one brand that sold particularly well, given the trust many Americans placed in her health advice.

The cereal wasn't just good with milk; young long-haired types discovered you could stick it in your knapsack for snacking on long hikes or road trips. In the early 1970s, granola was so connected to the underground that Seth Tibbott, founder of Tofurky, remembers buying it in head shops. In 1971, the *Ann Arbor Sun* published a news item about a high school principal in Minnesota who confiscated granola from one of his students, telling the kid: "Granola relates to drugs, drugs relate to hippies, hippies relate to (he holds his fingers in the peace sign), and the (peace sign) relates to an unjust peace."[41]

But the counterculture was never content to buy what they could make themselves. Another Adventist, Rosalie Hurd, included some of the first published recipes for modern granola in her popular 1968 vegetarian cookbook *Ten Talents*, and recipes proliferated. *Mother Earth News* published a recipe. So did scores of underground newspapers. By the mid-1970s, granola recipes appeared in *Joy of Cooking* and small-town newspapers like the *Yuma Sun* (Arizona). Almost every whole-grain bakery in the country supplemented its income by selling granola to local food co-ops and natural-foods stores; some also produced a non-cooked version they called "familia."

Granola was also one of the first health foods that big business co-opted. Pet Incorporated introduced the granola-like Heartland Cereal and Quaker Oats released 100% Natural Granola in 1972, both of which were so successful every major cereal company came out with its own version in the next couple of years.[42]

Crunchy Granola, the original brand, eventually faded away, perhaps doomed by the competition. But its memory slithered into the collective subconscious of Generation X, who would call anyone in possession of a tie-dye shirt and a COEXIST bumper sticker "crunchy" or "granola."

# 7

# Food Co-ops, Social Revolutionaries, and the Birth of an Industry

IN THE FALL OF 1976, BURGESS Jackson, Gary Newton, and the other founders of the Wheatsville Food Co-op decided that Austin's co-ops were doing everything wrong. To be more precise, Austin's food co-ops were doing everything *right*, just in the wrong way.

Evidence of the wrong way was all around them: in just five years, University of Texas students and free-floating longhairs had knotted together a net of interlocking cooperatives that housed hundreds of people, brought food from organic farms to the city, repaired cars, provided people with natural foods unavailable almost anywhere else, and even kept one another's books. It was a glorious effort, every step and misstep documented in the *Rag*, Austin's collectively run underground newspaper. Like a matchstick Eiffel Tower held together with strawberry jam, though, by 1976 the whole network was tottering.

The Inter-Cooperative Council, the housing co-op organization, had just staged a coup at the two existing food co-ops, taking over their finances. The small farms, who already operated on a shoestring, were complaining that they weren't being paid. Activists were burning out right and left.

Wheatsville, like thousands of buying clubs and food co-ops that had appeared across the country between 1969 and 1978, had every intention to reform America's food system and bring good food—whole grains and pulses, fresh organic vegetables—to the masses. The store's founders and customers, though, thought that was just the beginning. Like so many of this new wave of co-ops, Wheatsville's secondary goal was to establish a more human-centered economy outside the bounds of the current one, corrupted and exploitative as it was.

Unlike many in their cooperative community, Jackson and Newton believed they could use the tools of capitalism to dismantle the system from the inside out. "We were pretty arrogant guys," Jackson says now. "We were going to do it better."

BY THE TIME Wheatsville opened, the concept of cooperatively owned food stores was more than a hundred and thirty years old.

In 1844, a group of weavers in Rochdale, England, failed in their strike for better wages and conspired to flout poverty another way: if they couldn't increase their pay, they could decrease how much they paid for food and basic goods. The weavers pooled their money to open a store that stocked basics such as flour, butter, sugar, and oatmeal. The store shared its profits with its members, distributed according to how much money each had spent, and asked those who could to reinvest their dividends in the cooperative.

The Rochdale cooperative became internationally famous, and its "Rochdale rules" were copied all over Europe and North America.[1] Consumer cooperatives popped up around the United States all through the nineteenth century; most lasted no more than a few years. Much more durable were the farm cooperatives, whose numbers swelled as white farmers settled in the western states and the railroads connected rural areas to major cities. The farm cooperatives allowed individual farmers to pool their milk (Land O'Lakes, Tillamook), sell cranberries (Ocean Spray) or citrus fruits (Sunkist), and mill their grains (the Butte County Rice Growers' Association, which the Lundberg family abandoned in 1971 to go organic).

The next great wave of consumer co-ops crested in the Depression of the 1930s and crashed during World War II. In the postwar era, the ones that survived learned to compete against supermarkets and shopping malls. Though the co-ops, which identified themselves with the Twin Pines logo, were organized along the Rochdale principles and sold Co-op brand canned foods and household supplies, they looked just like grocery stores. In 1971, the Cooperative League of the USA reported the existence of 257 Twin Pines stores selling $441 million worth of food and home supplies.[2]

In the late 1960s, when the country inhaled the co-op spirit again, filling its towns and cities with a renewed passion for collective purchasing, most young Americans were half conscious of these older traditions, informed by their existence but ignorant of their successes and failures.

Austinites, in fact, were more familiar with the idea of a housing co-op than a co-op grocery store.[3] Texas's first student housing cooperatives first appeared in the 1930s. By the early 1970s, an estimated eight hundred people in Austin lived in cooperative housing, and two organizations—the Inter-Cooperative Council and College Houses—owned or rented buildings with names like the Ark, 21st Street College House, Stonehenge, and Nexus.[4] Some co-ops housed as few as twenty students, some as many as a hundred. Residents of the co-ops contributed both money and time in exchange for cheap room and board. A flat fee paid for monthly housing, upkeep of the houses, and meals. Most co-ops served dinner nightly, and students would sign up for a certain number of hours of work every week.

While the San Francisco Bay Area roiled in protests, Madison and Chicago rioted, and Minneapolis and New York spewed thousands of furious words on revolutionary ideas, Austin joined the movement in a more congenial fashion.

The city had around a quarter million residents by the late 1960s, some thirty thousand of them students at the University of Texas. "Austin at the time was a hotbed of both leftist political activism and hippie counterculture," says Bill Meacham, who moved there in 1968 to go to grad school and joined the *Rag* newspaper staff in 1969 (the newspaper collective's motto, he says, was "functioning anarchy"). "Sex, drugs, rock and roll—it was all together," Meacham says. "You'd go to a demonstration and then go to somebody's house to smoke dope and listen to music, then you'd go to the park and hang out and play guitars, then you'd go to another rally or political action."

That same loose-limbed activism gave birth to Austin's first food co-op in 1968 as a way, its organizers wrote, for students to get food on the cheap without having to cut their hair to get a job.

Organizers of the Milo Minderbinder Memorial Food Co-op, named after a character in Joseph Heller's *Catch-22*, bought food wholesale from railroad salvagers and drove a truck to the San Antonio produce market to pick up apples, tomatoes, dry beans, and onions. To the fresh food, Milo added stocks of brown rice, whole-wheat flour, corn meal, and turkey eggs, as well as a few racks of used clothing. "You went in, picked out what you wanted, and put what you could afford in the jar," one shopper remembered.[5]

Another wrote several years afterward:

> The first time we went, we missed it altogether, wandered through this amazing labyrinth of a houseful of dogs, derived psychedelic art, and purple this and that's to a somewhat less than well-kept kitchen to find a lone sewer who in late sixties

fashion murmured something about maybe some eggs and a few jars of yogurt someplace. We learned from those more coherent than the stoned sister of our first visit that the co-op had hours, or more precisely an hour or so every day or so, and that you needed to get there early.[6]

Milo sputtered into life, stopped, moved, renamed itself, spun off a short-lived branch, lost its location, and moved again. One former member remembered that, in true furry freak manner, the bookkeeping schedule observed the phases of the moon.[7] In October 1970, the *Rag* reported that the city had shut down Milo's final location—even though it only needed some broken glass replaced and a toilet and sink installed—after a neighbor complained about all the longhairs loitering around her neighborhood. An obituary, written three months later, sniped that Milo's ending was no loss because it had already been corrupted: "The co-op was so large that it was turning into a consumer relationship between the people and the co-op."[8]

That fall, however, a group of Austinites who had recently visited Berkeley replaced Milo with a longer-lasting organization that they called, in Berkeley fashion, a "food conspiracy." Where Milo sold health foods mixed in with whatever its members could afford, the food conspiracy narrowed its focus to healthy, ecologically sound natural foods.

THE BERKELEY FOOD Conspiracy was first plotted in June 1969 when "Vivian," "Jim," and "Anita" (food conspiracy members tended not to use last names, because they never knew who was going to rat them out) schemed up ways to drop out of the supermarket lines and turn themselves on to cheap food.[9] They handed out EAT TO CONSPIRE leaflets and tacked up posters looking for other people to join them.

So many people were living in communal households—already sharing rent, food, and cigarettes—that the idea of sharing vegetables took off.[10] As *The Food Conspiracy Cookbook* author, Lois Wickstrom, wrote, "There are those who live in communes for whom joining a conspiracy is as natural as making soup in a 10-quart pot."

The group first sent a VW van to the nearby Oakland farmers' market for produce once a week and returned to a driveway where they divvied it up. Several members talked a local cheese shop into selling them dozens of blocks, and on Friday night the cells would congregate for cheese-cutting sessions. So many households clamored to join that the conspiracy split in two, then divided by mitosis into four and then eight cells.

The idea jumped the bay to San Francisco and slid south down the peninsula, taking hold especially fast in the Haight-Ashbury, where a tightly linked web of communal houses had succeeded the raucous Summer of Love street scene. John Carter, a member of the Haight-Ashbury Food Conspiracy, told the *San Francisco Chronicle* twenty years later that the word *conspiracy* was always ironic: "a response to the Nixon-Agnew rhetoric of the time (which) had us all as communist conspirators against the state, the war and public morality. We tended to take the charge as a compliment."[11] They weren't just meeting to share cheese: another former conspirator says that when her cell would convene to place their orders or divvy up dry goods, they would schedule a lecture about some aspect of the food supply or pick a political topic to discuss.

True conspiracy or no, what was happening in the Bay Area was just the hippie manifestation of a much broader 1960s movement: food-buying clubs.

In the mid-1960s, civil rights leaders like Stokely Carmichael and Bob Moses promoted the idea of small buying clubs that would give African American communities some measure of economic independence from the system that was crushing them. It's hard to track how many formed, says co-op historian Dave Gutknecht, because most were short-lived.[12]

At the same time, young volunteers participating in Community Action Programs across the country, funded by President Johnson's Economic Opportunity Act of 1964 (the "War on Poverty"), helped set up dozens of buying clubs and small food co-ops in low-income urban neighborhoods. For example, in 1966 the *New York Times* wrote a small profile of a buying club that a man named Pedro Otero had organized in the Puertorriqueños Unidos center, supported by antipoverty programs and replicated at the nearby Negro Federation of the Lower East Side.[13] In Chicago, a retired Yugoslavian immigrant named Paul Horvat founded the Self Help Action Center, which organized close to four hundred buying clubs that would contract with midwestern farmers to sell them produce directly, often at shopping events the center called "farmers' food shows." It was no anticapitalist conspiracy. Horvat told the *Chicago Tribune* in 1974 that he saw his organization as an exercise of free-market economy that benefited both farmers and low-income consumers.[14]

The counterculture—largely white, more middle class, more educated—may have been aware of these efforts but were only in tangential contact with them. Good intentions aside, most of the young white hippies weren't immersed in African American and Latino neighborhoods. Buying clubs in those neighborhoods were primarily focused on securing inexpensive, fresh food and not about the hippies' concerns about organics and whole grains, or avoiding the evils of sugar and pesticides. (A few co-ops in large metropolitan areas, such as Detroit and Washington, D.C., were the exception to this; in fact, one of San Francisco's first natural-foods co-ops was Semillas de la Vida/Seeds of Life, located in the city's Latino district, and Bay Area co-ops made perhaps the most decisive effort in the country to engage Latino and Asian American shoppers.)

But the concept of collective buying, directly from suppliers, appealed to a generation that had been organizing for antiwar protests, direct actions, consciousness-raising groups, and communes since its teenage years. By 1974, the Berkeley Food Conspiracy had two thousand members and sixty different subgroups; seven hundred more people belonged to the Haight-Ashbury conspiracy alone. Many of the cells filed for business licenses and resellers' permits, going legitimate enough to keep the Man from squashing their movement. A representative from the U.S. Food and Nutrition Service—the feds!—even reached out to conspirators to show them how they could accept food stamps.

Often, the buying clubs' existence depended on the drive of one or two people, and the group would dissolve the moment a key coordinator burned out or moved away. Smart conspiracies accumulated enough money to cover each buy before they sent volunteers shopping, rotated duties frequently to avoid volunteer burnout, and charged members a small markup to cover gas, operational expenses, and even spoilage. Some buying-club members taught themselves how to break down sides of beef.

Gloria Stern, author of the 1974 *How to Start Your Own Food Co-op*, noted that the average life span of a small buying club was two years. Many of the food conspiracies and buying clubs grew big enough, complex enough, that they moved from garages and living rooms to church basements and rec centers. Then they swelled beyond those spaces, renting small storage rooms where they could install a few shelves and fit in a refrigerator or two. Some of these gave birth to retail stores. Other buying clubs opened their storerooms to get rid of leftover goods and found that their members liked shopping better than filling out order forms.[15]

Over the course of 1972 and 1973, one of Austin's Berkeley-inspired food conspiracies evolved into something much bigger: a retail store, named Woody Hills, but also the Austin Community Project, one of the country's most ambitious, interlocking local cooperative networks.

THE PERSON AT the center of that nexus was a twenty-six-year-old named John Dickerson.

Dickerson was a fifth-generation Texan, blond and lanky, with shoulder-length hair and a long face punctuated by round wire-framed glasses. Born at the vanguard of the baby boom, he had grown up in San Antonio and become so accomplished at playing French horn in high school that North Texas State offered him a music scholarship.

After a few years of practicing French horn eleven hours a day, he exchanged the instrument for a picket sign. "Playing a kind of museum instrument like the French horn was just not in the spirit of the times," Dickerson says. "I wound up getting more active in antiwar stuff and moved to Austin." He enrolled in classes at the University of Texas—psychology, American studies, history—and pursued them in desultory fashion. There were too many protests to go to, and then a restaurant to run.

Dickerson and a group of eight or nine friends took over an old Victorian in downtown Austin that had a restaurant on the ground floor and bedrooms above. They named the restaurant the Bo-Tree, after the tree in whose shade Buddha became enlightened. The Bo-Tree became a counterculture hub, and so many roommates crammed into the quarters upstairs that they located a more spacious two-story house in West Austin. They called it the Oakland House.

Given Austin's eighty-degree December days, swimming holes, and low-key vibe, the city was getting a reputation as the hippie Riviera, a winter escape for hitchhikers who were sick of snow. In the winter of 1972, Chuck Phenix, one of Dickerson's college friends, came back from Minneapolis for a few months to winter at Oakland House.

Phenix told Dickerson about all the natural-foods co-ops that were starting in the Midwest. In Madison, for instance, a group of activists and University of Wisconsin students had taken over a vacant grocery and canvassed their neighborhood, asking for $5 donations to open.[16]

Ann Arbor already had two year-old food co-ops: one was fetching vegetables from Detroit wholesalers to distribute to houses and communes, and the other sold dry goods in a small basement storefront after graduating up from a table in a head shop.[17]

Phenix talked most effusively about what was happening in the Twin Cities: About collective restaurants like the New Riverside Cafe, whose workers lived communally and could survive by paying themselves subsistence "people's wages." About the Cedar-Riverside People's Cooperative Center, which housed a free clinic and collective enterprises. About the burgeoning food co-op scene.

North Country Co-op, which had started in 1970, posted a sign near the cash register: IF THE LINE IS TOO LONG, START YOUR OWN CO-OP. Shoppers took the idea to heart. Within two years North Country was joined by Selby Co-op, Whole Foods Co-op, Mill City Co-op, and Southeast Co-op. A splinter group from North Country formed the People's Warehouse to supply all these new co-ops and restaurants with wholesale goods.

Listening to these stories, Dickerson got excited about doing something similar in Austin. The more the idea consumed him, the more he made contact with other people running collective enterprises in Texas. "There were quite a few people in Austin at the time who were doing similar things," he says. "There was a group that had an auto co-op where you could come in and work on your car. There were all those housing co-ops. There was a collective school called Greenbriar, in the woods thirty miles east of Austin; one hundred fifty kids lived out there and would go home on the weekends, and they had about twenty adult teachers and staff living in yurts. . . . A lot of people were having the same ideas and getting together to talk about them excitedly."

Inspired by Phenix, Oakland House pooled its money to buy a flatbed truck, which they would drive to the San Antonio produce market to buy vegetables and fruits for the Bo-Tree. The housing co-ops

signed on to this delivery service, giving the fledgling produce collective the volume to get better prices. Soon Dickerson was making
deliveries to a small for-profit natural-foods store called Good Food,
a smoothie shop, and Sattva, a new collective vegan restaurant in the
basement of the Hillel Center.

In those first few months, the produce collective would dump clumps
of wrinkled tens and twenties in a bag, take it to market to spend on
vegetables, and then collect more dollar bills from their customers. Theoretically, the profits would cover Oakland House's rent. Practically,
there was never any money left over.

"We weren't businesspeople, and nobody wanted to become one,"
Dickerson says. "I said, 'There's probably a reason that people keep
books.' So I went down to the Austin Public Library and checked out a
book on nonprofit corporation accounting, and I taught myself accounting." He learned to make budgets and cost projections. Surpluses finally
appeared.

One of the produce collective's early customers in 1972 was a newly
formed food conspiracy in the Berkeley mold that distributed food from
the basement of a Methodist church near Oakland House. Together, the
Oakland House activists and the buying club looked for a building the
club could transform into a retail store.

In 1973, they took over an old general store in the rolling hills west of
the University of Texas campus and painted WOODY HILLS FOOD CO-OP
onto its front window. Compared to the food conspiracy, Woody Hills
was a professional affair with a cash register, regular hours, and official
fees. Modeled after the other new food co-ops in other cities, members
paid dues in exchange for a steep discount. Their fees included a fifty-
cent lifetime membership charge, plus one dollar a month for each adult
for up to twenty months to give the new co-op a pool of money to expand its stock. Prices listed were the amount the co-op paid the wholesale supplier, and the cashier would tack on a 40 percent markup for

nonmembers and 20 percent for members, which covered the store's operating costs. Aside from its one paid staff "coordinator," all the workers were volunteers, members fulfilling their requirement to work at least two hours a month.

"Membership may mean a change in your diet," one Woody Hills member informed readers in the *Rag*. "We do not stock such items as meat, party crackers, or TV dinners. We do have fresh fruits and vegetables, whole grains and legumes, herbs and spices, cheese of all kinds, eggs, fruit juices and fruit butters, nuts and nut butters, unrefined oils, nutritional yeast, flours, breads, granola, and honey."[18] New customers were warned that they would have to bring their own jars, bags, and bottles.

AS WOODY HILLS was taking shape, John Dickerson was filling large black sketchbooks with diagrams and notes, a blueprint for a cooperative of cooperatives to concentrate all this collectivist energy. In the summer of 1972, Dickerson announced in the *Rag* that this group had a name—the Austin Community Project—as well as papers of incorporation, all the permits he could think of, and, of course, a manifesto, drafted in prose so overheated the page practically swooned:

> We must gain control over our own space. We must control over the productive consumptive processes which exist to serve our existence. We must vitally construct a whole system of life activities designed and/or evolved about a viable cultural center of our own determination. . . . Practically every time we rent, buy food, play a radio, go to school, buy a record, pay the water bill, practically every time we give our time and effort in the form of money, we reward the oppressors. We rob ourselves.[19]

Produce, Dickerson decided, was the link that could unite Austin's burgeoning cooperative scene into an alternative economy.

By 1974, the Austin Community Project drew into its network Woody Hills, the vegan restaurant Sattva, the off-campus housing co-ops, the auto co-op, the free school, plus a new whole-grain bakery that had set up shop next to Woody Hills. Dickerson's original produce-buying collective was now officially named AC Produce.

The Austin Community Project's leadership council met twice a month (at "7:30 hippie time," which meant whenever enough people straggled in) and held general membership meetings every three months. It formed working groups specializing in tools and accounting (the "Bookies") and announced that a journal of revolutionary theory, a credit union, and a land trust were in the works for the future.[20]

Austin Community Project funded all these actions from fees that each of the member cooperatives contributed; Woody Hills members, for example, each paid $2 a year. The income, particularly from the flush housing co-ops, was enough for ACP to open a small office and hire three or four staff. It could also afford to lend money to Woody Hills to move into a larger storefront and get the Avenues, a second food co-op north of campus, up and running in a permanent space.

ACP members agreed to a flat monthly "people's wage" for every participating collective worker: $212.50, after taxes. By that time, some staffers had already gone three months without a paycheck because they were so devoted to the cause. Nevertheless, just as the parents of the baby boom were convinced one joint would lead to a heroin overdose, to some ACP members, paying people wages veered close to outright capitalism.

At the same time that the Vermont back-to-the-landers in NOFA were contracting with New York City co-ops to deliver what they grew, the ACP arranged for four nearby back-to-the-lander farms outside Austin to supply its enterprises with organic eggs and goat milk, herbs, vegetables, and citrus fruits. In exchange for lower prices, each participating co-op would send four people once a week to one of the four farms to plant fields or mend fences. Some of the members formed a compost collective to take food waste from city co-ops to the farms to nourish their soils.

The group convinced the *Rag* to cover ACP activities, and Bill Meacham, a philosophy grad student, launched a weekly one-page co-op column. Meacham's column documented the logistical details of countless meetings, scolded co-ops that had fallen behind on fees and farm labor, and notified the public of economic shortfalls.[21]

Within a few columns, Meacham abandoned any pretext of objectivity. "By banding together co-op members discover the joy and relief of not being alone, pitted against a hostile, or at best indifferent, world by oneself," he wrote in September 1974. "Sharing, community, mutual concern—these are words for realities that aren't quite as tangible as cash in your pocket, but are more important."[22]

Over the next two years, the Austin Community Project came to represent hundreds of Austinites, involving a core group of forty to fifty volunteers and paid (but not very well-paid) staff. It also hooked into a national cooperative movement that was forming between cities.

Dickerson had no idea how big this new movement was until he and a few friends attended a national conference in Rochester, New York, loading their pickup truck with watermelons for the drive north. When the Austinites got to the Rochester Co-op, they found a hundred people who were just as shocked to see a crew of Texans as the Texans were to find one hundred like-minded people. "We wound up spending a month driving around to various places where the co-ops were," he says: "Buffalo, Ann Arbor, Madison, Minneapolis, bunches of little towns. We just rambled around for a month looking at places and talking." He invited everyone he met to Austin for the winter, and for years Oakland House would house twenty to thirty co-opers a year retreating from chillier states.

Conferences in Minneapolis and Fayetteville, Arkansas, followed, and Austin hosted its own. At one of the events, Dickerson remembers, a hundred conference attendees, exhausted from their day of meetings, collectively flopped onto couches, chairs, and plush rugs and turned off the lights. "We were all lying around, connected physically," he says. "Not in a group grope, but we were maybe holding hands or having an arm around a buddy. For about an hour, somebody would start talking about what they hoped all this would wind up being, and the kinds of things that they felt like we were all trying to do. There was this real sense that we were connected in this effort to make a better country. To make a more humane place. That was a thrilling moment, and there was a lot of those, a sense of a movement together and commonality."

But as Austin's web of co-ops flourished, its fissures also spread.

THE COOPERATIVE LEAGUE of the USA has estimated that over the course of the 1970s, the baby boomers spawned five thousand buying clubs and consumer cooperative retail stores.[23] This new generation of co-ops came up with a rallying cry—"Food for people, not for profit"—that would be printed on thousands of tote bags and posters, often with a graphic of a fist holding a carrot. As the 1970s progressed, this mantra would simultaneously propel the movement and vex it.

The operating principle behind the 1970s wave of consumer co-ops was to abandon hierarchy in favor of what the student movements of the 1960s called "participatory democracy." Worker collectives—like the New Riverside Cafe in Minneapolis—practiced participatory democracy by abandoning hierarchy. Consumer co-ops invited any member, and sometimes the general public, to determine how it should operate.

Hundreds of thousands of co-opers signed up for their volunteer shifts not just to earn their discount but to participate: to raise objections at meetings, poke around the shelves while sweeping, engage in debates over El Salvador with the cheese-cutting crew, and make the most of their cash register stint by flirting with customers.

Many volunteered for extra shifts because they *had* the time. "People were willing to put in a lot of volunteer time because they didn't have [today's] pressures and anxiety about trying to work a lot," says Jim Jones, a former Austin housing cooperative activist. "Communications were in person, and that sense of building something for the future as a group was really a very strong way of bonding."

Most co-ops became communication hubs for the community. Shoppers made their first stop at the bulletin board near the entryway to flip through notices for yoga classes and cooking workshops, or jot down the number on a local gardener's business card. The bulletin boards advertised rallies and jobs, screeds and apartment listings.[24]

Almost every established storefront, as well as some of the larger networks like ACP, published newsletters that listed their profits and losses, urged volunteers to sign up for shifts, engaged in Maoist self-criticism, and provided recipes for all the new products that they were carrying. The newsletters reminded their readers: You aren't just a member, you are a member-owner. You are privy to information about the store finances and decisions the paid staff is making so you can help the store make informed decisions.

The thrill—as well as the bedevilment—of member meetings was that they gave every person who attended a voice. In practice, that meant that when debates erupted over the future of the store and the products it carried, everyone could have their say, sometimes saying it very loudly and for very long.[25]

A generation that had come to see food as political, thanks in part to Frances Moore Lappé, became consumer activists through the co-ops. Most co-op newsletters ran articles supporting the United Farm Workers' strikes, and resulting boycotts, against table grape farms (1968–1970) and iceberg lettuce growers (1970–1975) in California.

But members could also obsess over every ingredient. Should we carry products made with white flour and sugar? (The answer, in those early days, was almost always no.) What about coffee, cashews, or bananas, given the exploitative conditions that farm workers in the developing world endured? What about cucumbers coated in a wax that was rumored to be carcinogenic, given that waxless cucumbers were only available a few months of the year? Should we stock Saran Wrap, which was made by Dow Chemical Company, which made some of the components in napalm, or Jarlsberg cheese, manufactured by a subsidiary of Nestlé, which was campaigning in developing companies for women to abandon breastfeeding in favor of its infant formula?[26]

One of the biggest political debates in Austin erupted in 1974 when John Dickerson raised the question of whether Woody Hills and the Avenues should carry meat. One of their organic farms had been raising cattle—on pastureland, so the animals were no protein factory in reverse—and the animals were ready to slaughter. The fight hinged on concerns that the pasture they grazed should have been planted with cereals for humans instead of grass.[27] Ultimately, a few households decided to break from the ACP to buy the beef, and the group collectively agreed not to protest.[28]

For all their antihierarchical rhetoric, co-op meetings favored the strident. And as Kathy Sharp wrote in one co-op newsletter, too often that meant male voices:

> The meetings feel competitive and it's sometimes hard to get a word in edgewise. Many times men are interrupting each other. There's much intellectualizing and redundancy, and people aren't sensitive to the fact that there are others in the room (of either sex) who haven't said a word and the same folks are continuing to talk. . . . Women don't often speak up at meetings because they

are frequently interrupted, attacked or simply not given the space to speak.[29]

More and more, too, the conversation pivoted around a central argument: Should the co-ops serve cheap food or should they serve good food?

As the collective authors of the 1975 *Food Co-op Handbook* would put it, in tones so prim you can almost hear their lips squeaking as they struggled to move:

> Co-ops should accept their responsibility to safeguard their members' health by not carrying junk foods, and to educate them about nutrition by carrying whole unprocessed foods and by posting recipes, articles, and nutrient charts on co-op walls and in newsletters. The buying policy of the co-op can be an effective educational tool in itself. If the majority of the members decide they want air-filled white bread, TV dinners, and tortilla chips, it's the responsibility of the minority to try to educate them and try to change the policy.[30]

Other groups, though, felt that this purist stance was isolating the co-ops from the broader community. Jackie Byars, a key member of the ACP "bookies," published an open letter in the *Rag* in 1975 after she saw one Woody Hills co-op member yelling at another for bringing "shit food" in the form of Sta-Krisp potato chips into the store:

> I've become more and more cynical about the kind of people that are involved in these hippie health food co-ops. There has been controversy about whether to expand the kind of items carried so as to attract a wider variety of people. Our neighborhood is made up of white, older people, white middle-class

hippies, older Chicanos, and blacks of all ages. The only group
the store appeals to is the hippies. "Food is the hippie religion."
That's another of my latest theories.[31]


DESPITE THEIR CONCERNS, hippies weren't the only ones looking for an
escape from the food industry. Soon after the co-op boom of the 1970s
began, outrage over high food prices drove middle-class shoppers to the
new natural-foods co-ops. So did fears of pesticide poisoning, chemical
additives, and the flurry of environmental scandals.

The consumer price index was already shooting up in the early 1970s,
averaging 10 percent per year over the decade. Driven primarily by oil
prices and bad weather, the price of food rose 29 percent between the
fourth quarter of 1972 and the end of 1974. The rise slowed for a few
years, but spiked another 22 percent between fourth quarter 1977 and
fourth quarter 1979.[32] President Gerald Ford recognized inflation as the
"nation's biggest problem" in 1974.

Mainstream magazines and newspapers all over the country warily
proposed joining a food co-op to compensate for rising food prices. In
March 1975, for example, *Good Housekeeping* offered a short how-to on
starting a food co-op, telling readers, "The goal must be to save money.
This sounds obvious, but often co-ops have failed because members lost
sight of the fact that they were banded together to save, not for social
reasons."[33] The *Boston Globe* cautioned readers curious about the idea of
joining a food co-op, arguing that even if they saved 20 to 40 percent on
food costs, the price was that they would have to work, cooperatively,
with the other members.[34]

In 1974, the fear of contaminated milk drove a young mother named
Suzanne Caya to a food-buying club in Wyandotte, Michigan, a suburb
of Detroit, and then to an organization that would demonstrate just how
far outside the counterculture the co-op movement could reach.[35]

That spring, the *Detroit Free Press* reported that the Michigan Department of Agriculture had quarantined fifteen herds of cattle after tests found their milk was contaminated with a flame retardant. More than forty-five hundred dairy cattle and five hundred beef cattle were affected. Despite the fact that children living at the affected farms were breaking out in blotches and losing hair, the secretary of agriculture reassured the public that the contaminated milk had been blended in with so much other milk that the public shouldn't worry.[36]

Caya and her then husband had two toddlers and a newborn son, and the contaminated milk scandal shocked them into searching out sources for clean foods. Through friends of friends, she learned of the Wyandotte buying club and placed orders for oats, cheese, and flour in bulk. "For people downriver of Detroit, there was absolutely nothing," she says. "There were no GNCs, no pseudo-health-food stores, nothing. So we had no recourse but to buy that way.

"My family thought we were dabbling in hippie stuff," she says. Yet, "so many mainstream people became patrons of the co-op movement that it transcended that." Though the couple were in their twenties, the two were far from hippies—Caya raised her kids at home, and she swears she had no involvement with patchouli or Ram Dass.

She was a natural organizer, though; within a short time, she was hosting the club's monthly pickups in her garage and coordinating orders for fifty families. "A lot of women experienced managing a buying club co-op as empowering," she says. "There were still a lot of women [like me] who were full-time mothers and working only inside the house. Stepping up and stepping out was empowering."

Besides, the more she talked and read about the movement, the more she was drawn to what it represented. "I liked the idea of the co-op, the principles—that we all owned this and were all responsible, and the beneficiaries of the co-op were its stakeholders, not some anonymous people," she adds.

The buying club was how she came to be involved, first as a volunteer and then as a board member and staffer, with the Michigan Federation of Food Co-ops in Ann Arbor.

The federation had begun in 1972 after the city's brand-new People's Food Co-op realized the young, volunteer-run operation couldn't supply all the small buying clubs around the state who were calling to place orders. It called a meeting of twenty co-ops and buying clubs from all over Michigan—co-ops from college towns like East Lansing and Kalamazoo, back-to-the-land communes in the middle of the state, and groups in small cities like Petoskey and Ypsilanti. Inspired by the North Country People's Warehouse in Minneapolis, the group established a collectively run wholesale food supplier. Like the Austin Community Project, the Michigan Federation of Food Co-ops would be a cooperative of cooperatives; one of these cooperatives would be its own "People's Wherehouse." (If that sounds convoluted, you're not alone: it was to the federation members, too.)[37]

In the first five years of the 1970s, Minneapolis inspired like-minded collective warehouses in Portland (Oregon), New York City, Tucson, Chicago, Madison, Seattle, San Francisco, and Vermont, among others. These small distributors, as well as a host of collectively run trucking companies, formed the internal machinery of the new co-op movement. They brought natural foods—as well as the ideas behind them—to every corner of the country.

As the Wherehouse's stock list grew, all the new foods the federation sold made their way into the homes of people who had never cooked with bulgur, tahini, soy grits, granola, mung beans, flaxseeds, quinoa, seaweed, or yogurt before. Many of the buying club members had read about these strange new foods in books like *Diet for a Small Planet* and *Ten Talents*, but couldn't find them in their local grocery. The Michigan Federation of Food Co-ops wasn't merely the best supplier of natural foods. For many people in the Midwest, it was the *only* supplier. "For a long time we had a monopoly," Caya says.

The Michigan Federation of Food Co-ops (MFOFC) also made it possible for tiny, collectively run food businesses to thrive by distributing their products all over Michigan, Ohio, Indiana, and Illinois. Ann Arbor's Grainola Collective, for instance, supplied breakfast cereal and roast nuts. The Soy Plant supplied tofu.[38] Organic farmers from southeast Michigan sold dry beans, soft wheat, and rye. The Daily Grind, located inside the Wherehouse, operated a flour mill. Co-op warehouses from the Twin Cities to southern Ohio linked with the MFOFC to form a massive regional network.

The longer Suzanne Caya was active on the board of the federation—eventually becoming its president—the more she engaged the broader questions the co-op movement was tackling. Some of them were practical, say, quizzing the producers they bought from on their farming and labor practices. "Members of the collective did that, board members did that, people in their local buying clubs did that, people in the retail co-ops did that: asking more and more questions and sharing the answers," Caya says.

As in Austin, though, the federation debated whether it should carry cheap food for all or pure food for some. By carrying a small and exclusive inventory, one member argued in the *MFOFC News,* "we fail to reach a large number of potential members who aren't familiar with the foods we now carry (we tend to take whole grains, beans, nuts and cheese for granted) or find it too inconvenient to make a second shopping trip."[39]

Should co-ops be open to all or should they provide a much-needed alternative for people who wanted to eat, and organize, in a different way? Shouldn't they be accessible to working-class people? This debate grew heated in cities all over the country in the mid-1970s, sucking into its vortex more minor arguments over sugar, white flour, canned goods, and meat.

But only in the Twin Cities did the debate turn violent.

THE "CO-OP WARS," as they would come to be called, broke out in the country's most robust co-op scene: more than a dozen retail food co-ops, two collective bakeries, the North Country People's Warehouse, and the New Riverside Cafe.[40]

In March 1975, a Marxist-Stalinist group that would take the name Co-op Organization (CO) took over the Beanery, a failing co-op in Minneapolis, and put out a manifesto defining its new modus operandi. "The Beanery serves the working class," the manifesto proclaimed, "the class whose labor produces and maintains the materials necessary for human survival." It then issued a long-winded condemnation of the cooperative movement and the white counterculture, calling it elitist and bourgeois.[41]

That same month, one of the CO's core members boiled down the argument for the *Scoop*, the Twin Cities cooperative newsletter: "Changing diet is an escape route that few can afford," she said. "Concentrating on diet and nutrition satisfies a few and diverts fire from the attacks on the economic system."[42] The CO took up the flag of the working class, arguing that the food co-ops existed to fight capitalism and to invite the working class into the revolution. Just as the Beanery was now doing, co-ops should provide inexpensive staples instead of esoteric whole foods.

A flurry of position papers and flyers emerged in response to the manifesto, starting with back-to-back articles in the *Scoop* over the ethics of selling canned food. (Pro: "A person would have to be hypocritical to reject tin cans, but not plastic Continental yogurt containers"; Con: "Any buying from Agribusinesses supports them materially and panders to our dependence on 'conveniences.' "[43]) The rhetoric quickly grew baroque, with one statement issued by "The Revolutionary Marxist Study Group of the Fourth International" and another statement titled "On the Radish Threat to the Process of Dialectical Self-Interpretation in the Co-op Movement: A Coughing Spasm."

Almost everyone in the Twin Cities counterculture was forced to take a side. Three CO members within the New Riverside Cafe collective, for example, turned its weekly Monday-night meetings into great arguments over the restaurant's genial brown-rice anarchism. The Stalinists argued that the working class wanted to eat meat, not soyburgers, and that blue-collar diners were put off by the café's ferns and stained-glass windows and would prefer utilitarian white walls.

As former *Scoop* journalist Craig Cox later documented in his 1994 book, *Storefront Revolution*, the practice of participatory democracy—a co-op's members are its owners, after all—gave the CO the means to act. What had been a war of ideas became a brutal fight for control.

As the CO bloc swelled, it piled into co-op membership meetings, assuming leadership of a few of the stores and pressuring dissenting staff to leave. The Stalinists' greatest upset took place in May 1975, after the bloc had stormed out of the monthly meeting of the People's Wherehouse, which had become an economic juggernaut in the Twin Cities. Over the next two nights, the CO returned in the early hours, first to whisk away the Wherehouse's checkbook, then to physically expel opponents who camped in the building.

The co-ops that had resisted the Marxist takeover scrambled to set up a new wholesale supplier and drain the once-thriving People's Wherehouse of its business. As the war escalated, one CO opponent's car was set on fire and a Molotov cocktail was thrown through his store's window. On another occasion, the two sides squared off outside a co-op, fifty CO members chanting protest songs and attempting to enter, to be rebuffed by two hundred anti-Stalinists who threw sticks of butter at them.[44]

The Twin Cities co-op war lasted a year, the violence subsiding into shouting matches and ending when the CO members slipped away to Chicago. The war ripped apart communes, destroyed friendships, and scuttled thriving businesses. Given the Twin Cities' prominence in the co-op movement—and the charges of elitism that the CO leveled—alternative newspapers all over the country printed news of the war.

"The basic theoretical struggle is important and relevant to Austin," Bill Meacham wrote in the *Rag* in May 1975 as he reported on Minneapolis. "Should co-ops be just 'us' serving ourselves or should they try to serve all the people in the neighborhoods where they are? Should the co-ops compromise their effort to market good food, produced in an ecologically sound manner, to try to involve more people than hip whites?"[45] He noted that Woody Hills was located in a historically African American neighborhood, but few black folks shopped there. The store and the bulk of its shoppers were too funky, he suggested, the food, perhaps, too unfamiliar.

But ACP and Austin's food co-ops soon became too embroiled in their own economic crises to carry the debate further.

THE FIRST SIGNS of trouble appeared in June 1975, when the *Rag* reported that Woody Hills was on the precipice of going under. Despite the dedication of its members, years of amateur bookkeeping and unstable crews of volunteers had left the co-op's bank account perpetually overdrawn. When Jackie Byars, a member of the ACP "bookies," studied the books, she found that Woody Hills owed $2,700 to the ACP, farms, and suppliers.[46]

Both Woody Hills' and the Avenues' economic struggles came to a head in March 1976. Jim Jones, head of the Inter-Cooperative Council, the big off-campus housing co-op, was chatting with a Woody Hills volunteer that month who told him the co-op was going well except its checking account was always in the red. Thankfully, she mentioned, the council he ran was guaranteeing Woody Hills' overdrafts so they weren't awash in fees.[47]

Jones, alarmed, discovered that the major housing cooperatives had signed paperwork making them legally responsible for both Woody Hills' and the Avenues' bank accounts. The stores were collectively $3,900 in the red. Within the week, he called a massive come-to-Jesus meeting that became known as the "Wednesday Night Massacre." The housing co-op staff told eighty assembled co-opers they were taking control of both stores' finances until they got them in order. "It was very bloody and a lot of people didn't like the process," Jones says (the blood: strictly metaphorical). "It wasn't exactly democratic."

It didn't work, either. By October 1976, the Avenues had disbanded and Woody Hills had decided to reincorporate in a new neighborhood, shaking off the control of the housing co-ops. The next month, the Austin Community Project, weakened by the loss of income from both enterprises, followed in their wake. The *Rag*'s functioning anarchy stopped functioning around the same time, and only a dozen or so issues would trickle out over the next year. Then the newspaper folded, too.[48]

A "study group" of former Austin Community Project members wrote an apologia for their dead organization in the *Rag* that could double as an elegy to the early days of 1970s co-ops:

> We got involved in the co-op movement primarily because we were interested in changing society. That is, we saw the purpose of co-ops as agents of social change and revolution. We tried to teach people and raise their consciousness about the world around them and what they could do about it. We tried

to provide good food at a good price and to educate people about the food they ate. We promoted natural food, organic gardening, small farms, urban/rural cooperation, and people-oriented economics. But we were always aware of the need to organize people for a revolution.

We tried to build a small human society in the midst of a monstrous, inhumane one. We failed. We now realize how incredibly naive we were in our attempts. But the problems that led us to work in the co-op movement and to want to change the world still exist.[49]

AGAINST THE BACKDROP of financial turmoil, another split in the cooperative movement emerged, a philosophical rift that could also be defined as dueling personality types. In Austin, the two camps called themselves the Wheelies (from "wheeler-dealers") and the Feelies.

"The Wheelies were the pragmatists and the Feelies were the purists," says Wheatsville cofounder Burgess Jackson, speaking as a Wheelie. Wheelies found consensus exhausting, while Feelies believed that good decisions only came by valuing community above efficiency. Wheelies examined numbers, set up committees, wrote bylaws, and demanded structure. Feelies abhorred hierarchy and loved the loose, impromptu nature of co-op decision making. Wheelies believed that, to build a new economy based on cooperatives, it was critical to draw mainstream shoppers to stores. Feelies demanded that pure, healthy food was the top priority, and they'd be harming the general public if they supplied it with trash food.

John Dickerson says today that the divide between the Wheelies and the Feelies was partly at fault for the collapse of his dream. By 1976 the core members of the Austin Community Project had been courting burnout for years, and they finally succumbed.

But burnout wasn't the only factor. "We were also hitting our thirties, and getting married and having kids, and thinking, 'Do I want to buy a house? I'm not going to do that if I keep doing this.' What also happened was that the Vietnam War ended. I think that had a huge impact. It was like this burr under everybody's saddle, and when it stopped, you didn't have that bleeding sore getting punched, emotionally, every day. That took the urgency out of our effort, at the same time that people were making this generational shift," he says.

"At some point, I got the sense that where those co-ops were going was to create a cultural space for [the counterculture] to live," he adds. "That's fine, but it was going to be one-half of 1 percent of society. It wasn't going to change people's work, our livelihoods, how society really functions." Dickerson, a self-professed Wheelie, wanted more. He took six months off to travel the United States, then enrolled in grad school to study business.

Starting in the mid-1970s, co-op organizers and volunteers all over the country were having the same doubts as Dickerson. In fact, these doubts were shared by the communard farmers in rural Vermont, the Boston macrobiotic study houses, the Dire Wolf anarchist collective in Minneapolis, and the Source Family stuck in Hawaii after Father Yod's death: If we can't remake the world, where do we go from here?

For co-ops, the question became: If we can't overturn capitalism, how do we survive within it? "While co-ops attempt to create an alternative food system beyond the control of the food-industry octopus," wrote Daniel Zwerdling in a 1979 assessment of the food co-op movement, "they need precisely the same nourishment that Safeway does. That's money—lots of it." Co-ops were too small to achieve the economies of scale required to keep the prices low, and the effort to keep price-comparison shoppers away from the supermarkets was taking a toll on co-op workers who accepted punishingly low wages. Zwerdling concluded:

New wave food co-ops have tangled with the realities of doing
business in the United States. The result: even the most politi-
cized and radical co-op activists are becoming more pragmatic.
In fact, many of the new co-ops are raising the same battle cry
of the corporate food industry they are struggling against: get
bigger. Build bigger co-op stores, build more co-op stores.[50]

JUST AS THE Austin Community Project was falling apart, a few members of the Wheelie contingent decided to try again, but this time with a
little professionalism.

Burgess Jackson, a slow-talking charmer from Louisiana, had graduated from Louisiana State University and moved to Austin in 1974 to
study law at the University of Texas, but, in his own words, was having
too much fun to graduate. He'd seen a poster for the Austin Community
Project and got sucked in, he says, by its vision of a better society. He
joined the co-op life, moving into a housing co-op and volunteering at
the Avenues.[51]

At parties and meetings he befriended another activist, Gary Newton, who oversaw ACP's communications and education working
group. Newton, Jackson says, was a dynamic guy who never shied from
a rancorous discussion, which both former debate-team members enjoyed. "Gary's the kind of person who starts things," Jackson says. The
two bonded over their Wheeliedom.

When Newton invited Jackson over one September afternoon in 1975
to propose they start a new food co-op west of campus that would re-
dress the flaws at Woody Hills and the Avenues, Jackson immediately
signed on. "We wanted a larger store with more square footage," Jackson says. "We wanted it to be more inclusive, to have things that the
people who were shopping at the Avenues and Woody Hills couldn't
get, so they'd get them at some other place. . . . We wanted real business

practices. We didn't want to decide based on the astrological alignments of the planets."

They called the new store the Wheatsville Food Co-op and assembled a core working group of ACP activists, many of whom lived together at the Nexus Co-op, to plot its future. The group collectively pooled together $5,000 and secured another $3,000 loan from the Inter-Cooperative Council—with luck, just a few months before its head discovered the financial mismanagement at Woody Hills and the Avenues.

One of the Wheatsville steering committee members, Audrey Eggar, was also on the University of Texas Student Senate. Eggar told them that the senate had come into a windfall that year. The Cultural Entertainment Committee had signed a small bluesy rock band from Houston named ZZ Top to perform at its annual back-to-school fund-raiser, and between the contract signing and the concert, the band had blown up. The massive crowds at the September 1974 ZZ Top First Annual Rompin' Stompin' Barndance & Barbecue were almost too stompin' to be a romp, complained the *Austin American-Statesman*. It made the senate a lot of money.[52]

Jackson and Newton put together a prospectus—a prospectus!—with impressive-looking financial projections they concocted around the dinner table. At the dog and pony show they gave to the senate, they explained their business model, which followed after successful consumer cooperatives they'd read about in British Columbia: a direct-charge system, in which every member would put down a big membership fee and pay $6 a month in dues, but there would be no markup over the wholesale prices. The structure, they thought, would encourage members to buy most of their food at the co-op. The pitch was convincing enough that the senate loaned them $5,000, interest-free.[53]

With $13,000 in hand, the Wheatsville group secured a three-thousand-square-foot space in a former carpet warehouse—double or three times the size of any of the other co-ops and natural-foods stores in town—and opened in March 1976. It had bare floors, cinder-block-and-plank shelves, a wraparound mezzanine with no guardrail, and no air-conditioning. In the summers, when Austin temperatures stay in the triple digits for months, the walk-in cooler would be so covered in sweat that it required frequent rubdowns.

All the traditional bulk bins were there, as well as whatever organic vegetables and fruits Jackson and Burgess could source. Perhaps even more shockingly, shoppers could find beef and chickens from local farms in the freezer, along with bags of sugar and bottles of wine—even Coca-Cola—on the shelves.

Wheatsville's shelves were a library of all the foods that the counterculture had adopted, reclaimed, and invented over the past decades: packaged foods from health-food-era brands such as Hain and Dr. Bronner's; grains from Texas's Arrowhead Mills, which had built its business selling to *Organic Gardening and Farming* types; macrobiotic staples from Michio and Aveline Kushi's Erewhon Foods; and products from new hip capitalist enterprises like Celestial Seasonings teas. Wheatsville was as close to a full-service natural-foods co-op as anyone had seen in Austin—in fact, in most U.S. cities at the time. The founders posted a sign over the checkout counter: THE FUTURE WILL BE WHAT THE PEOPLE STRUGGLE TO MAKE IT.[54]

And in the beginning, Wheatsville did struggle, rarely selling more than $50 worth of goods a day. Customers who didn't respect Wheatsville's decision to stock meat and canned goods stuck to Woody Hills and the Avenues, still open at the time. A local Stalinist faction marched into the store one day to argue with Newton over Wheatsville's business model, calling him, as a departing shot, "a barking dog of imperialism." More critically, the $6 monthly fee and the member stocking charge kept University of Texas students away. An MBA student Jackson and Newton knew suggested Wheatsville waive the fee for a one-day open house and advertise it in the school newspaper. The event packed the store and saved the business. Within a few years, Wheatsville remained the last food co-op standing in Austin.[55]

Like most of the co-op stores that survived into the late 1970s, Wheatsville was also discovering the flaw in the co-op movement's "food for people, not for profit" ethos. It took very little money to start a food-buying club or a co-op. It was easy to acquire food at wholesale prices, gather together a bunch of like-minded volunteers, and keep your labor costs at a minimum. But when the Marxist revolution didn't materialize, "food for people, not for profit" wasn't sustainable in a capitalist economy.

"We decided to go into one of the most competitive businesses in America that operates on incredibly low margins," John Dickerson, who joined Wheatsville's board of directors, says. "We were saying, 'We're going to beat the hell out of the prices in grocery stores.' You wound up finding out that if you do, you won't get paid your salary."

In 1979, the store went through one last great ideological spasm. For all its bylaws and boards of directors, Wheatsville was run like its predecessor co-ops: through nonhierarchical meetings, large crews of volunteers (called "Turnips," because they turned up to work), and discussions that needed to end in consensus.

The crew of paid staff complained to the board of directors that they were tired of attending endless meetings, often off the clock, to decide every little detail. The board was butting into their jobs, and some Turnips spent their volunteer shifts pestering workers. The staff—well, most of the staff—wanted a manager. So the board of directors hired one.

All hell broke loose.

For three months, the weekly *Wheatsville Breeze* newsletter was anything but breezy. Turnips protested they were being pushed out of their jobs. "This we oppose; give us a co-op, not a dues-paying Kash-Karry!" one wrote.[56]

Two weeks later, staffer Kathy Wall wrote a three-page resignation letter, titled "I QUIT," that ran on the front page of the newsletter. "The management system had not been in effect long before I began to feel a loss of power in decision-making," she sniped. In the following weeks, the newsletter ran angry resignation letter after angry resignation letter, ending with one from the new manager, who was fed up by the turmoil. By July, the newsletter estimated that 60 percent of the staff had quit, and board member Hunter Ellinger pleaded for the resignations to stop:

> I do not want any more staff members to quit. It would probably be an economic disaster for the co-op; but, more than that, I see it as unnecessary, and think it would poison the political process in the co-op. These people (and their many allies on the Board and in the membership) are not our enemies. They are not crypto-capitalists or enemies of the people. They, and all of us, are people betrayed by an inadequate political process, a process that was not their responsibility to develop. I don't want to chase out the "professionals" or even hold them back; I want to catch up with them.[57]

The fighting came to a head when one remaining staffer who was deeply committed to the idea of a professional hierarchy spotted a particularly strident member of the other faction walking into the store. Fed up with her protests, the worker dumped his mop bucket over her head. John Dickerson, who was head of the Wheatsville board, called an emergency meeting. "We posted our statement on the window, like Martin Luther on the gates of the cathedral, that we'll fire any staffer who does something like this and we'll initiate expulsions against any member who does these kinds of things," he says.

He thought he'd just unleashed the nuclear arsenal. The opposite happened. "I'd walk around the store, waiting to have somebody throw something at me, and everybody just shopped and smiled and went away. I think it was one of the first times I realized that every now and again, people in a crisis just want somebody to be an adult."

From that day on, Wheatsville was owned by its members but was no longer run by them. It had become a professional operation—and just in time to compete with a new store in Austin that would help reshape America's natural-foods industry.

THE TEXAS CAPITAL'S tiny for-profit natural-foods stores—the descendants of the vitamin-dominated health-food stores, now selling whole-grain foods and organic produce—were multiplying, but they could never match the co-ops for low prices and customer loyalty. Burgess Jackson and Gary Newton didn't even consider them competitors per se—in fact, Wheatsville joined forces with two stores, named SaferWay and Clarksville Natural Grocery, to order truckloads of organic produce from California, which gave all three a regular supply of this rare commodity at affordable prices.

Then, in 1980, the two for-profit stores merged. Owners John Mackey, Renee Lawson, Craig Weller, and Mark Skiles secured $45,000 in funding—a windfall compared to the start-up capital most co-ops raised—to renovate a ten-thousand-square-foot nightclub, opening in the fall of 1980 with nineteen employees, some of them recruited from the ranks of Wheatsville Turnips.[58]

They called the new store Whole Foods.[59]

Despite the fact that Mackey, who would come to run the company, was only twenty-five at the time, Whole Foods was no hippie enterprise. Where Wheatsville's founders were using the tools of capitalism to build a new economy, Mackey retooled the food co-op ethos to sell it to capitalists.

At Whole Foods, there were no membership fees, no volunteer shifts to schedule, no unwieldy meetings to sit through. The person at the cash register was a trained employee. So was the butcher. So was the person who stood in the produce section handing slices of some unusual fruit to try. You weren't forced to join the community. You could just shop.

And the shopping, compared to co-ops like Wheatsville, was grand. Whole Foods was bigger, of course, but it also conveyed abundance. The bulk herbs and tubs of grains were there. So were dog food, sugar, toilet paper, loofah sponges, and after the first year, a café. The produce section was stacked high with attractive displays of organic vegetables, tropical fruits, Japanese mushrooms, and several kinds of sprouts.

"We wanted a store where people could do their entire shopping," Mark Skiles would tell the *Austin American-Statesman* in 1982. "In the past, the majority of people would go to a natural food store for certain things, and then would go on to a grocery store for the rest."[60]

The newspaper, in turn, called Whole Foods "the Cadillac of natural foods stores." It repackaged all the foods that had been so fringe just a decade before for upscale shoppers, and added gourmet cheeses, small-batch ice cream, and the accoutrements of a healthy, upper-middle-class lifestyle. Burgess Jackson says he would drive by Whole Foods in its early years and marvel over the Mercedeses in the parking lot.

Both stores achieved a success that surpassed what anyone might have expected. Wheatsville has stayed open for forty years—and Whole Foods dominates the natural-foods industry.

# CONCLUSION

·····································

The world was not ready for Utopia yet, and those who attempted
to found it only got laughed at for their pains. In other days, men
could sell all and give to the poor, lead lives devoted to holiness
and high thought, and after the persecution was over, find themselves honored as saints or martyrs. But in modern times those
things are out of fashion. To live for one's principles, at all costs,
is a dangerous speculation; and the failure of an ideal, however
humane and noble, is harder for the world to forgive and forget
than bank robbery or the grand swindles of corrupt politicians.
—Louisa May Alcott, *Transcendental Wild Oats* (1873)[1]

THE REVOLUTION FAILED. THE REVOLUTION SUCCEEDED.

The 1980s and 1990s saw so many of the counterculture's gains
stagnate or reverse themselves. Communes disbanded. Homesteading
farmers, after years of failing to turn a profit on their five acres, returned to the city. Macrobiotics briefly flared in the public consciousness after Michio and Aveline Kushi trumpeted it as an anticancer diet,
then it faded into obscurity. Despite the success of *Diet for a Small
Planet*, meat consumption ticked upward.

"Food for people, not for profits" proved the food movement's greatest strength and its biggest weakness. The organic farmers, co-op organizers, macrobiotic students, and "right livelihood" entrepreneurs who introduced the general public to brown rice, tofu, whole-wheat bread, alfalfa sprouts, and hosts of natural foods saw in these foods a reflection of their anticommercial values. They worked for very little or volunteered their time to make natural foods affordable, their efforts eased by low operating costs and the freedom of youth. They rejected the workings of the for-profit marketplace, trusting instead in the bonds that linked their communities and the conviction of their ideals.

Yet the great alternative economy powered by co-ops, supplied by back-to-the-land farmers, and linked together by cooperative suppliers and distributors never materialized, damned in part by financial naiveté and in part by laws and financial institutions that did not adequately support cooperative enterprises. According to Dave Gutknecht, longtime editor of the trade magazine *Cooperative Grocer,* there were as many as five hundred natural-foods co-ops by the end of the 1970s, as well as thousands of buying clubs and fifty cooperative natural-foods distributors like the Michigan Federation of Food Co-ops. By the early 1990s, the buying clubs had evaporated, and the number of stores had shrunk to less than three hundred. By 2003, the fifty distributors had consolidated into five. A few years later, the five folded into one: United Natural Foods Incorporated, a publicly owned, for-profit company based in Providence, Rhode Island.

Mass-market co-optation certainly played a role in these reversals, too: Grocery stores saw that there were profits to be made in rice cakes and whole-wheat bread. Major food companies concocted sugary granola bars and fruit-on-the-bottom yogurts that seduced mainstream consumers away from their cognates at natural-foods stores.

Tastes changed, too. As crusty white French baguettes supplanted dense oatmeal ryes in the public imagination and as Tuscan risottos edged out brown-rice pilafs, the mainstream media, which had always treated natural foods with pursed-lip amusement, blithely followed the zeitgeist. Restaurants like the New Riverside Cafe floundered after twenty-some years (a good run nevertheless) and closed. The food the hippies ate became "hippie food," scorned by the very children who had grown up eating it. Children like me.

And yet.

Just as the Reagan-Bush era didn't kill off the political Left, the food that the 1970s counterculture brought into the mainstream never went away. Carob brownies, bean-and-walnut loaves, and avocado-and-sprout sandwiches may have faded away, but the ingredients to make these foods never disappeared from grocery stores and home kitchens.

In the past decade, fashion has found them again.

Just as the 1970s interest in whole foods sent longhairs into tiny health-food stores, the Paleo, vegan, and gluten-free movements of the early twenty-first century have sent people to food co-ops and natural-foods stores, where contemporary shoppers have taken bulk-bin staples and used them to their own ends.

Living in the San Francisco Bay Area, I can't walk a mile in any direction without passing the spiritual descendants of Gypsy Boots and the Source Family: stores that sell green juices, protein smoothies fortified with almond "mylk" and flaxseeds, and granola bowls with yogurt and berries. Gayelord Hauser's five superfoods (blackstrap molasses, brewer's yeast, skim milk powder, wheat germ, and yogurt) qualify as merely muscular compared to maca, chia, açai berry, and turmeric, if we believe the claims made of their powers. We still embrace any new food that some *New York Times* article—or that woman we were talking to at yoga yesterday—suggests is magical enough to brighten our eyesight, or smooth over our cellulite, or give us that Hollywood glow. Only now, the words we throw out to characterize these magical properties, like *phytonutrients* and *antioxidants*, sound like we came across them while reading scientific journals.

Macrobiotics has flared into common consciousness again in the form of grain bowls (sometimes called "macro bowls") and a line of MacroBars that would enrage George Ohsawa, based as they are on tropical ingredients like cashews and coconut. Thanks in part to the gluten-free movement—a growing awareness of celiac sprue and gluten sensitivity, amplified by a generalized and unstudied anxiety over wheat—I can find baked goods made with any number of whole grains in my local grocery store.

The portion of the U.S. population that is vegetarian is holding steady at 5 percent. Not only can I order tofu burritos at Chipotle and pick up packages of Tofurky-brand sliced tempeh at my local Whole Foods, Frances Moore Lappé's core argument in *Diet for a Small Planet* has resurfaced in the rhetoric of venture-capital-backed firms like Impossible Foods and Beyond Meat, which are engineering new meat substitutes, they claim, to conserve natural resources and feed a population that has topped 7.5 billion.

It may have become harder to be a food revolutionary, but it has become a hell of a lot easier to shop like one.

Through the 1980s and 1990s, mainstream supermarkets all across the country added natural-foods sections, and for-profit natural-foods groceries like Bread & Circus, Mrs. Gooch's, and Wild Oats grew steadily, to be acquired by Whole Foods in the progress of its Manifest Destiny. For all of Whole Foods's success—it reported $15.4 billion worth in sales in 2015, closing out the year with 431 stores[2]—the co-op movement did not die off, either.

The three-hundred-some stores that made it through the gauntlet of the 1980s and 1990s moved into larger locations, and expanded from bulk bins and sweaty coolers, adding aisles of packaged foods and freezers, gourmet cheese stations, and espresso bars. In fact, according to *Cooperative Grocer* editor Gutknecht, at least fifty of them have expanded into multiple locations—Wheatsville Food Co-op in

Austin, for instance, added a second one in 2013. Not only that, Gutknecht says, but over the past ten years the United States has seen
the largest wave of new co-ops since the 1970s, even though now the
process of opening a co-op starts with market feasibility studies, fund-
raising campaigns, and business plans, not renting out a church basement for a few bucks a month.

To trace the natural-foods movement from 1980 to the present is a
dull slog compared to the foment of the 1960s and 1970s: an interminable string of start-ups and acquisitions, legislative gains and losses,
changes often measured in million-dollar increments.

Many of the oldest natural-foods brands belong to the country's largest corporations now. General Mills owns Cascadian Farm and Muir
Glen. J. M. Smucker owns Santa Cruz Organic. Danone bought the
majority stake in Stonyfield from Samuel Kaymen and his partners in
2004. Then there's the Hain Celestial Group, which began in the 1920s
as Hain Pure Foods, a tiny Los Angeles company known for jarred
juices. The owners of early organic powerhouses like Arrowhead Mills
and Walnut Acres sold their businesses to Hain. Then it acquired hip
businesses of the 1970s like Celestial Seasonings and Westbrae, as well
as Rice Dream, Garden of Eatin', MaraNatha, Terra Chips, Spectrum,
and two dozen other household names. The corporation reported $2.7
billion in net sales in 2015.[3]

The growth of the organic marketplace is even more spectacular.
Organic food is, arguably, the most visible legacy of the 1970s food
movement.

By the end of 2015, the U.S. National Agricultural Statistics Service
counted 12,818 certified organic farms on 4.4 million acres of land, up
from 915,000 acres in 1995. Only 1 percent of American farmland is
certified organic, it's true, but that's enough land to produce $6.2 bil-
lion worth of produce, dairy, eggs, meat, and fiber. Seventy-five percent of organic farms sell at least some of what they produce directly to

customers through farm stands and the thousands of farmers' markets that the founders of the organic movement could justifiably claim responsibility for.[4]

Farmers weren't the only ones to apply for organic certification. According to the Organic Trade Association, sales of organic products hit $43.3 billion in 2015, up 10 percent from the year before and twelve times the size of the market in 1997. The trade association reported that 75 percent of American households buy some amount of organic foods.[5]

JUST HOW DID hippie food spread out from the longhair enclaves to small midwestern cities like the one I grew up in? After five years of research, I was able to answer that initial question: Through the tiny vitamin shops and health-food stores that predated the 1970s. Through recipes, nonfiction books, and newspaper articles. Most significantly, through the testaments of millions of people: the back-to-the-landers brought their strange tastes to rural towns across the country; the organizers of food conspiracies roped in their neighbors, sneaking millet and tofu into the Trojan horse of lower prices; food co-ops exposed anyone who braved them to legions of unfamiliar foods and ways of thinking.

The answer to the question of *why* hippie food spread so far, insinuating itself in the kitchen cabinets of people who would never have cooked cheesy millet-lentil loaves, is more of a subjective one. Over the course of the last five years, I have asked the hundreds of people I interviewed why they thought the movement had been successful in changing the way so many of us eat. Four common threads emerged.

One was that the fears scaring young freaks and back-to-the-landers away from plastic food weren't exclusive to the counterculture. After Rachel Carson's bestselling exposé, *Silent Spring,* was published, the congressional debates that resulted in a prohibition against DDT were well chronicled. Newspapers in the tiniest towns in America reported on the FDA's bans on saccharin and red dye number 2, pesticide poisonings, and food contamination scares. By the mid-1970s, anyone terrified enough over the safety of their food to search out cleaner alternatives could find them in the resources young Americans had published and the nationwide supply chain they had established.

Another reason hippie food survived: just as the 1969 trope "the personal is political" took hold, so, too, did the idea that food choices were political. Buying vegetables grown without chemical fertilizers and pesticides became a political act. Shopping at a community-owned market became a political act. Making your own bread or yogurt could be seen as a political act: a denial of a morally bankrupt, capitalist system that prized profits over nutrition.

Almost five decades later, a good-sized segment of the population finds the subject of food even more fraught with political implications than ever. Activists all over the country are pressuring local and state governments to bring nutritious food to neighborhoods abandoned by grocery chains. As consumers, many of us freeze up in the supermarket aisles, worrying: Does eating produce airlifted from Chile bankrupt local family farms? If I buy this chocolate, am I condoning child labor in West Africa? By shopping at Walmart, am I supporting the exploitation of workers who make minimum wage? To think through these issues means grappling with the far-reaching and subtle effects of globalization. It can torque us into neurotic knots, or by contrast, fill us with pride and righteousness—in both the good sense and the bad—when we make the "right" choices. At the same time, the debate over whether it is elitist to privilege pure food over cheap food is just as trenchant as it was in 1976.

A third reason is that cookbooks like *Moosewood Cookbook* and *The Tassajara Bread Book* stuck around because their recipes were easy to make. By and large, the 1970s natural-foods movement was a grassroots one: a cuisine created in the home and spread largely by home cooks to home cooks. Anyone who adopted its guidelines—using whole grains instead of refined, substituting honey or molasses for white sugar, cooking with fresh vegetables—found they were loose enough to play with.

The hippie food of the 1970s, as I see it, was a collective effort to come up with a healthier, more environmentally responsive, *everyday* cuisine for the twentieth century and beyond. It was simple and straight-forward. It took no special equipment. The recipes, even the most elaborate, were easy for beginning cooks to tackle, as long as they could shake off a reflexive fear of millet.

Cooks at collective restaurants like Moosewood and the New River-side Cafe refined this new cuisine—how could they not, after spending forty to eighty hours a week thinking and tasting?—but the recipes that came out of these restaurants could easily be scaled down for six-person households.

It was the last grassroots cooking movement to have widespread effect until, perhaps, social media changed the way we learned about food. If you look at how culinary culture in America evolved from the 1980s on, so much of it has come out of restaurants, professional bakeries, and gourmet food suppliers. Some of that is logistical: in 1970, a quarter of our household spending was on food "eaten away from home," as the U.S. Economic Research Service likes to classify food prepared in restaurants, schools, hotels, and other institutions. That percentage rose to 43 by 2012.[6]

As dining out became entertainment, many Americans looked to chefs—in both professional kitchens and television studios—to teach them how to eat and cook. The world of food came to resemble the world of fashion, new ideas emerging from the creative elite and trick-ling down to the hoi polloi. A chef like Paul Prudhomme, who helped popularize Cajun cooking at his New Orleans restaurant K-Paul's, introduced a new dish like blackened redfish (fish coated in spices and seared). The *New York Times* covered it. Chefs in other cities copied it. By the 1990s, Red Lobster had adopted the technique; by that time, haute cuisine had moved on.

In California, chefs like Alice Waters, Jeremiah Tower, Michael Mc-Carty, and Wolfgang Puck solicited farmers (many of them back-to-the-landers) to cultivate better-tasting vegetables and fruits that increased in rarity, such as mixed baby greens, Yukon Gold potatoes, and heirloom tomatoes. Diners discovered these new varieties at their restaurants and then at the farmers' markets, and they slowly made their way to grocery chains over the course of decades.

Americans didn't just become familiar with luxury lettuces and professional cooking techniques like braising beef and caramelizing onions through restaurants. We learned about one another's culinary backgrounds as well. The effects of the 1965 loosening of the immigration laws could be seen in our dining options as well as elementary classrooms: Korean, Mexican, a clutch of regional Chinese cuisines, Salvadoran, Ethiopian, Filipino, Lebanese, Japanese, Thai.

IN THE PAST decade, the New Hippie Food, as I tend to call it—almond-milk chia puddings, avocado toast, grain bowls, and so, so many kale salads[7]—has incorporated all these later culinary shifts.

The New Hippie Food isn't just found at juice shops and salad bars but at soigné restaurants like San Francisco's Bar Tartine, where chefs Nick Balla and Cortney Burns turned DIY crafts like pickling and fermenting into a high art and served dishes like sprouted mung-bean fritters with herbed yogurt sauce that were so deeply flavorful that they transcended 1970s nostalgia.

New Hippie Food cookbooks have landed on the bestseller lists, among them Heidi Swanson's *Super Natural Cooking*, Jessica Koslow's *Everything I Want to Eat* (based on her popular Sqirl restaurant in Los

Angeles, New Hippie Food par excellence), and queen of the movement
Gwyneth Paltrow's *It's All Good* and *It's All Easy*.[8]

Counterculture staples from the 1970s such as yogurt, lemon-tahini
dressing, millet, and seeds appear in recipe after recipe in cookbooks
and blogs. But the dishes they're worked into are often colorful, light,
and unreservedly bourgeois.

The recipes in books like *Super Natural Cooking* and *It's All Good* call
on European vegetables and heirloom varietals that only a few back-to-
the-land farmers might have read about in their seed catalogs in 1973.
Gourmet produce, such as arugula and figs, is now considered mainstream. So are spice blends like harissa and baharat, which only the most
dogged of cookbook scholars would have encountered in 1978. To cook
the New Hippie Food requires shopping trips to high-end natural-foods
stores and, as many of Paltrow's critics have complained, expensive
products like cold-pressed coconut oil and almond meal.

For its spelt flour cookies and sprouted-chickpea falafel, the New
Hippie Food is more colorful and often tastier than its predecessor cuisine. Now that getting enough protein isn't task number one of any
chef, whole grains and legumes are woven into dishes with brighter and
bolder-tasting ingredients. Hefty doses of cheese, eggs, and dairy aren't
required to make the food satisfying. Basic French culinary techniques,
like sautéing aromatics or blanching green vegetables, that make a huge
difference in the outcome of the dish are now standard.

The New Hippie Food, I have to confess, has become my own everyday cuisine. Forty years after I groused about my mother's lentil stews
and whole-wheat bread, I now make them more often than she does.


THE FINAL, AND most significant, reason that hippie cuisine has endured
is that the 1970s counterculture succeeded in selling America on its concept of healthy food.

Well into the 1970s, the food industry, the media, and many nutrition experts pooh-poohed advocates of whole, unprocessed foods as fantasists, nutritional neurotics who thought they needed to chew, chew, chew their way to health. Then they discovered fiber.

Starting in the mid-1970s, a series of articles about the benefits of fiber emerged in the popular press. New research suggested that higher-fiber diets could help control obesity and reduce colon cancer. In a May 1975 article titled "Fiber: The Forgotten Nutrient," for instance, Harvard nutritionist Jean Mayer summarized these new studies and concluded that Americans should eat more fruits, vegetables, and whole grains. "Once again, the better part of wisdom seems to be to return to a simpler, less processed diet." Considering the director of Mayer's department at Harvard was America's number one critic of natural foods, Frederick J. Stare, this was a cannon-shot across the bow of the disbelievers.

The news set off a fiber craze. "People who once described bran as the closest thing to cattle feed are happily eating like their four legged friends," Jane Brody wrote in the *New York Times* in 1977. "Last year, the fiber fad resulted in a shortage of bran in the United States."[9]

Even as Americans choked down bran cereal and squinted at food labels to read the fiber content, the acknowledgment of fiber's importance signaled the start of a shift in how the nutritional establishment—academic dietitians, the USDA, and other health authorities—would treat the foods that the counterculture was eating and its critique of the country's meat-centered, heavily processed diet.

You can see the shift in the USDA's first Dietary Guidelines, published in 1980 and updated every five years, when the agency recommended, albeit tepidly, that Americans eat less meat and more whole-grain foods. The 1995 guidelines finally recognized, "You can get enough protein from a vegetarian diet as long as the variety and amounts of foods consumed are adequate." The 2005 recommendations got more specific: from here on out, the USDA would tell us that half the grain-based foods that we consume, such as breads and rice dishes, should be whole grains.

If you scoff at the notion that Americans observe the USDA Dietary Guidelines as religiously as they do the Ten Commandments, you're probably not wrong: according to the Economic Research Service, by 2010, Americans were only eating 26 percent of the whole grains their government advised them to.[10] In 2014, Centers for Disease Control and Prevention researchers found that 13 percent of Americans followed the USDA's daily recommendations for fruits (one and a half to two cups a day) and only 7 percent ate all the vegetables (two to three cups) they were supposed to.[11]

And yet, few nutritionists now disagree with the fact that Americans should eat less red meat, significantly less sugar, more vegetables, more fruits, more whole grains, and more unprocessed foods. Tofu and soy milk are no longer for bizarre food faddists, either—since 2000, the USDA agrees that they're healthful sources of protein.

The Dietary Guidelines may not be influencing our dinner plate, but they *do* shape public policy. The moment it hit me that hippie food had become the gold standard for nutrition was the day in 2014 I attended a taste test at Gordon J. Lau Elementary School in San Francisco.

Revolution Foods, an Oakland company that provides lunch for more than two thousand schools across the country, had invited me, as a reporter for the *San Francisco Chronicle* food section, to observe the company run a new breakfast dish past a final board of critics: second graders.

I took my seat in the school cafeteria as company representatives, including cofounder Kirsten Saenz Tobey and corporate chef Amy Klein, fussed over the contents of a portable food warmer and taped butcher paper on the pale blue walls. Then, with the school's principal playing sheepdog, twenty seven- and eight-year-olds bumbled into the lunchroom and squirmed their way onto the benches.

The Revolution Foods team handed them paper cups of the test dish. "I know it looks yummy, but try to resist eating," one told the students. The strain was great enough that one girl pushed her cup away and hid her eyes.

Klein stood up and introduced herself to the group. "As your chef, I've been working in my kitchen," she told them. "I have pots so big I think I could put you in those pots. I make rice in those pots, and noodles, and sauce. How many of you have had rice with soup for breakfast?" Hands went up. Almost all the children at the table were Chinese American, many of them learning to speak English at school.

The chef asked the kids to identify the vegetables they saw in their rice—green beans! carrots!—and told them the rice also had a tiny link of smoked chicken sausage in it. After she unleashed their appetites and before she quizzed them on whether they thought the rice was not spicy enough or too spicy, one of the staff brought me a cup.

Inside it was a half cup of brown rice (from a local Japanese American farmer, I was later told) cooked with diced vegetables, scrambled eggs, vegetable broth, and just enough tamari to deepen its beige color. Its familiarity startled me. Take out the chicken sausage, and this dish, which the students collectively named "Sunshine Breakfast Bowl," might be the New Riverside Cafe's signature Brown Rice and Vegetables.

Revolution Foods, which Tobey founded with Kristin Groos Richmond in 2006, was one of the first school lunch providers in the country to adopt brown rice and whole-wheat baked goods, as well as to ban preservatives, artificial colorings and flavorings, nitrates, and milk from cows given the growth hormone rBST. "We have a list of ingredients that we don't allow, which is similar to the list you'd see at Whole Foods," Tobey told me later.

For Revolution Foods's first years, many school districts considered them starry-eyed Bay Area foodies, overprotective and fussy. That was before Congress passed the 2010 Healthy, Hunger-Free Kids Act. Based in part on the USDA Dietary Guidelines, the act required schools to serve fruits or vegetables to students at every meal and make sure 51 percent of grain-based foods are whole grains. (A 2013 update allowed tofu and soy milk as well.)

The act was greeted with outrage. The National School Lunch Program feeds 30.5 million children every day at one hundred thousand schools across the country. Many schools responded to the new requirements by ordering processed foods with barely tweaked specs. "Kraft comes in with a mac and cheese that's whole grain, and Tyson comes up with chicken nuggets that are whole grain," explains Ann Cooper, head of the Boulder Valley School District food services and founder of the Chef Ann Foundation, which helps schools switch to cooking fresh, healthy foods.

At the time this book was printed, the fate of the Healthy, Hunger-Free Kids Act's new regulations under the Trump administration was uncertain, and 20 percent of all school districts had been granted some form of exemption from its requirements. Yet the act also galvanized some school districts across the country to do away with processed foods and return to scratch cooking, just as Cooper has in Boulder. "Most school districts since 2010 have started down the road of serving healthier food," she adds. Tobey says that since the act passed, Revolution Foods has fielded dozens of calls from other school districts asking for advice.

Tobey says that Revolution Foods has tried to make all these new foods palatable to students by pairing the unfamiliar with flavors that kids recognize. "We call it having a foot in the familiar," she says. That means serving Mexican-style brown rice flavored with tomato and paprika, whole-wheat calzone with cheese and soy pepperoni, and "firecracker chicken" with sesame whole-grain noodles. Where white hippies once used non-European seasonings to make natural foods tasty,

Revolution Foods uses them because so many of the children the company feeds were raised on those very flavors.

The Sunshine Breakfast Bowl isn't hippie food, old or new. It's more like hippie adjacent. But watching twenty second graders—who must count, collectively, as the country's pickiest eaters—down their rice bowls and give Tobey the thumbs-up, I was struck that second graders in the 2010s were eating the same foods I had forty years earlier, at the peak of my parents' co-op shopping days.

When they're a decade or two older, these same second graders may reminisce about their cafeteria's bean-cheese burritos on whole-wheat tortillas with the same disdain-tinged fondness that my friends do our parents' food. Like my generation, too, tomorrow's adults may find these flavors so familiar that they weave through their memories in ways they can't consciously identify. They slip into the meals we throw together after a long workday or call to us from the take-away cases at the airport. Like a twist of melody that leaps from a car window and sets us humming, these flavors belong to us and, in turn, soothe us with a sense of belonging.

When brown rice reminds us all of our childhoods, then the hippie food revolution will finally be won.

# ACKNOWLEDGMENTS

THE RULE WITH FIRST BOOKS, I think, is to thank everyone in the universe.

First off, thanks to the people who made this book happen: to my agent, Nicole Tourtelot, who immediately got where I was going and blazed a trail for me to get there. Much gratitude to Trish Daly, who believed in this book enough to convince William Morrow to publish it; to Margaux Weisman, who offered wise counsel and wiser edits throughout the writing process; and to Kara Zauberman, who so ably ushered it through to publication.

Thanks to friends who looked over rough drafts: Christopher Tradowsky, Rachel Khong, Jon Bonné, you have no idea how much each of you helped. To Tara Austen Weaver, who set me back on the road after I'd steered into a ditch. To Scott Hocker and Geoff Bartakovics, who gave me the time to work on the proposal while I was at Tasting Table. And to Kitty Morgan, Paolo Lucchesi, and Audrey Cooper, my editors at the *San Francisco Chronicle*, who backed me wholeheartedly and let me take a few months off to finish this book, not to mention my colleagues in the food section who covered for my absence and, at other points, my exhaustion.

Every chapter in *Hippie Food* was possible only through the efforts of a few superconnectors, people who opened the door to their entire community: Laurie Praskin, Deborah Koons Garcia, Patti Smith, Bill Meacham, Carolyn Brown Zniewski and Erik Riese, Jodi Wille, Alex Gyori, and Bill Nowak. Other superconnectors: librarians, a.k.a. the information superheroes, who hooked me up with resources I could never have found on my own.

I could have spent a few months just digging through the files of the Soyinfo Center; thanks to William Shurtleff for sharing his time, his books, and his archives. Thanks to Isis Aquarian for preserving Father Yod's legacy, and to Akasha Richmond and Gordon Kennedy for first making the connections between Los Angeles and health food. Thanks to Mollie Katzen, Seth Tibbott, and especially the Lundberg clan for talking to me so early on and assuring me that this was a rich and fascinating topic. Thanks to Edward Brown, whose words on bread and Zen practice have inspired me for decades. And to Frances Moore Lappé, who changed the world in 1971 and whose work today still drives me to think differently.

In the process of writing this book, I feel so fortunate to have encountered hundreds of people who shared their time, their life stories, their thoughts, and their encouragement. In order to turn a sprawling movement into a legible narrative, I wasn't able to mention more than a handful of names in the text, but every tale is constructed of dozens of others, some of which are so fantastic I wish I could publish a second book of outtakes (Olive Ylin, Steve Bellock, and Cynthia Bates would each get their own chapter).

I particularly want to thank a few people who inspired me and this book in ways that transcended the simple sharing of anecdotes: Paul Bantle and Annie Elder, the generous macrobiotic memoirist Peter Milbury, Peter Gould (your next reading assignment: seek out his memoirs), Eve MacLeish, Pam Peirce, David Hirsch, Odessa Piper, Jack Lazor, Ginny Callan, Warren Weber, Amigo Bob Cantisano, and Bruce Curtis.

Thanks to my family—the Kauffmans, the Bourneufs, and the Rummells—who have offered unconditional love and deep wells of sympathy these past five years. To Jennifer Coffey for her near-boundless generosity. To fellow deadline-racer and black-humor-texter Jessica Battilana. To Jennifer Snyder for her enthusiasm and curiosity. To Pat Walsh, who lent me a house at the most critical moment. And much love to my friends who kept our connection alive during the months when I had no time to devote to friendship, and who let me vent in the rare moments when I did.

This book might not have existed without two people: Kara Platoni, who traveled this road before me and called out all the bumps so I would see them coming, then edited me and cheered me on every time I felt lost. And most especially my beloved husband, Christian Rummell, who held us together, mind and body, every damn day. We had no idea that dissertations and books were two-person tasks, did we?

# NOTES

## Introduction

1. Dorothy B. Marsh, ed., *The New Good Housekeeping Cookbook* (Harcourt, Brace and World, 1963).

2. Lizzie Collingham, *The Taste of War: World War II and the Battle for Food* (Penguin Books, 2012).

3. FAO AGRostat database, via Lisa Clark, "Organic Limited: The Corporate Rise and Spectacular Change in the Canadian and American Organic Food Sectors" (Ph.D. dissertation, Simon Fraser University, 2007).

4. U.S. Department of Agriculture, downloaded from http://www.earth-policy.org/datacenter/pdf/book_fpep_ch3_all.pdf.

5. U.S. Department of Labor, "100 Years of U.S. Consumer Spending: Data for the Nation, New York City, and Boston" (U.S. Bureau of Labor Statistics, 2006).

6. Harvey Levenstein, *Paradox of Plenty: A Social History of Eating in Modern America*, rev. ed. (University of California Press, 2003).

7. Tribal Council Food Committee, "Eat to Get High," *Ann Arbor Sun*, September 1, 1972.

8. Tom Murtha, "Scenes: 1958–73: Escaping Conformism," *Insider*, February 1973, pp. 94–99.

9. John Leggett, "Metamorphosis of the Campus Radical," *New York Times*, January 30, 1972.

## 1. Fruits, Seeds, and (Health) Nuts in Southern California

1. Interview with Bart and Wendy Baker, May 1, 2015.
2. Health Hut menu, circa 1957. Property of Dan Bootzin.
3. Emily Abel, *Suffering in the Land of Sunshine: A Los Angeles Illness Narrative* (Rutgers University Press, 2006).
4. Tom Zimmerman, *Paradise Promoted: The Booster Campaign That Created Los Angeles, 1870–1930* (Angel City Press, 2008). See also Emily Abel, *Tuberculosis and the Politics of Exclusion* (Rutgers University Press, 2007).
5. This section owes a debt to James C. Whorton's *Nature Cures: The History of Alternative Medicine in America* (Oxford University Press, 2002).
6. Philip Lovell, "Care of the Body," *Los Angeles Times*, December 16, 1928; Lee Shippey, "The Lee Side o' LA," *Los Angeles Times*, December 17, 1927.
7. Vera Richter, *Mrs. Richter's Cook-Less Book with Scientific Food Chart* (Hale Publications, 1948). In *Mrs. Richter's Cook-Less Book,* Vera Richter gives recipes that alternate between the timelessly appealing and the repellent: shucked fresh corn with green onions and parsley, tomato-celery soup with peanut butter and garlic, dehydrated carob-date bread.
8. Gordon Kennedy's fascinating 1998 book *Children of the Sun: A Pictorial Anthology from Germany to California, 1883–1949* (Nivaria Press, 1998) traces the figures who brought the *naturmenschen*, and their Teutonic proto-hippiedom, to Southern California.
9. Arnold Ehret. *Professor Arnold Ehret's Rational Fasting for Physical, Mental & Spiritual Rejuvenation* (reprint: Summertown, Tenn.: Ehret Literature, 2013).
10. The weak were allowed to cheat with a potato, but better still would be some toasted grains or crispbread, which had no paste-building characteristics.
11. Ingredients: senna, buckthorn, psyllium husk and seed, aniseed, and fennel seeds.
12. For example, the True Light Beaver commune in Woodstock, New York, which published a 1972 cookbook titled *Eat, Fast, Feast,* repeated Ehret's instructions for fasting.
13. Heather Addison, *Hollywood and the Rise of Physical Culture* (Routledge, 2003).
14. "Hollywood Warns Film-Struck Girls," *New York Times*, December 4, 1923, as cited in Addison, *Hollywood and the Rise of Physical Culture.*
15. Macfadden, who was based in New York, was one of the most powerful publishers of his day and helped give birth to the physical culture movement of the early twentieth century that gave rise to every CrossFit class and running-shoe company. More than a few books have been written about his amazing

life; the most entertaining may be Mark Adams's *Mr. America: How Muscular Millionaire Bernarr Macfadden Transformed the Nation Through Sex, Salad, and the Ultimate Starvation Diet* (Harper, 2009).

16. "Be Young at 70!" [advertisement]. *Oakland Tribune*, October 3, 1930.

17. Wheatgrass juice didn't make inroads in the United States until the later 1960s, popularized by a Boston naturopath named Ann Wigmore, who in her 1964 biography *Why Suffer?* claimed to have discovered the wheat variety with the most vitality by offering her pets the choice of which sprouts to nibble on.

18. Akasha Richmond, *Hollywood Dish* (Penguin, 2006). Richmond's cookbook is the best existing survey of Los Angeles's health-food prophets and pioneers, including Arnold Ehret, Gayelord Hauser, Paul Bragg, Otto Carqué, and Jim Baker. See also Catherine Carstairs, "'Look Younger, Live Longer': Ageing Beautifully with Gayelord Hauser in America, 1920–1975," *Gender & History* 26, no. 2 (August 2014).

19. You may never have heard of Gayelord Hauser, but you may have encountered two of his products. Swiss Kriss is a laxative, apparently much loved by Louis Armstrong. Spike is a line of salt substitutes that can still be found in grocery stores across the country.

20. Michael Ackerman, "Interpreting the 'Newer Knowledge of Nutrition'" (Ph.D. dissertation, University of Virginia, 2005).

21. Gayelord Hauser, *Look Younger, Live Longer* (Fawcett Crest, 1951).

22. All products and stores were advertising in 1957 issues of *Let's Live*, the Los Angeles–based health-food magazine.

23. "Myth of the Wonder Foods," *Science Digest*, January 1952. (Reprinted from *Changing Times: The Kiplinger Magazine*.)

24. Gordon Greer, "Just How Healthy Are Health Foods?" *Better Homes and Gardens*, March 1963.

25. Harry Nelson, "Quackery in Nutrition Field Assailed by Medical Groups," *Los Angeles Times*, November 8, 1964.

26. David Ferrell, "Gypsy: At 75, 'Nature Boy' Is a Free Spirit with a Healthy Sense of Humor," *Los Angeles Times*, April 20, 1986.

27. Interviews with Dan and Alex Bootzin as well as Gordon Kennedy, longtime friend of Gypsy Boots.

28. *You Bet Your Life*, April 7, 1955. YouTube video, https://www.youtube.com/watch?v=UgWjPVGmxDA.

29. Marla Matzer Rose, *Muscle Beach* (LA Weekly Books/St. Martin's Griffin, 2001).

30. Ibid.

31. Ibid.

32. "Nature Boy," words by eden ahbez.

33. Undated 1959 episode of *On the Go*. University of California, Los Angeles Television Collection.

34. This section relies heavily on Isis Aquarian and Electricity Aquarian's *The Source: The Untold Story of Father Yod, Ya Ho Wa13 and the Source Family* (Process, 2007), as well as Jodi Wille's 2012 documentary *The Source Family* (Drag City, 2013).

35. Their friendship was confirmed in Jack LaLanne, *The Jack LaLanne Way to Vibrant Good Health* (Prentice Hall, 1960). Also see Joseph Garretson, "Muscle Contest," *Cincinnati Enquirer*, September 18, 1947. Similar articles in the *Enquirer* claimed Baker was a world heavyweight jujitsu champion.

36. Interview with Bart and Wendy Baker, May 1, 2015.

37. Ibid.

38. Telephone interview with Elaine and Wendy Baker, July 7, 2015.

39. Jim later told the Source Family the first customer was Greta Garbo, who did become a regular later.

40. Gypsy Boots with Jerry Hopkins, *Bare Feet and Good Things to Eat*, 7th ed. (Self-published, n.d.). Hopkins was the producer from the *Steve Allen Show* who recruited Gypsy for the show.

41. Ibid. Courtesy of Gypsy Boots, LLC.

42. Joseph Finnegan, "Boots Leaves Tree House to Become Folk Singer," *Albuquerque Journal*, November 21, 1963.

43. William Shurtleff interview, Soyinfo archives.

44. In a 2003 article, Gordon Kennedy, author of *Children of the Sun*, claimed that the Los Angeles hippies took their penchant for long hair and beards from the Nature Boys; apparently Sky Saxon, guitarist for the early psychedelic rock band the Seeds and later a member of the Source Family, was friends with Gypsy Boots. See Gordon Kennedy and Kody Ryan, "Hippie Roots and the Perennial Subculture," *Hippyland*, May 13, 2003. Accessed at http://www.hippy.com/modules.php?name=News&file=article&sid=243.

45. Tom Nolan, "The Health-Food Restaurateur Who Decided to Be God," *Los Angeles Magazine*, June 1980.

46. Roger Vaughan, "The Mad New Scene on Sunset Strip," *Life*, August 26, 1966.

47. "Father Yod-Ya Ho Wha's Morning Meditations, series II," recording 8–12–73B (Global Recording Artists, 2014).

48. Wille, *The Source Family* documentary; Steve Allen, *Beloved Son: A Story of the Jesus Cults* (Bobbs-Merrill, 1982).

49. Rather than folding, the Old World spawned locations all over Southern California and inspired legions of imitators.

50. Biographical details taken from Szekely's three-part biography, *Search for the Ageless* (San Diego: Academy Books, 1977), and summarized online at http://communiu.home.xs4all.nl/Studymat/Brimasters/B03profes.htm.

51. Edmond Bordeaux Szekely, *The Essene Gospel of Peace: The Aramaic and Old Slavonic Texts*, 17th ed. (Academy of Creative Living, 1971). You can also read the full text of the gospel online at http://essene.com/GospelOfPeace/peace1.html. In fact, I insist you do.

52. Per Beskow, *Strange Tales About Jesus*, English translation (Fortress Press, 1983).

53. Edmond Bordeaux Szekely, *The Essene Science of Life According to the Essene Gospel of Peace* (International Biogenic Society, 1978).

54. Conversation with Richard Moon and Rochelle Karr, the two hippies present at the event, on May 22, 2015.

55. Philip Deslippe, "From Maharaj to Mahan Tantric: The Construction of Yogi Bhajan's Kundalini Yoga," *Sikh Formations*, December 2012.

56. In 1974, Dick Gregory—who by then had become one of America's best-known African American comedians, published numerous books, attended "every major" civil rights march, and run for both mayor of Chicago and president—published *Dick Gregory's Natural Diet for Folks Who Eat*. Gregory made national news in 1972 for doing a forty-day juice fast to protest the war in Vietnam, and he claimed that he lost 180 pounds, dropping to 97 pounds.

When Gregory embarked on the Vietnam fast, he put himself under the care of Alvenia Fulton, a former Baptist minister and naturopathic doctor in Chicago who ran the Fultonia Health Food Center and told Ebony in 1974 that she was a "dietician to the stars" (Ruby Dee and Ossie Davis were also clients). Fulton taught Gregory how to subsist on juices and, more critically, schooled him in the mysteries of the colon that he devoted most of his book to explaining.

"Cooked, devitalized foods passing through the colon leave a coating of slime on the walls like plaster on the walls of a house," he wrote. He frequently called this slime "mucus," though he never referenced Arnold Ehret either in the text or his lists of resources. To rid the body of feculant phlegm, Gregory explained, we would have to eat only raw fruits and vegetables, juice incessantly, get regular enemas and colonics, and fast on a regular basis.

Gregory, who gave up comedy for advocacy in 1973, criticized soul food for being too fatty and meaty: "I personally would say that the quickest way to wipe out a group of people is to put them on a soul food diet," he wrote. He also emphasized the links between diet and civil rights. "Just as individual Americans need to realize the beauty and marvel of their own bodies and clean out their systems, the national body must realize that its own system needs cleaning," he wrote.

Thousands of Gregory's fans, black and white, bought Gregory's book; in a 1974 feature on African American vegetarians, *Ebony* called it a "zinging best-seller." Natural Diet quickly went out of print, but it influenced a later generation of African American food activists and instilled disgust in millions of readers who had never given any thought to the mucus flowing through their intestinal tracts.

57. This section relies on interviews with Robert Quinn, Isis Aquarian, Damian Paul, and Bart and Wendy Baker, as well as the Isis and Electricity Aquarian book and Jodi Wille documentary cited above.

58. "Spiritual shock troops" is how Isis Aquarian, chronicler of the family, now thinks of the Source Family.

59. Allen, *Beloved Son*. Allen's son Brian belonged to the Love Israel family in Seattle, which briefly considered joining with the Brotherhood of the Source. You can listen to the recordings yourself; the high-pitched cooing and gasps that greet every utterance from Father Yod are, well, remarkable.

60. So claims Damian Paul, the brother who ran the restaurant.

61. Display ad, *Evening Gazette* (Xenia, Ohio), September 10, 1920.

62. "Alfalfa Tea Is Popular in Texas," *San Antonio Evening News,* November 24, 1922.

63. Display ad, *Arkansas City Traveler,* May 27, 1953.

64. Betty Harris, "Just Between Girl Shoppers" [display ad], *Pasadena Star News,* May 20, 1957.

65. "Alfalfa Sprouts Keep Gloria Swanson Young in the Absence of Love," Wilmington, Delaware, *News Journal,* February 14, 1958. A syndicated story that appeared in papers all across the country.

66. "On Sprouting Beans," *Quicksilver Times,* January 30, 1971.

## 2. Brown Rice and the Macrobiotic Pioneers

1. Gay Talese, "One Year Later, Still No Bomb," *Esquire,* May 1963.

2. Taken from the August 1961 issue of *Unique Principle* (macrobiotic newsletter), but reprinted in many, many places.

3. George [Georges] Ohsawa, *Zen Macrobiotics*, pocketbook edition (The Ohsawa Foundation, 1965). Note: George Ohsawa lived in France before coming to the United States, and used "Georges Ohsawa" as his pseudonym in some of his earliest American publications.

4. Depending on which macrobiotic scholar you ask, the term may have come from Hippocrates or a nineteenth-century German physician named Christoph Wilhelm von Hufeland.

5. Much of the details of Ohsawa's biography, and the evolution of his philosophy, comes from Ronald E. Kotzsch, *Macrobiotics: Yesterday and Today* (Japan Publications, 1985).

6. Interview with Dick Smith, March 13, 2013.

7. Ohsawa, *Zen Macrobiotics*.

8. A quick digression: It was critical that Smith and Kennedy find short-grain rice, macrobiotic historian Peter Milbury has told me. Not only was it the kind of rice Ohsawa and his Japanese students were accustomed to, short-grain rice was considered more yang than long-grain rice. The more yang, the better. In the early years, Ohsawa connected with Koda Farms, a Japanese American family farm in the San Joaquin delta; with Ohsawa's imprimatur, the Kodas supplied many of the early macrobiotic enterprises with unmilled rice, but they refused to go organic. These days, of course, they produce a wonderful organic brown rice.

9. Kennedy, Ohsawa told Wolfe, was *sanpaku*, which meant the whites of his eyes showed on three sides of his irises. It was a sign of a dangerous imbalance, both physical and cosmological. Also *sanpaku*: Gandhi, Abraham Lincoln, and Brigitte Bardot. The term hit the counterculture like a cloud of nerve gas after William Dufty published *You Are All Sanpaku*, a reworking of *Zen Macrobiotics*, in 1965, sending millions of eighteen-year-olds and perhaps a hippie-food historian who should know better to the mirror to stare urgently at their irises.

10. Robert Christgau, "Beth Ann and Microbioticism," *New York Herald Tribune*, January 29, 1966. Yes, this is the same Robert Christgau who became a rock critic at the *Village Voice*.

11. George Ohsawa, "A Poor Victim of Americanized Macrobiotics," *The Macrobiotic Monthly*, November 1965.

12. Ohsawa assigned many of his followers in Japan Western names, some of them rather fanciful.

13. Interview with Alex Jack, longtime Kushi collaborator.

14. Many details about the history of Erewhon come from William Shurtleff's

wonderful sourcebook *History of Erewhon: Natural Foods Pioneer in the United States, 1966–2011,* (Soyinfo Center, 2011), e-book.

15. Kotzsch, *Macrobiotics Yesterday and Today,* p. 173.

16. Dufty, whose before-and-after photographs of the physical transformation that macrobiotics accomplished were the book's greatest calling card, later married silent-film star Gloria Swanson, who had long been Hollywood's most vociferous health-food advocate. Dufty followed up *You Are All Sanpaku* with an influential tirade against refined sugar called *Sugar Blues,* and the couple became prominent in macrobiotic circles.

17. Aveline taught a few classes in how to make futons, traditional Japanese bedding. One of the Boston residents, a former costume designer named Carol Schoeneberger, reengineered the thin futon that Aveline showed her how to sew into a thicker, more Western-style mattress. Schoeneberger ended up opening the United States' first futon stores and invented the futon frame that folds into a couch. You owe the decor of your first apartment to Aveline Kushi.

18. Though the column was only attributed to St. Hieronymous Press, it was actually a collaboration between a young cook and activist named Alice Waters, who would go on to open Chez Panisse in Berkeley in 1971, and lithographer David Lance Goines, who would illustrate her menus and books for forty-plus years. The series became Goines's legendary art folio, *Thirty Recipes Suitable for Framing.*

19. Another *Good Times* column, Jeannie Darlington's "Grow Your Own," became a bestselling book for nascent organic gardeners.

20. Mary Schooner, "Eat and Enjoy," *Good Times,* January 15, 1970.

21. Mick Wheelock, "The Viet Cong Walks Strong," *Los Angeles Free Press,* August 29, 1969. The article unwittingly echoed arguments made a generation before about the nutritional paucity of American white bread compared to muscly Russians' dark brown bread.

22. Mick Wheelock and Lini Lieberman, "Ecological Cookery," *Los Angeles Free Press,* June 19, 1970. Side note from the last chapter: one column explains Arnold Ehret's mucusless diet to the next generation. Thanks to Steve Finger for his help locating two years' worth of Mick and Lini's columns in the *Los Angeles Free Press.*

23. Editor's introduction to "Food Thing," by Mick Wheelock and Lini Lieberman, *Kaleidoscope* (Milwaukee), October 19, 1970.

24. Michio Kushi, *The Book of Macrobiotics: The Universal Way of Health and Happiness* (Japan Publications, 1977).

25. Theoretically, you could balance out an ultra-yang food like beef by consuming it with über-yin wine. But such a balancing act would be precarious. As Michel Abehsera reported in his book *Zen Macrobiotic Cooking* (University Books, 1968), Ohsawa said, "It is better to avoid eating beef than think to balance it."

26. Most macrobiotic students I interviewed gave up the diet long ago, but almost all of them say that the main lesson they took from it was observing how their body responded to what they ate, and becoming aware of the subtle shifts in their energy and mood that food could bring on.

27. Paul Hawken, "Erewhon: A Biography," *East West Journal* 3, no. 8 (August 1973): 11–16.

28. Floyd Allen, "Raising Rice the Right Way," *Organic Gardening and Farming*, July 1971.

29. Interview with Homer and Wendell Lundberg, October 24, 2012. Eldon and Harlan Lundberg died in the early 2000s, and Wendell Lundberg died in 2016.

30. Peter Milbury, "Brown Rice, Organic Brown Rice, and Macrobiotics: A Personal Journey" (unpublished memoir manuscript), p. 21. In his memoir and interviews, Milbury was a rich source for information about Chico-San, Kennedy, and Smith.

31. In 1984, after opening two additional plants in Mississippi and New Jersey and two decades of fifteen-hour days, Kennedy and Smith learned that Quaker Oats was going to muscle into the rice-cake business. It was a good time to retire, they decided, and sold Chico-San to H. J. Heinz for a gratifying sum. At the time of the sale, Heinz made what amounts to a costly decision. Chico-San was still producing small amounts of its "Yinnies" brown-rice syrup, primarily for the macrobiotic market. However, it had just contracted production of the syrup to a company called California Natural Products, which figured out how to use enzymes to culture the rice instead of the traditional koji spores. Heinz didn't know what to make of this bizarre product, so it paid off California Natural Products and broke the contract. Brown rice syrup is now an integral part of rice milk and rice-milk ice cream, salad dressings, and most of the energy bars you'll find on store shelves.

32. The Kushis, who continued to be the formal owners of Erewhon, were not businesspeople, and as the 1970s became the 1980s, Erewhon sold off its L.A. store, purchased a giant warehouse it couldn't afford, botched an effort to block the unionization of its staff, filed for bankruptcy, and was sold in 1983. The Kushis then turned their attention to preaching macrobiotics as a cure for cancer and AIDS.

33. Shurtleff, *History of Erewhon*.

34. Abercrombie, "Abercrombie Acquires Too Many Carob Pods," *Los Angeles Times*, August 10, 1945.

35. "'Wild Locusts' Fit for Food," *Los Angeles Times*, November 6, 1914; "Sugar from Carobs," *Los Angeles Times*, August 1, 1920.

36. Philip Lovell, "The Care of the Body," *Los Angeles Times*, June 26, 1932.

37. V. Meldo Hillis, "The Chocolate Tree," *Los Angeles Times*, November 8, 1953.

38. Julie Jordan, *Wings of Life: Vegetarian Cookery* (Crossing Press, 1976); Jordan ran the well-loved Cabbagetown Café in Ithaca, New York, a friendly competitor to Moosewood Restaurant.

39. Cooperative Whole Grain Educational Association, *Uprisings: The Whole Grain Bakers' Book* (Uprisings Publishing, 1983). Aside from the carob, this is a trove of excellent whole-grain recipes.

40. Maureen Goldsmith, *The Organic Yenta* (Atheneum, 1972).

## 3. Brown Bread and the Pursuit of Wholesomeness

1. Charles Perry, *The Haight-Ashbury: A History* (Wenner Books, 2005).

2. The material for background information on the Diggers and Emmett Grogan comes from a number of sources, primarily: Emmett Grogan, *Ringolevio* (New York Review Books, 2008); Perry, *The Haight-Ashbury*; David Talbot, *Season of the Witch* (Free Press, 2012); *Les Diggers de San Francisco*, directed by Céline Deransart and Alice Gaillard (La Seine Planete, 1998); Peter Coyote, *Sleeping Where I Fall* (Counterpoint, 2009); and documents from the online Digger Archives at diggers.org.

3. The standard explanation for the name was that Grogan and Murcott were naming themselves after a seventeenth-century Protestant movement in England, but others suggest that the two originally meant "those who dig it," and later adopted the loftier etymology.

4. David Swanston, "The Diggers' Mystique," *San Francisco Chronicle*, January 23, 1967.

5. Interview in *Les Diggers de San Francisco*.

6. Merla Zellerbach, "Bread—The Staff of Love and Life," *San Francisco Chronicle*, July 12, 1968.

7. Digger spectacles could be pure, anarchic hedonism, like the time they picked up five hundred pounds of frozen meat from a University of California marine lab in Bodega Bay, which had butchered a beached whale, and held a giant

whale barbecue in the park, complete with fake snow for snowball fights
and alcoves where people could have sex. The whale, Simpson and Lapiner
confess, tasted god-awful.

8. "Bake-In Spreads Love in the Haight," *Berkeley Barb,* June 30, 1967.

9. "Lots of Bread's Good for All," *Berkeley Barb,* July 14, 1967.

10. Much of the material for my writing about Sylvester Graham comes from
the following sources: James C. Whorton, *Crusaders for Fitness: The History
of American Health Reformers* (Princeton University Press, 1982); Stephen
Nissenbaum, *Sex, Diet, and Debility in Jacksonian America* (Greenwood Press,
1980); Gerald Carson, *Cornflake Crusade* (Rinehart, 1957); and Sylvester Graham,
*Lectures on the Science of Human Life* (Office of the Health Reformer, 1872).

11. Aaron Bobrow-Strain, *White Bread: A Social History of the Store-Bought Loaf*
(Beacon Press, 2012).

12. Sylvester Graham, *Treatise on Bread and Bread-Making* (Light & Stearns,
1837).

13. Ibid.

14. Bobrow-Strain, *White Bread.*

15. Frank Murray, *More Than One Slingshot: How the Health Food Industry is
Changing America* (Marlborough House, 1984).

16. Ackerman, "Interpreting the 'Newer Science of Nutrition.'"

17. A wonderful source for information on the scientific discovery of vitamins and
how marketers sold Americans on vitamin pills is Catherine Price, *Vitamania:
Our Obsessive Quest for Nutritional Perfection* (Penguin, 2015).

18. Adding to their conviction: In the earliest days of vitamin research, wheat
germ—which is removed from commercially milled white flour—was found
to contain significant amounts of vitamins B and E, and some of the earliest
commercial supplements were made from wheat germ. Other "natural"
sources for vitamin supplements: brewer's yeast, cod liver oil, and rose hips.

19. James Rorty and N. Philip Norman, *Tomorrow's Food* (Devin-Adair, 1956).

20. Bobrow-Strain, *White Bread.*

21. "Will Offer Bread Vitamin-Enriched," *New York Times,* January 30, 1941.

22. In fact, many experts credit enriched flour with the eradication of pellagra in
the South.

23. Catharine Carstairs, "'Our Sickness Record Is a National Disgrace': Adelle
Davis, Nutritional Determinism, and the Anxious 1970s," *Journal of the
History of Medicine and Allied Sciences,* July 2014. Also, Daniel Yergin,
"Supernutritionist," *New York Times Magazine,* May 20, 1973. Davis died of
cancer not long after the profile appeared.

24. Adelle Davis, *Let's Eat Right to Keep Fit*, rev. ed. (Harcourt Brace Jovanovich, 1970); Adelle Davis, *You Can Get Well* (Benedict Lust Publications, 1975).

25. Ackerman, "Interpreting the 'Newer Science of Nutrition.'"

26. More than one former hippie told me of downing her yeast-and-molasses smoothies, shivering in disgust, and shrugging: Adelle said it was healthy, so it *had* to be good for you.

27. *The Tonight Show with Johnny Carson*, May 19, 1972 [episode downloaded from Amazon Video].

28. Adelle Davis, *Let's Cook It Right* (Harcourt, Brace, 1947).

29. Ibid.

30. Reminiscences from Thomas Morris in "Digger Bread and the Free Bakeries," Digger Archives. Downloaded from www.digger.org, August 6, 2015.

31. Bob Buyer, "Food Revolution Has Consumer on Cows' Side," *Buffalo Evening News*, January 6, 1968. The story was about a new dairy analogue called "Melloream" that was projected to replace up to 40 percent of our milk. Why? The article didn't say.

32. William Longgood, *The Poisons in Your Food* (Simon and Schuster, 1960).

33. Gene Marine and Judith Van Allen, *Food Pollution: The Violation of Our Inner Ecology* (Holt, Rinehart and Winston, 1972).

34. Longgood, *The Poisons in Your Food*.

35. Elijah Muhammad, *How to Eat to Live*, book 1, Sectarius MEMPS Ministries, 1967. Accessed online at http://www.seventhfam.com/temple/books/eattolive_one/eat1index.htm.

36. Alex Haley, "Playboy Interview: Malcolm X," *Playboy*, May 1963.

37. Elizabeth Mehren, "Secrets of Shabazz," *Washington Post*, January 4, 1973.

38. "Gotta Get Some C," *Kaleidoscope*, January 8, 1971.

39. This section on plastic versus natural, as well as some aspects of the brown-versus-white debate, is indebted to Warren J. Belasco's wonderful *Appetite for Change: How the Counterculture Took On the Food Industry*, 2nd ed. (Cornell University Press, 2006).

40. Beatrice Trum Hunter, *Beatrice Trum Hunter's Whole-Grain Baking Sampler* (Keats Publishing, 1972). Hunter also published a series of bread recipes in *The Natural Foods Cookbook* (Simon & Schuster, 1961). Just as Adelle Davis was the link between the health-food movement and scientific nutrition, Hunter was a muckraking journalist who wrote about pollution, ecology, gardening, natural foods, and baking.

41. Anonymous, "Spirit of Love Bread." *Carolina Plain Dealer* 2, no. 11 (1972).

42. Mick Wheelock and Lini Lieberman, "Food for Thought: The Art of Making Bread—Part I," *Los Angeles Free Press*, January 23, 1970.

43. Ita Jones, *The Grub Bag* (Vintage Books, 1971); the book is a compilation of Jones's syndicated columns.

44. Bill Farthing, *Odiyan Country Cookbook* (Dharma Publishing, 1977).

45. Macrobiotics did come to shape the artisanal baking movement, but only after a half century. Ohsawa and the Kushis endorsed sourdough bread, even though they obviously didn't know how to harness wild yeasts to their own ends. Other bakers did, however. The macrobiotic Lima Bakery, based in Ghent, Belgium, unearthed an almost forgotten Low Countries method of fermenting whole-grain breads to produce airy, robust, and terrifically long-lived breads, a style it called *desem*. Bakers in Los Angeles, Massachusetts (baby boomers there may remember Baldwin Hills), and Chico produced this whole-grain sourdough, some traveling to Ghent to apprentice. Laurel Robertson, Carol Flinders, and Bronwen Godfrey, authors of the 1984 *Laurel's Kitchen Bread Book*, learned of desem, too, and may have been the first to publish a recipe for it in English. The method endured at Berkshire Mountain Bakery, whose baker, Richard Bourdon, emigrated from Canada to Massachusetts at the behest of Michio and Aveline Kushi, and at Great Harvest Bread in Chico, California, whose baker trained with a macrobiotic sourdough master. Desem also influenced the rustic, whole-grain, naturally leavened breads at the megainfluential Tartine Bakery in San Francisco, whose owners, Chad Robertson and Liz Prueitt, founded it after Robinson apprenticed with Bourdon in his twenties. (Robertson tells some of this story in *Tartine Book No. 3*.)

46. Edward Espe Brown, *The Tassajara Bread Book* (Shambhala Publications, 1970); Alicia Bay Laurel, *Living on the Earth* (Vintage Books, 1971).

47. See Jane Nickerson, "More Nutrition in Bread Is Advocated; Professor Says Cost Would Be Slight," *New York Times*, April 19, 1949.

48. Cornell bread enjoyed a slight renaissance in the early 1970s as well, with recipes appearing in publications as varied as the *New York Times* and *Mother Earth News*.

49. The information in this section comes from a September 23, 2015, interview with Edward Espe Brown, as well as two of his books: *The Tassajara Bread Book* (Shambhala Books, 1970) and *Tomato Blessings and Radish Teachings: Recipes and Reflections* (Riverhead Books, 1997).

50. Full disclosure: I am a member of the San Francisco Zen Center, though I have never interacted with Brown through Zen channels.

51. Brown remembered their last names, but not the exact spelling.

52. This actually would have been a savvy move; a few years later, hand-lettered books such as Alicia Bay Laurel's *Living on the Earth* and Mollie Katzen's *Moosewood Cookbook* became best sellers, partly because they looked so homespun.

53. Brown, *Tassajara Bread Book*.

54. Members of the SUNY Buffalo American Studies Program, "Down and Out in America," *New York Times Magazine*, February 9, 1975.

55. Edward Glaeser, "Can Buffalo Ever Come Back?" *New York Sun*, October 19, 2007. Accessed September 26, 2015, at http://www.nysun.com/opinion /can-buffalo-ever-come-back/64879/.

56. Much of this section was based on interviews with Bill Nowak on July 20, 2015, Josh Ingram on July 27, 2015, and a group of former Yeast West and Greenfield Street restaurant employees on September 19, 2015.

57. Janice Okun, "For the Bakers at Yeast-West [*sic*] Food Is Part of Their Philosophy," *Buffalo Evening News*, March 30, 1977.


## 4. Tofu, the Political Dish

1. Frances Moore Lappé's recollections come from two sources: an interview conducted on May 9, 2013, and the "My Story" chapter of the 1982 revised edition of *Diet for a Small Planet* (Ballantine Books).

2. Paul R. Ehrlich, *The Population Bomb* (Ballantine Books, 1968).

3. Ibid.

4. If you're curious, they were mid-1960s reports from the U.N.'s Food and Agricultural Organization and a 1965 book by A.M. Altschul titled *Proteins, Their Chemistry and Politics* (Basic Books).

5. L. C. Gray, O. E. Baker, F. J. Marschner, B. O. Weitz, W. R. Chapline, Ward Shepard, and Raphael Zon, "The Utilization of Our Land for Crops, Pasture, and Forests," in *United States Department of Agriculture, Agriculture Yearbook, 1923* (Department Printing Office, 1924); Otto Carqué, *The Key to Rational Dietetics* (Health Research, originally published 1930; republished 1970).

6. Lappé says that in 2013, she drove to Woodstock, New York, to pay tribute to Betty Ballantine, then in her eighties, and ask her a question that had been nagging at her for years: "Betty, why did you take a chance on this kid who'd never written anything?" Lappé asked her. She says Ballantine replied, "Frankie, it was the ideas! It was the ideas! I figured if you couldn't write, I could do that part!"

7. Frances Moore Lappé, *Diet for a Small Planet* (original edition Ballatine, 1976).

8. Lappé has taken a lot of flak over the years for misleading the public about complementary proteins, but she emphasizes today that her understanding was based on the available research at the time. She retracted the amino-acid charts from the 1975 edition, and in the 1982 edition issued a mea culpa for creating another myth. "With three important exceptions, there is little danger of protein deficiency in a plant food diet," she wrote. "The exceptions are diets very heavily dependent on *fruit* or on some *tubers,* such as sweet potatoes or cassava, or on *junk food* (refined, flours, sugars, and fat) [italics mine]."

9. Lappé, *Diet for a Small Planet,* 1971.

10. William Shurtleff and Akiko Aoyagi, *The History of Tofu and Tofu Products: 963 CE to 2013* (Soyinfo Center, 2013). Accessed via Google Books at https://books. google.com/books?id=gGrUNvZt0_YC&dq=history+tofu&source=gbs _navlinks_s.

11. Lappé, *Diet for a Small Planet* (Ballantine, 1971).

12. James Shaub, W.C. McArthur, Duane Hacklander, Joseph Glauber, Mack Leath, and Harry Doty, *The U.S. Soybean Industry* (USDA Economic Research Service report no. 588, May 1988).

13. Frances Moore Lappé, *Diet for a Small Planet: 10th Anniversary Edition* (New York: Ballantine Books, 1981), pp. 23–24.

14. Jill Betts, "Diet for a Small Planet," republished in the *Great Speckled Bird* (Atlanta), March 20, 1972.

15. Jacket copy for Lappé's 1977 book *Food First.*

16. Multiple people I spoke to told me they gave up meat for a few years after reading *Diet.*

17. The sources for this section were multiple telephone and in-person interviews I conducted with William Shurtleff from 2013 to 2015 and a telephone interview with Akiko Aoyagi Shurtleff in 2015, with help on specific dates from "Chronology of Soyinfo Center," an undated document produced by Shurtleff's organization and archives. Also, Akiko Aoyagi uses the formal name Akiko Aoyagi Shurtleff, but for clarity's sake I use Aoyagi in this chapter to refer to her.

18. Diana Waggoner, "With His Book on Tofu, William Shurtleff Hopes to Bring Soy to the World," *People Weekly,* October 13, 1980.

19. Shurtleff and Aoyagi, *The History of Tofu and Tofu Products.*

20. William Shurtleff and Akiko Aoyagi, *The Book of Tofu: Food for Mankind* (Autumn Press, 1975).

21. Ibid.

22. Ibid., p. 16.

23. This section is based on interviews with Farm residents, both present and past: Laurie Sythe Praskin, Ellen Schweitzer, Paul and Mary Schweitzer, Michael Halpin, Cynthia Bates, Judith Dodge, Louise Hagler, Stephen Huddleston, Michael Traugot, Darryl Jordan, and Alan Praskin. Factual details were compared against two theses: Pat Ledoux, "The History of a Hippie Commune: The Farm" (Ph.D. dissertation, Middle Tennessee State University, 1992); and Kevin Mitchell Mercer, "The Farm: A Hippie Commune as a Countercultural Diaspora" (master's thesis, University of Central Florida, 2012).

24. Stephen Gaskin, *The Caravan* (Random House, 1972).

25. Quoted in the "Foodage" chapter of Gaskin, *The Caravan*.

26. Lappé, *Diet for a Small Planet*, 1971.

27. Textured vegetable protein is made from the solid residues from pressing soy oil, through a technologically complex and chemical-assisted process. It was already used as a meat extender throughout the food industry, and by the 1970s, Adventist vegetarians had long made prepackaged products like steaks out of it.

28. Interview with Cynthia Bates, one of the scurvy survivors.

29. *Hey Beatnik! This Is the Farm Book* (The Book Publishing Co., 1974). Also quoted verbatim by multiple Farm members.

30. Brewer's yeast—bitter and nasty tasting, since it was cultured on hops, but nutritious—was readily available in health-food stores. The Farm located a source of *Saccharomyces cerevisiae* grown on molasses, and not bitter in the least. They later marketed it as Good Tasting Nutritional Yeast.

31. Just to close another small-world circle, they learned to make yeast sauces from the *Ten Talents* cookbook (see pages 214–215).

32. On the Farm, they pronounce *tempeh* "tempee," like the city in Arizona.

33. Stephen and the Farm *Hey Beatnik! This Is the Farm Book* (Book Publishing, 1974).

34. Rupert Fike, ed., *Voices from the Farm: Adventures in Community Living* (Book Publishing, 1998).

35. Several years later, Shurtleff and Aoyagi published *The Book of Tempeh*.

36. Shurtleff, *History of Tofu and Tofu Products,* record no. 3173.

37. The tour also took Shurtleff and Aoyagi to Mill Valley, just north of San Francisco, where they talked to the Farm members who had been sent to California to set up a short-lived "soy deli" and factory making tofu and Ice

Bean. The operation was one of the first large-scale moneymaking businesses that the community engaged in; unfortunately, internal struggles doomed the operation before it had a chance to succeed. Sometime around then, they helped Praskin secure an internship at the Japanese American San Jose Tofu Company.

38. Shurtleff, *History of Tofu and Tofu Products*, record no. 9145. The date range he gives is 1974–1984.

39. Ibid., record no. 13297.

40. Samuel Fromartz, for example, devotes a chapter to the influence of Frances Moore Lappé and *The Book of Tofu* on White Wave and founder Steve Demos in *Organic, Inc.: Natural Foods and How They Grew* (Harcourt, 2006).

41. Praskin says the shop is still in existence.

42. As of 2014, Turtle Island Foods had sold 3.4 million of them.

43. According to the USDA, Americans consumed an average of 161.2 pounds of meat per person per year in the 1960s, 177.2 pounds per person per year in the 1970s, and 182.2 per person per year in the 1980s. USDA, "Profiling Food Consumption in America," *Agricultural Factbook*. E-book accessed September 12, 2016, at http://www.usda.gov/factbook/chapter2.pdf.

44. 2013 figures courtesy of Katahdin Ventures, reported by the Soyfoods Association of North America. Accessed September 9, 2016, at http://www .soyfoods.org/soy-products/sales-and-trends.

## 5. Back-to-the-Landers and Organic Farming

1. Information about Samuel Kaymen's early life comes from an interview with Samuel Kaymen, April 6, 2017, as well as from J. Tevere MacFadyen, "Samuel Kaymen's Journey to the Center of the Earth," *New Roots*, December 1980. See the Northeast Organic Farming Association Records, Special Collections and University Archives, W. E. B. Du Bois Library, University of Massachusetts Amherst.

2. Sources for much of the biographical information: interviews with Samuel Kaymen, April 22, 2016, and April 6, 2017; Samuel Kaymen, December 1998 oral history, Northeast Organic Farming Association Records, Special Collections and University Archives, W. E. B. Du Bois Library, University of Massachusetts Amherst.

3. Edward Hyams, *Soil and Civilization* (Thames and Hudson, 1952), p. 81.

4. Kaymen, 1998 oral history.

5. His work on wheat was successful enough to earn him the knighthood and gave his radical ideas somewhat more credibility in the scientific community.

6. Information about Sir Albert Howard comes primarily from three sources: Suzanne Peters, "The Land in Trust: A Social History of the Organic Farming Movement" (Ph.D. dissertation, McGill University, 1979); Lisa F. Clark, "Organic Limited: The Corporate Rise and Spectacular Change in the Canadian and American Organic Food Sectors" (Ph.D. dissertation, Simon Fraser University, 2007); and Samuel Fromartz, *Organic, Inc.: Natural Foods and How They Grew* (Harcourt, 2006).

7. Recollections of Kaymen's library come from conversations with Samuel Kaymen and Howard Prussack.

8. Sources for biographical information on J. I. Rodale and the founding of Rodale Publications: Carlton Jackson, *J. I. Rodale: Apostle of Nonconformity* (Pyramid Books, 1974); Andrew N. Case, "Looking for Organic America: J. I. Rodale, the Rodale Press, and the Popular Culture of Environmentalism in the Postwar United States" (Ph.D. dissertation, University of Wisconsin-Madison, 2012).

9. Robert Rodale, "Prevention Is One Man—J. I. Rodale," *Prevention,* June 1970.

10. To briefly and grossly summarize the core of anthroposophy, Steiner taught that our human sense organs, the ones that intercepted and interpreted rays of light and the chemical compounds that formed smells and tastes, had another parallel in the human spirit. These organs within our inner beings could perceive "astral-aetherial" forces. Steiner studied folk practices, which he believed could shape and direct these astral-aetherial forces, with the same intensity he did the modern plastic sciences.

11. Information for the Steiner section primarily comes from Peters, "The Land in Trust."

12. Jackson, *J. I. Rodale.*

13. A court of appeals eventually dismissed the FTC complaint in 1968 after four very expensive years of trials.

14. Quoted in Jackson, *J. I. Rodale,* p. 129.

15. Case, "Looking for Organic America," p. 156.

16. Sources for the section on Carson include Mary A. McCay, *Rachel Carson* (Twayne Publishers, 1993) and Frank Graham Jr., *Since Silent Spring* (Fawcett Publications, 1970).

17. James Whorton, quoted in McCay, *Rachel Carson.*

18. Adam Rome, *The Genius of Earth Day: How a 1970 Teach-In Unexpectedly Made the First Green Generation* (Hill and Wang, 2013).

19. The phrase *back to the land* may be as old as the industrial revolution, says University of Vermont history professor Dona Brown, author of *Back to t/.: Land: The Enduring Dream of Self-Sufficiency in Modern America* (University of Wisconsin Press, 2011), which chronicles back-to-the-land migrations in the 1910s, 1930s, and 1950s. The hippie kids weren't doing anything new; they were just doing it in bigger numbers.

20. Benjamin Huffman, *The Vermont Farm and a Land Reform Program*, vol. 1 (State of Vermont Planning Office, June 1973).

21. "Sounds from the Seed-Power Sitar," *San Francisco Oracle*, issue 6 (February 14, 1967). Also quoted in Perry, *The Haight-Ashbury*.

22. *Ebony* magazine ran a profile of one African American woman who had settled on a rural commune in Colorado that was as much about her decision to live collectively with white people as it was about the commune's geodesic dome, organic gardens, and rock band. Louise Robinson, "Life Inside a Hippie Commune," *Ebony*, November 1970.

23. The Tick Creek Tribe, "Livin' on the Farm," *Carolina Plain Dealer*, October 1972.

24. Mark Kramer, *Mother Walter & the Pig Tragedy* (Alfred A. Knopf, 1972).

25. Robert Houriet, *Getting Back Together* (Coward, McCann & Geoghegan, 1971). Two other beautifully written chronicles of New England communes that may convince you to buy a Vanagon and leave for the country: Mark Kramer, *Mother Walter & the Pig Tragedy*, and Stephen Diamond, *What the Trees Said: Life on a New Age Farm* (Dell Publishing, 1971).

26. The seventy-five figure comes from a 2008 online article on the Vermont news site *Seven Days* (http://www.sevendaysvt.com/vermont/hippie-havens /Content?oid=2134607); the two hundred figure, from a study quoted by Timothy Miller in *The 60s Communes: Hippies and Beyond* (Syracuse University Press, 1999).

27. The estimate most frequently cited, from a study by Jeffrey Jacob (see note below), is one million. *Back to the Land* author Dona Brown argues that it is based on fantasy math. Grassroots movements: so hard to quantify!

28. U.S. Census Bureau, "Population: 1790 to 1990" [table]. Downloaded May 14, 2016, from https://www.census.gov/population/www/censusdata/files /table-4.pdf. Note: Part of that growth may be attributed to urban workers buying homes in the exurbs; the Census Bureau changed its definition of *urban* in 1950 to accommodate suburban populations. However, the 1970–1980 shift in the rural population is even more impressive when you compare these figures against the growth of the overall population: they are almost equal (11.1 percent vs. 11.4 percent); the last census findings that showed

rural areas growing at the same rate as the rest of the country were in 1820
(33.2 percent growth in the rural population vs. 33.1 percent overall).
Comment about the exurbs courtesy of Jeffrey Jacob, *New Pioneers:
The Back-to-the-Land Movement and the Search for a Sustainable Future*
(Pennsylvania State University Press, 1997).

29. Matthew Vita, "New Breed Giving Farms Young Face," *Burlington Free Press*,
AP wire story, September 21, 1980.

30. Correspondence from April and May 1971 between the public and the
Vermont governor's office over the "hippie invasion." Collected by the
Vermont Historical Society as part of its "Vermont in the 1970s" project
(http://vermonthistory.org/research/vermont-1970s).

31. "Statement from Governor Davis," unpublished press release, May 19, 1971.
Collected by the Vermont Historical Society.

32. Eleanor Agnew makes this argument most convincingly in *Back from the
Land: How Young Americans Went to Nature in the 1970s, and Why They Came
Back* (Ivan R. Dee, 2005).

33. Houriet, *Getting Back Together.*

34. *Mother Earth News,* whose circulation jumped from 147 in 1970 to 250,000 in
1975, facilitated the back-to-the-land movement with a section of classified-
style announcements called "Positions and Situations." At least a third of
them were personal ads, men and women (usually men) looking for a suitable
mate to move onto their rural property or find one to move to. Some ads sold
homesteads far from the city, others were posted by want-to-be-homesteaders
advertising their search for twenty acres. They posted from every state in the
nation: Washington, Arizona, New York, Florida, North Carolina. It was a
measure of how ubiquitous this movement was.

35. Rob Johnston, who would break away from both Erewhon Farm and NOFA
in 1973 to found Johnny's Selected Seeds, is now one of the largest suppliers of
organic seeds in the country.

36. Packer Corners was Vermont's most famous commune, chronicled in Ray
Mungo's *Famous Long Ago* and *Total Loss Farm,* Verandah Porche's poems,
and the collectively written *Home Comfort,* a book of stories, recipes, and tips
for other aspiring back-to-the-landers. It's a lovely read.

37. This section was based in large part on interviews with organic farmers in
Vermont: Howard Prussack (High Meadows Farm), Jake and Liz Guest
(Killdeer Farm), Joey Klein (Littlewood Farm), Olive Ylin (who no longer
raises goats but was an early NOFA member), Robert Houriet, Jack Lazor

(Butterworks Farm), and Alan LePage (LePage Farm). Also contributing to my understanding of back-to-the-land organic farmers were Eliot Coleman (Four Season Farm) and Jim Gerritsen (Wood Prairie Farm) in Maine and, in California, Warren Weber (Star Route Farms) and Amigo Bob Cantisano (organic farming consultant).

38. Jeff Cox, "The Political Implications of Organic Farming," *WIN*, July 1972. Incidentally, the founder of *WIN* was Martin Jezer of Packer Corners.

39. Martin Jezer, "How Many Harvests Have We Left?" *Mother Earth News*, July–August 1970.

40. This section comes from an April 12, 2016, interview with Robert Houriet as well as a December 1998 oral history interview from the Northeast Organic Farming Association Records, Special Collections and University Archives, W. E. B. Du Bois Library, University of Massachusetts Amherst.

41. Quoted in William Ronco, *Food Co-ops: An Alternative to Shopping in Supermarkets* (Beacon Press, 1974).

42. Jane Pyle, "Farmers' Markets in the United States: Functional Anachronisms," *Geographical Review* (April, 1971), pp. 167–197; Allison Brown, "Counting Farmers Markets," *Geographical Review* (October 2001), pp. 655–674.

43. "Farmers Markets Report Rising Demand," *Natural Farmer*, August 1977.

44. Hank Burchard, "The Big Organic Boom," *San Francisco Chronicle*, July 19, 1972.

45. Geof Hewitt, *Working for Yourself: How to Be Successfully Self-Employed* (Rodale Press, 1977).

46. "Reality Food: Menu, Recipes, Tips for an Organic Dinner," *Vogue*, November 15, 1971.

47. "Organic Shops Move into the Big Stores," *Business Week*, July 10, 1971.

48. Gene Logsdon, "Organic: Magic Word at the Food Counter, Many Doubts on the Farm," *Farm Journal*, December 1971.

49. Editors of *Organic Gardening and Farming* and *Prevention*, *The Organic Directory* (Rodale Press, 1971).

50. Sylvia Porter, "Organic Foods and Shopper Traps," *San Francisco Chronicle*, February 8, 1972.

51. "Organic Shops Move into the Big Stores," *Business Week*; Harold Seneker, "Growing Up Among the Bean Sprouts," *Forbes*, March 19, 1979.

52. Jean Hewitt, "Organic Food Fanciers Go to Great Lengths for the Real Thing," *New York Times*, September 7, 1970.

53. See Logsdon, "Organic: Magic Word at the Food Counter"; Arthur J. Snider, "Beware Back-to-Nature Fads," *Science Digest*, September 1972; Butz quoted in Frederick Stare and Elizabeth M. Whelan, *Panic in the Pantry* (Atheneum, 1975).

54. Natalie Gittelson, "The $2 Billion Health Food . . . Fraud?" *Harper's Bazaar*, November 1972.

55. Details for the section on Grace Gershuny come from interviews in March and May 2016 and her book, *Organic Revolutionary: A Memoir of the Movement for Real Food, Planetary Healing, and Human Liberation* (Joes Brook Press, 2016).

56. Gershuny, *Organic Revolutionary*.

57. Websites for all groups, as well as "Organic Farming Groups in Regional Action," *Organic Gardening and Farming*, August 1976.

58. "Organic Foods: Not All That Pure," *Business Week*, February 12, 1972; Harold Faber, "Farmers Study Organic Market," *New York Times*, January 30, 1972.

59. "A History of Oregon Tilth," Sunbow Farm, http://www.sunbowfarm.org /tilth.php. Downloaded May 30, 2016.

60. Burchard, "The Big Organic Boom."

61. Gershuny says that Prussack liked to grumble about the seal in the early years. "I'm not selling NOFers," he'd tell her.

## 6. Vegetarians on the Curry Trail

1. Interviews conducted in the summer of 2016 with collective members Bill Teska, Ralph Wittcoff, Carolyn Brown Zniewski, Eve MacLeish, Ruth Ann Tortenson LeMasters, Margaret Connoy (Gracie Schwartz), Erik Riese, Chrycinda Bourdon, and Jeff Garetz.

2. Teska's ordination ceremony at Riverside Park in the summer of 1969 was a spectacle, the bishop driven to the ceremony by the young priest's friend Ralph Wittcoff in a purple top hat, riding in a limousine trailed by forty bikers.

3. For more detailed information about this initiative, which resulted in one high-rise complex that is now the center of Minneapolis's Somali community, see Randy Stoecker, *Defending Community: The Struggle for Alternative Redevelopment in Cedar-Riverside* (Temple University Press, 1994).

4. Articles providing contemporary source material on the West Bank and the founding of the New Riverside: Ralph Wittcoff and Nancy Belding Brochin,

"Standing Firm on the West Bank," *North Country Anvil*, January–February 1978; Sheryl Wohlers, "New Riverside—A Cafe Collective," article from unknown magazine, circa 1973, found in the New Riverside Collection, Minnesota Historical Society, Saint Paul, Minnesota.

5. This wasn't limited to Farm members. I talked to several other people who stopped eating meat as a result of an acid trip; some were still vegetarians, fifty years later.

6. Lucy Horton, *Country Commune Cooking* (Coward, McCann & Geoghegan, 1972). I don't know how many of the recipes I'd make, but this is one of the most colorful, engaging documents of how the counterculture ate in the early 1970s. If you ever spot a used copy, buy it.

7. Susan Nelson, "So You Want to Be a Vegetarian?" *Chicago Tribune*, July 11, 1971.

8. Jean Hewitt, "Teen-agers Choose the Meatless Diet," *New York Times*, June 5, 1972.

9. "Vegetarianism Gains Popularity on Campus," *Los Angeles Times*, October 24, 1971.

10. Small-world alert: one of the Jook Savages who moved to Los Angeles, Richard Moon, was the early Source Restaurant employee who turned Jim Baker on to Yogi Bhajan. Swear to god.

11. There were a few years when they'd serve hamburgers on April Fool's Day, but that hardly counts.

12. Ronald L. Numbers, *Prophetess of Health: Ellen G. White and the Origins of Seventh-Day Adventist Health Reform*, rev. ed. (University of Tennessee Press, 1992). Also James C. Whorton, *Crusaders for Fitness: The History of American Health Reformers* (Princeton University Press, 1982), pretty much the most entertaining scholarly work on health food ever published.

13. E. G. Fulton, *Vegetarian Cook Book: Substitutes for Flesh Foods* (Pacific Press Publishing, 1914).

14. One side note: a Seventh-day Adventist cook named Mary Burgess published the first vegetarian soul-food cookbook, *Soul to Soul*, in 1976, that reworked dozens of African American and southern classic dishes with Adventist fake meats and vegetarian broths.

15. Familia probably took its name from Bio-Familia, the Swiss company that first sold mass-market muesli in the United States; the corporate brand may be why "familia" fell out of use by the 1990s.

16. The collective say they enjoyed the discomfort the slogan evinced, but eventually put up a sign with suggested prices, ranging from nearly free for homeless kids to extravagant sums for the bourgeoisie. The collective, Eve

MacLeish also adds, felt the need to use its nightly deposits to school the bank on the evils of capitalism. "There were a number of people in the collective who would write all over the envelope 'Fuck money!' 'Smash the state!'" she says. "Then Dave Cleveland, the banker, said, 'C'mon, you guys, I'm on your side! It's really offensive.'"

17. Brown Zniewski says that the catering operation specialized in hippie weddings and Jewish parties, since vegetarian food was kosher. The café offered a bonus program for longhair weddings: *You supply the pot, we bake it into the cake.* Once, a big bag of loose leaves arrived at the back door to be baked the next day, and Brown Zniewski was paranoid that they'd get raided. She dumped it into a big canister, labeled it WEED, and shoved it on the herb shelf. The next morning, she came in to work, and a coworker called her over. "I'm trying to make dill miso soup but I can't taste the dill, no matter how much I add," he said. She looked at the canister and sighed. They served the soup anyway, but Brown Zniewski made him draw a poster warning customers that it had magic properties, on it a big pot whose steam tendrils formed a marijuana leaf.

18. Polly Vollmar-Heywood, Facebook comment to my own query about New Riv food, March 23, 2016.

19. Between 1960 and 1980, for example, the number of Americans who had been born in China, Taiwan, and Hong Kong almost quadrupled and the population of Filipinos quintupled. The population of Indians, Pakistanis, and Bangladeshis increased fifteenfold and that of South Koreans by a factor of twenty-five. The later 1970s saw the beginning of mass immigrations of Iranians and Southeast Asians, whose populations had been almost nonexistent before the start of the decade. Before 1965, most of the Latino population was concentrated in California and Texas. Between 1960 and 1980, though, the number of Americans who had been born in Mexico almost quadrupled, to 2.2 million people. Central Americans arrived in small numbers in the late 1970s, then flooded into the country in the 1980s, driven north by war. Source: Campbell Gibson and Kay Jung, "Historical Census Statistics on the Foreign-Born Population of the United States: 1850 to 2000" (Population Division working paper no. 81), U.S. Census Bureau, 2006. Accessed online August 5, 2016, from http://www.census.gov/population/www/documentation/twps0081/twps0081.pdf.

20. "Fast Growth of Air Travel: Report on a Nonstop Boom," *U.S. News & World Report,* September 5, 1966, pp. 51–53; "Revolution in Air Travel About to

Start," *U.S. News & World Report,* May 9, 1966, pp. 52–53.

21. David T. Courtwright, *Sky as Frontier: Adventure, Aviation, and Empire* (Texas A&M University Press, 2005).

22. Robert Lindsey, "Airlines, in Flight of Fancy, Offer Under-26 Travelers Rock and Organic Food," *New York Times,* July 13, 1972.

23. "Summer '70: Young Americans Abroad," *Newsweek,* August 10, 1970.

24. Anthony J. Despagni, "Card-Carrying Americans Crowd the Rails of Europe," *New York Times,* September 20, 1970. The *Times* reported that Eurail passes saw a 45 percent jump in sales between 1969 and 1970 alone.

25. Dori Lundy, "Vagabond Youth: Financial Miracle in Europe," *Los Angeles Times,* October 4, 1970, p. 16.

26. Jack McDonald, "San Miguel—Mexican Town That Agrees With Americans," *Boston Globe,* February 15, 1970; "Hippies Must Clean Up for Mexican Tourist Card," *Christian Science Monitor,* July 21, 1969 (similar stories ran in other newspapers through the early 1970s); "Mexicans Rounding Up Hippies," *Austin Statesman,* July 12, 1969; "Mexico Hard on 'Hippie,'" *Austin Statesman,* August 29, 1971.

27. Southern California seemed to draw Indian spiritual teachers the most strongly: Swami Prabhavananda, Krishnamurti, Yogananda (who called Los Angeles "the Benares of America" in 1925), Swami Muktananda, and Jim Baker's guru, Yogi Bhajan, all settled there for at least a spell. See Philip Goldberg, *American Veda: From Emerson and the Beatles to Yoga and Meditation: How Indian Spirituality Changed the West* (Crown Archetype, 2010).

28. Lewis Lapham chronicled the Beatles' visit and the attendant news glut in "There Once Was a Guru from Rishikesh," a two-part series in *Saturday Evening Post,* May 4 and 11, 1968.

29. "Year of the Guru," *Life,* February 9, 1968.

30. For more information on the Hippie Trail, read Rory MacLean, *Magic Bus: On the Hippie Trail from Istanbul to India* (Penguin Books, 2007). See also Tony and Maureen Wheeler, *Unlikely Destinations: The Lonely Planet Story* (Periplus, 2005) and Patrick Marnham, *Road to Katmandu* (G. P. Putnam's Sons, 1971).

31. David Tomory, *A Season in Heaven: True Tales from the Road to Kathmandu* (Lonely Planet Publications, 1998). Later in the 1970s, Tomory writes, they would be eclipsed by Western Europeans by as much as three to one.

32. San Francisco cookbook author Joyce Goldstein, who taught cooking classes

throughout the 1960s, says that almost all her clients were middle-class women who wanted to learn showpiece French recipes to impress friends or their husbands' coworkers. "It was the era of the competitive dinner party," she says. "I actually enrolled in Gestalt therapy classes so that I could deal with the emotionality that came out in a cooking class."

33. There's a story there, of course: read more in chapter 7.

34. Most of this section is based on an interview with Mollie Katzen, May 30, 2013.

35. Bill Stevenson, "Moosewood's Good," *Cornell Daily Sun*, March 21, 1974.

36. Martha Espedahl, "Restaurant Success Results in Health Food Cookbook," *News Journal* (Wilmington, DE), February 9, 1977.

37. Mary Flachsenhaar, "Meat-Eaters Have a Bone to Pick," *Detroit Free Press*, July 11, 1978.

38. Scott Bruce and Bill Crawford, *Cerealizing America: The Unsweetened Story of American Breakfast Cereal* (Faber & Faber, 1995).

39. "History of Muesli," Evoke Foods. Accessed September 7, 2016, at http:// www.evokefoods.com/history-of-muesli/.

40. Michael Kernan, "Is Granola Overrated as a Health Food?" *Los Angeles Times*, October 19, 1972.

41. "Granola Outlawed in Minneapolis," *Ann Arbor Sun*, June 11, 1971.

42. Joe Klein, "A Social History of Granola," *Rolling Stone*, February 23, 1978.

## 7. Food Co-ops, Social Revolutionaries, and the Birth of an Industry

1. The Co-op Handbook Collective, *The Food Co-op Handbook* (Houghton Mifflin, 1975). The rules were: open membership; democratic control based on one member, one vote (this included women as well as men); promotion of education; dividends in proportion to purchases; limited interest on capital investment, and limit on number of shares any member can own; political and religious neutrality; cash trading, no credit; and active cooperation among cooperatives.

2. CLUSA factsheet, quoted in Ronco, *Food Co-ops*.

3. The UT student store is also a cooperative, but the counterculture wrote it off as a faceless capitalist enterprise.

4. Information about Austin's housing cooperatives comes from Jim Jones, *Many Hands: A History of the Austin Cooperative Community* (Allen Creek Media, 2013). See also "Co-ops News [*sic*]," *The Rag*, June 5, 1972.

5. Paul Spencer, "Cooperative Store-y," *The Rag*, September 16, 1968; Bill

Meacham, "Co-ops: A Way of Life in Austin," *The Rag*, September 3, 1974.

6. Kick Kingsley, "Obit," *First Flower* (newsletter), September 1973, quoted in Jones, *Many Hands*.

7. Ibid.

8. Anonymous, "The Many Lives of Milo," *The Rag*, January 25, 1971.

9. We're not just talking about the health authorities. Many of the food conspiracy members were active in leftist circles, where FBI plants and informants were legion and the underground newspapers regularly outed any they identified.

10. Sources on the Berkeley Food Conspiracy: Lois Wickstrom, *The Food Conspiracy Cookbook: How to Start a Neighborhood Buying Club and Eat Cheaply* (San Francisco: 101 Productions, 1974). See also Pam Peirce, "A Personal History of the San Francisco People's Food System," in *Ten Years That Shook the City: San Francisco 1968–1978*, ed. Chris Carlsson (City Lights Publishers, 2011); Shanta Nimbark Sacharoff, *Other Avenues Are Possible: Legacy of the People's Food System of the San Francisco Bay Area* (PM Press, 2016).

11. Laurel Rosen and Sally McGrane, "The Revolution Will Not Be Catered," *San Francisco Chronicle*, March 8, 2000.

12. The Co-op Handbook Collective, *Food Co-op Handbook*.

13. Bernadette Carey, "Mrs. Garcia Shops: Arroz, Papas, Sal," *New York Times*, November 26, 1966.

14. Angela Parker, "Buying Clubs Weld Small Farmers, Needy," *Chicago Tribune*, May 13, 1971; "This Solution Should Be Easy," *Chicago Tribune*, October 26, 1974.

15. Gloria Stern, *How to Start Your Own Food Co-op: A Guide to Wholesale Buying* (Walker and Company, 1974); interview with Matthew Lind, an early coordinator at the Centre-In Food Co-op, Goshen, Indiana.

16. You can find an incomplete but entertaining history of the Mifflin Street Food Co-op at http://www.waxingamerica.com/2006/05/history_of_the_.html.

17. More information on Ann Arbor comes from Patti F. Smith, *A History of Ann Arbor's People's Food Co-op* (People's Food Co-op, 2016).

18. "Who Is Woody Hills?" *The Rag*, March 25, 1974.

19. John Dickerson, "ACP," *The Rag*, June 28, 1972.

20. Bill Meacham, "Our Town: Co-op News," *The Rag*, June 3, 1974.

21. My favorite: in an October 21, 1974, item subtitled "The Continuing Saga of Sattva," he wrote, "Last week several people were disappointed because the stuffed grape leaves promised in the weekly menu didn't happen. That's because the person who was to cook them had to leave suddenly, and other people didn't know how to cook them. The staff apologizes."

22. Meacham, "Co-ops: A Way of Life in Austin."

23. Quoted in Daniel Zwerdling, "The Uncertain Revival of Food Cooperatives," in *Co-ops, Communes and Collectives*, eds. John Case and Rosemary C. R. Taylor (Random House, 1979); CLUSA actually speculated that it was five thousand to ten thousand, but David Gutknecht, longtime editor of the *Cooperative Grocer* magazine, has argued that the lower number is the correct one.

24. True story: I found my first apartment in San Francisco in 1991 via the bulletin board at my local co-op.

25. Olive Ylin, founding member of a co-op in Iowa City, told me meetings were so long that she had to entertain herself by embroidering a pair of jeans or a workshirt.

26. The debates over cashews and bananas took place in Minnesota co-ops, coffee at the New Riverside Cafe, cucumbers at Wheatsville. The Jarlsberg example comes from the Wheatsville newsletter, the Saran Wrap example from Anne Meis Knupfer, *Food Co-ops in America: Communities, Consumption, and Economic Democracy* (Cornell University Press, 2013).

27. These days, most politically motivated shoppers know that pastureland is often not suitable for growing grains or vegetables, but this was the early 1970s.

28. AC News & Co-op Report, *The Rag*, November 4 and December 2, 1974.

29. Kathy Sharp, "Women: Been to Any Good Meetings Lately?" *Scoop*, January 1979.

30. The Co-op Handbook Collective, *Food Co-op Handbook*.

31. Jackie [Byars], "Co-ops or Social Change?" *The Rag*, September 8, 1975. (The "Food is the hippie religion" quote is one widely attributed to Timothy Leary.) In another, more troubling, incident, one member of the Ann Arbor People's Food Co-op remembers a time when an Asian student from the University of Michigan approached the register to ask where the white rice was. "We don't carry *shit* food," the volunteer hissed back.

32. Alan S. Blinder, "The Anatomy of Double-Digit Inflation in the 1970s," in *Inflation: Causes and Effects*, ed. Robert E. Hall (University of Chicago Press, 1982).

33. "How to Start a Food Co-op," *Good Housekeeping*, March 1975.

34. Gail Perrin, "Food Co-ops—The Price of Survival Is Work," *Boston Globe*, January 29, 1975.

35. Much of the detail in this section comes from interviews with Suzanne Caya on August 4 and 14, 2016, as well as interviews with Earl Goddin, Paul Brown, David Corsa, Bruce Curtis, Carol Collins, and Felicity Mildner.

36. William Meek, "State Quarantines 15 Contaminated Dairy Herds,"
    *Detroit Free Press*, May 14, 1974; Susan Ager, "Answers on Tainted
    Meat—No Real Danger Seen," *Detroit Free Press*, July 14, 1974. The
    contamination happened when the Michigan Farm Bureau mistook bags
    of bromide for magnesium oxide, a "common additive to improve milk
    production," then sold tons and tons of contaminated feed to farmers
    all across the state. The agriculture secretary reassured consumers
    again when it became clear some farmers had sold their cattle to
    slaughterhouses, bucking the quarantine.

37. Information about the founding of the People's Wherehouse comes from
    "History," *Michigan Federation of Food Co-ops Newsletter*, April 1976, as well
    as documents obtained from the "People's Wherehouse" collection at the
    Joseph A. Labadie Collection, University of Michigan Special Collections
    Library, Ann Arbor.

38. The Soy Plant started after the founders devoured Bill Shurtleff and Akiko
    Aoyagi's *Book of Tofu*, naturally.

39. Phil Shaw, "Do We Need More Items?" *MFOFC News*, January 1976.
    Michigan Federation of Food Co-operatives newsletter collection. Bentley
    Historical Library, University of Michigan, Ann Arbor.

40. Unless specified, much of the detail on the co-op wars comes from Craig Cox,
    *Storefront Revolution: Food Co-ops and the Counterculture* (Rutgers University
    Press, 1994), the defining work of journalism on the war, as well as John Curl,
    *For All the People: Uncovering the Hidden History of Cooperation, Cooperative
    Movements, and Communalism in America* (PM Press, 2009).

41. Quote from Curl, *For All the People*.

42. Quote from Cox, *Storefront Revolution*.

43. Essays from David Olmschid and Marcia [no last name], "On the
    Controversy" [series of essays], *Scoop*, March 1975.

44. Why? I don't quite know.

45. Bill Meacham, "Co-ops in Crisis," *The Rag*, May 12, 1975.

46. Bill Meacham, "ACP," *The Rag*, July 23, 1975; Bill Meacham, "Woody Hills
    in Struggle!" *The Rag*, September 8, 1975.

47. Sources for information on this episode: interviews with Jim Jones and Bill
    Meacham, as well as Jones's book, *Many Hands*.

48. Just as a side note, sometime around 2013 former *Rag* editors digitized eleven
    years' worth of issues and posted them online at http://rag.tlok.org/issues
    .php. Clear your schedule before you type that URL into your browser,
    though.

49. The Gung Ho Collective, "Austin Co-ops in Crisis? Or Stage Two in Our Study!" *The Rag,* October 26, 1976.

50. Daniel Zwerdling, "The Uncertain Revival of Food Cooperatives."

51. The story of the founding of Wheatsville was based primarily on multiple interviews with Burgess Jackson, Gary Newton, John Dickerson, and Jim Jones.

52. Marjorie Hoffman, "Crowd Jams Rock Concert," *Austin American-Statesman,* September 2, 1974.

53. Details on the financial arrangements are from "Wheatsville: Austin's New Food Co-op," *The Rag,* May 3, 1975.

54. Details from Fran Fulwiler, "Wheatsville: A Food Co-op With a Difference," *Austin American-Statesman,* June 11, 1976.

55. After the Avenues and Woody Hills closed, a group of Woody Hills members opened another co-op in South Austin with an attached restaurant. A few years into Wheatsville's run, the co-op's insurance broker called Burgess Jackson up to suggest that he could get much better rates if he enrolled in a group policy with the South Austin co-op. Jackson drove over to the new store to propose the scheme to the store manager. "He looks me in the eye," Jackson recalls, "and says, 'We don't need insurance because accidents are a result of karma. We don't have insurance because we don't have bad karma. You need insurance because you carry meat.'" A few months later, Austin's hippie community was hit with a hepatitis outbreak. Health inspectors traced it back to watercress that amateur foragers had gathered from the banks of a contaminated stream and sold to the South Austin co-op's restaurant. The inspector shut it down, and the store soon followed.

56. Tony Switzer, "Cashier Turnips: Don't Squeeze Us Out," *Wheatsville Breeze,* April 13, 1979.

57. Hunter Ellinger, "Some Thoughts on Cooperating," *Wheatsville Breeze,* August 7, 1979.

58. "Rethinking the Social Responsibility of Business," *Reason Online,* October 2005.

59. R. Michelle Breyer, "All-Natural Capitalist," *Austin American-Statesman,* May 10, 1998. See also Nick Paumgarten, "Food Fighter," *New Yorker,* January 4, 2010. Some of the Wheatsville founders say Mackey was a co-op member, but this was unconfirmed.

60. Linda Anthony, "A Couple of Naturals," *Austin American-Statesman,* February 23, 1982. Skiles would leave the company a few years later.

## Conclusion

1. *Transcendental Wild Oats* was Alcott's satire about the short-lived vegetarian commune her father, Bronson Alcott, dragged the family to live on in 1843.

2. Whole Foods, *2015 Annual Report*. Accessed September 29, 2016, at http://investor.wholefoodsmarket.com/investors/financial-information/annual-reports-and-proxy/default.aspx.

3. *HAIN 2015 Annual Report*. Accessed September 27, 2016, at http://ir.hain.com/phoenix.zhtml?c=87078&p=irol-reportsannual.

4. Results of the 2015 Certified Organic Survey reported in the National Agricultural Statistics Service, *NASS Highlights*, September 2016. Accessed September 29, 2016, at https://www.nass.usda.gov/Publications/Highlights/2015_Certified_Organic_Survey_Highlights.pdf. The 1995 figure comes from Economic Research Service statistics. Accessed September 29, 2016, at http://www.ers.usda.gov/data-products/organic-production.aspx.

5. Organic Trade Association, "2016 State of the Industry" [factsheet].

6. U.S. Department of Agriculture, Economic Research Service, "Food-Away-from-Home" and "Food Expenditures." Accessed at https://www.ers.usda.gov/topics/food-choices-health/food-consumption-demand/food-away-from-home.aspx and https://www.ers.usda.gov/data-products/food-expenditures.aspx.

7. McDonald's added a kale salad to its menu in 2016. Need I say more?

8. Looking outside the United States, you could also add the British Anna Jones's *A Modern Way to Cook* and the Australian Lola Berry's *The Happy Cookbook: 130 Wholefood Recipes for Health, Wellness, and a Little Extra Sparkle*.

9. Jane Brody, Personal Health, *New York Times*, March 30, 1977.

10. Biing-Hwan Lin and Rosanna Mentzer Morrison, "ERS's Food Consumption and Nutrient Intake Data—Tools for Assessing Americans' Diets," *Amber Waves*, October 6, 2014; Melanie Warner, *Pandora's Lunchbox: How Processed Food Took Over the American Meal* (Simon & Schuster, 2014).

11. Reported in Kathryn Doyle, "Few U.S. Adults Meet Fruit, Vegetable Intake Guidelines" Reuters, July 17, 2015. Accessed September 27, 2016, at http://www.reuters.com/article/us-health-nutrition-fruit-vegetables-idUSKCN0PR26N20150717.

# BIBLIOGRAPHY

**A note about sources:**

Research for this book was based on three kinds of sources: (a) interviews with more than a hundred people, a quarter of them multiple interviews; (b) secondary histories published in the trade press as well as academic dissertations; and (c) contemporary accounts from the 1960s and 1970s, including cookbooks, memoirs, and many periodicals. Oral history is a tricky pursuit, as anyone who's tried interviewing their grandparents has experienced. After forty or fifty years, memories turn into imprecise sketches, and we humans unconsciously fill in gaps with details from unrelated events. I found it most helpful to use oral history to flesh out the character of a story whose facts I could trace through documentary sources. I also tried to cross-check details one source would report against the memories of other sources before reporting them as fact, though there were some bits too juicy or vivid to leave out, in which case I attributed them to the speaker. Please take them for what they are: a portrait of a time, not provable fact.

One of my primary sources for tracking how ideas were phrased and circulated among the counterculture was the underground press, which started at the Vietnam War and blew up by 1970; many newspapers only lasted a few issues or years, but several dozen still publish.

As someone who began his career in journalism writing for alternative newspapers—three of them, in fact, from 1999 to 2012—I want to say how much I loved this part of the research, and how proud I am of this tradition in journalism, now on the wane. Interspersed among the thousands of crappy poems and awkward line drawings was an incredible body of smart, wiseass, urgent reporting and social criticism. I raise my fist in salute.

Abel, Emily. *Suffering in the Land of Sunshine: A Los Angeles Illness Narrative*. Rutgers University Press, 2006.

——. *Tuberculosis and the Politics of Exclusion*. Rutgers University Press, 2007.

Ackerman, Michael. "Interpreting the 'Newer Knowledge of Nutrition.'" Ph.D. dissertation, University of Virginia, 2005.

Adams, Mark. *Mr. America: How Muscular Millionaire Bernarr Macfadden Transformed the Nation Through Sex, Salad, and the Ultimate Starvation Diet*. Harper, 2009.

Addison, Heather. *Hollywood and the Rise of Physical Culture*. Routledge, 2003.

Agnew, Eleanor. *Back from the Land: How Young Americans Went to Nature in the 1970s, and Why They Came Back*. Ivan R. Dee, 2005.

Allen, Steve. *Beloved Son: A Story of the Jesus Cults*. Bobbs-Merrill, 1982.

Apple, Rima D. *Vitamania: Vitamins in American Culture*. Rutgers University Press, 1996.

Aquarian, Isis, and Electricity Aquarian. *The Source: The Untold Story of Father Yod, Ya Ho Wa13 and the Source Family*. Process, 2007.

Belasco, Warren J. *Appetite for Change: How the Counterculture Took On the Food Industry*. 2nd updated ed. Cornell University Press, 2006.

Beskow, Per. *Strange Tales About Jesus*. English translation. Fortress Press, 1983.

Bobrow-Strain, Aaron. *White Bread: A Social History of the Store-Bought Loaf*. Beacon Press, 2012.

Boots, Gypsy [Robert Bootzin]. *The Gypsy in Me!* Golden Boots Company. Self-published, 1993.

Boots, Gypsy, with Jerry Hopkins. *Bare Feet and Good Things to Eat*. 7th ed. Self-published, n.d.

Briarpatch Community. *The Briarpatch Book*. New Glide/Reed, 1978.

Brown, Dona. *Back to the Land: The Enduring Dream of Self-Sufficiency in Modern America*. University of Wisconsin Press, 2011.

Carlsson, Chris, ed. *Ten Years That Shook the City: San Francisco 1968–1978*. City Lights Publishers, 2011.

Carqué, Otto. *The Key to Rational Dietetics*. Health Research, originally published 1930; republished 1970.

Case, Andrew N. "Looking for Organic America: J. I. Rodale, the Rodale Press, and the Popular Culture of Environmentalism in the Postwar United States." Ph.D. dissertation, University of Wisconsin-Madison, 2012.

Clark, Lisa F. "Organic Limited: The Corporate Rise and Spectacular Change in the Canadian and American Organic Food Sectors." Ph.D. dissertation, Simon Fraser University, 2007.

Collingham, Lizzie. *The Taste of War: World War II and the Battle for Food*. Penguin Books, 2012.

Co-op Handbook Collective. *The Food Co-op Handbook*. Houghton Mifflin, 1975.

Coyote, Peter. *Sleeping Where I Fall*. Counterpoint, 2009.

Davis, Adelle. *Let's Eat Right to Keep Fit*. Rev. ed. Harcourt Brace Jovanovich, 1970.

Deutsch, Ronald M. *The Nuts Among the Berries: An Exposé of America's Food Fads*. Rev. ed. Ballantine, 1967.

Diamond, Stephen. *What the Trees Said: Life on a New Age Farm*. Dell Publishing, 1971.

*Organic Gardening and Farming* and *Prevention*. *The Organic Directory*. Rodale Press, 1971.

Ehrlich, Paul R. *The Population Bomb*. Ballantine Books, 1968.

Fike, Rupert, ed. *Voices from the Farm: Adventures in Community Living*. Book Publishing, 1998.

Fromartz, Samuel. *Organic, Inc.: Natural Foods and How They Grew*. Harcourt, 2006.

Gardner, Marvin. *Fads & Fallacies in the Name of Science*. Dover Publications, 1957.

Gaskin, Stephen [as "Stephen"]. *The Caravan*. Random House, 1972.

Gaskin, Stephen, and the Farm. *Hey Beatnik! This Is the Farm Book*. Book Publishing, 1974.

Gershuny, Grace. *Organic Revolutionary: A Memoir of the Movement for Real Food, Planetary Healing, and Human Liberation*. Joes Brook Press, 2016.

Graham, Frank, Jr. *Since Silent Spring*. Fawcett Publications, 1970.

Grogan, Emmett. *Ringolevio*. New York Review of Books, 2008.

Guthman, Julie. *Agrarian Dreams: The Paradox of Organic Farming in California*. 2nd ed. University of California Press, 2014.

Hauser, Gayelord. *Look Younger, Live Longer.* Paperback ed. Fawcett Crest, 1951.

Houriet, Robert. *Getting Back Together.* Coward, McCann & Geoghegan, 1971.

Hyams, Edward. *Soil and Civilization.* Thames and Hudson, 1952.

Iacobbo, Karen, and Michael Iacobbo. *Vegetarian America: A History.* Praeger, 2004.

Jackson, Carlton. *J. I. Rodale: Apostle of Nonconformity.* Pyramid Books, 1974.

Jones, Jim. *Many Hands: A History of the Austin Cooperative Community.* Allen Creek Media, 2013.

Kaiser, Charles. *1968 in America: Music, Politics, Chaos, Counterculture, and the Shaping of a Generation.* Weidenfeld & Nicolson, 1988.

Kennedy, Gordon. *Children of the Sun: A Pictorial Anthology from Germany to California, 1883–1949.* Nivaria Press, 1998.

Knupfer, Anne Meis. *Food Co-ops in America: Communities, Consumption, and Economic Democracy.* Cornell University Press, 2013.

Kotzsch, Ronald E. *Macrobiotics: Yesterday and Today.* Japan Publications, 1985.

Kramer, Mark. *Mother Walter & the Pig Tragedy.* Alfred A. Knopf, 1970.

Kushi, Aveline, with Alex Jack. *Aveline Kushi's Complete Guide to Macrobiotic Cooking.* Warner Books, 1985.

Kushi, Michio. *The Book of Macrobiotics: The Universal Way of Health and Happiness.* Japan Publications, 1977.

Kushi, Michio, with Alex Jack. *The Cancer Prevention Diet: Michio Kushi's Nutritional Blueprint for the Relief and Prevention of Disease.* St. Martin's Press, 1983.

Lappé, Frances Moore. *Diet for a Small Planet.* Ballantine Books, 1971.

———. *Diet for a Small Planet.* Rev. ed. Ballantine Books, 1975.

———. *Diet for a Small Planet: 10th Anniversary Edition.* Ballantine Books, 1981.

Ledoux, Pat. "The History of a Hippie Commune: The Farm." Ph.D. dissertation, Middle Tennessee State University, 1992.

Lee, Martin A., and Bruce Shlain. *Acid Dreams: The Complete Social History of LSD: The CIA, the Sixties, and Beyond.* Rev. ed. Grove Press, 1994.

Levenstein, Harvey. *Paradox of Plenty: A Social History of Eating in Modern America.* Rev. ed. University of California Press, 2003.

Longgood, William. *The Poisons in Your Food.* Simon and Schuster, 1960.

MacLean, Rory. *Magic Bus: On the Hippie Trail from Istanbul to India.* Penguin Books, 2007.

Marine, Gene, and Judith Van Allen. *Food Pollution: The Violation of Our Inner Ecology.* Holt, Rinehart and Winston, 1972.

Marnham, Patrick. *Road to Katmandu.* G. P. Putnam's Sons, 1971.

McCay, Mary A. *Rachel Carson*. Twayne Publishers, 1993.

McKenzie, Shelly. *Getting Physical: The Rise of Fitness Culture in America*. University Press of Kansas, 2013.

Mercer, Kevin Mitchell. "The Farm: A Hippie Commune as a Countercultural Diaspora." Master's thesis, University of Central Florida, 2012.

Miller, Timothy. *The 60s Communes: Hippies and Beyond*. Syracuse University Press, 1999.

Murray, Frank. *More Than One Slingshot: How the Health Food Industry Is Changing America*. Marlborough House, 1984.

Numbers, Ronald L. *Prophetess of Health: Ellen G. White and the Origins of Seventh-Day Adventist Health Reform*. Rev. ed. University of Tennessee Press, 1992.

Ohsawa, George [a.k.a. Nyoiti Sakurazawa], and William Dufty. *You Are All Sanpaku*. University Books, 1965.

Ohsawa, Georges [George]. *Zen Macrobiotics: The Philosophy of Oriental Medicine, Volume 1*. Pocketbook ed. Ohsawa Foundation, 1965.

Perry, Charles. *The Haight-Ashbury: A History*. Wenner, 2005.

Peters, Suzanne. "The Land in Trust: A Social History of the Organic Farming Movement." Ph.D. dissertation, McGill University, 1979.

Price, Catherine. *Vitamania: Our Obsessive Quest for Nutritional Perfection*. Penguin, 2015.

Richmond, Akasha. *Hollywood Dish*. Penguin, 2006.

Ronco, William. *Food Co-ops: An Alternative to Shopping in Supermarkets*. Beacon Press, 1974.

Rorabaugh, W. J. *American Hippies*. Cambridge University Press, 2015.

Rorty, James, and N. Philip Norman. *Tomorrow's Food*. Devin-Adair, 1956.

Rose, Marla Matzer. *Muscle Beach*. LA Weekly Books/St. Martin's Griffin, 2001.

Sacharoff, Shanta Nimbark. *Other Avenues Are Possible: Legacy of the People's Food System of the San Francisco Bay Area*. PM Press, 2016.

Shurtleff, William. *History of Erewhon: Natural Foods Pioneer in the United States (1966–2011)*. E-book. Soyinfo Center, 2011.

Shurtleff, William, and Akiko Aoyagi. *History of Tofu and Tofu Products (963 CE to 2013)*. Soyinfo Center, 2013.

Smith, Patti F. *A History of Ann Arbor's People's Food Co-op*. People's Food Co-op, 2016.

Stern, Gloria. *How to Start Your Own Food Co-op: A Guide to Wholesale Buying*. Walker and Company, 1974.

Stoecker, Randy. *Defending Community: The Struggle for Alternative Redevelopment in Cedar-Riverside*. Temple University Press, 1994.

Szekely, Edmond Bordeaux. *The Essene Gospel of Peace: The Aramaic and Old Slavonic Texts*. 17th ed. Academy of Creative Living, 1971.

———. *The Essene Science of Life According to the Essene Gospel of Peace*. International Biogenic Society, 1978.

Talbot, David. *Season of the Witch*. Free Press, 2012.

Tomory, David. *A Season in Heaven: True Tales from the Road to Kathmandu*. Melbourne: Lonely Planet Publications, 1998.

Warner, Melanie. *Pandora's Lunchbox: How Processed Food Took Over the American Meal*. Scribner, 2013.

Wheeler, Tony, and Maureen Wheeler. *Unlikely Destinations: The Lonely Planet Story*. Periplus, 2005.

Whelan, Elizabeth M., and Frederick Stare. *Panic in the Pantry*. Atheneum, 1975.

———. *The 100% Natural, Purely Organic, Cholesterol-Free, Megavitamin, Low-Carbohydrate Nutrition Hoax*. Atheneum, 1983.

Whorton, James C. *Crusaders for Fitness: The History of American Health Reformers*. Princeton University Press, 1982.

———. *Nature Cures: The History of Alternative Medicine in America*. Oxford University Press, 2002.

Wickstrom, Lois. *The Food Conspiracy Cookbook: How to Start a Neighborhood Buying Club and Eat Cheaply*. 101 Productions, 1974.

Wizansky, Richard, ed., and the members of the Packer Corners community. *Home Comfort: Life on Total Loss Farm*. Saturday Review Press, 1973.

Zimmerman, Tom. *Paradise Promoted: The Booster Campaign That Created Los Angeles, 1870–1930*. Angel City Press, 2008.

## Cookbooks

Abehsera, Michel. *Zen Macrobiotic Cooking*. Carol Publishing Press, 1968; paperback ed., 1991.

alicia bay laurel. *Living on the Earth*. Vintage Books, 1970.

Bloodroot Collective. *The Political Palate: A Feminist Vegetarian Cookbook*. Sanguinaria Publishing, 1980.

Bragg, Paul C. *Paul C. Bragg's Four Generations Health Food Cook Book and Menus*. Health Science, 1966.

———. *Professor Bragg's Live Food Cook Book and Menus*. National Diet and Health Association of America, 1930.

Brock, Alice May. *Alice's Restaurant Cookbook*. Random House, 1969.

Brown, Edward Espe. *The Tassajara Bread Book*. Shambhala Books, 1970.

————. *Tassajara Cooking*. Shambhala Publishing, 1973.

————. *Tomato Blessings and Radish Teachings: Recipes and Reflections*. Riverhead Books, 1997.

Burgess, Mary. *Soul to Soul: A Vegetarian Soul Food Cookbook*. Woodbridge Press, 1976.

Davis, Adelle. *Let's Cook It Right*. Harcourt, Brace, 1947.

Dotzler, Louise, ed. *The Farm Vegetarian Cookbook*. Book Publishing, 1975.

Dragonwagon, Crescent. *The Commune Cookbook*. Simon & Schuster, 1972.

Farthing, Bill. *Odiyan Country Cookbook*. Dharma Publishing, 1977.

Fulton, E. G. *Vegetarian Cook Book: Substitutes for Flesh Foods*. Pacific Press Publishing, 1914.

Goldbeck, Nikki. *Cooking What Comes Naturally*. Cornerstone Library, 1972.

Goldsmith, Maureen. *The Organic Yenta*. Atheneum, 1972.

Hauser, Gayelord. *The Gayelord Hauser Cookbook*. Coward-McCann, 1946.

Holt, Calvin, and Patch Caradine. *Brown Rice & Love: A Zen Macrobiotic Cookbook*. Pyramid Books, 1971.

Hooker, Alan. *Vegetarian Gourmet Cookery*. 101 Productions, 1970.

Horton, Lucy. *Country Commune Cooking*. Coward, McCann & Geoghegan, 1972.

Hurd, Frank, and Rosalie Hurd. *Ten Talents*. Dr. and Mrs. Frank J. Hurd, 1968.

Hunter, Beatrice Trum. *Beatrice Trum Hunter's Whole-Grain Baking Sampler*. Keats Publishing, 1972.

————. *The Natural Foods Cookbook*. Simon & Schuster, 1961.

Jones, Ita. *The Grub Bag*. Vintage, 1971.

Jordan, Julie. *Wings of Life: Vegetarian Cookery*. Crossing Press, 1976.

Katzen, Mollie. *Moosewood Cookbook*. Ten Speed Press, 1977.

LaLanne, Jack. *The Jack LaLanne Way to Vibrant Good Health*. Prentice Hall, 1960.

The Ohsawa Foundation. *Zen Cookery: Practical Macrobiotics*. Ignoramus Press, 1966.

Richter, Vera. *Mrs. Richter's Cook-Less Book with Scientific Food Chart*. Hale Publications, 1948.

Robertson, Laurel, Carol Flinders, and Bronwen Godfrey. *Laurel's Kitchen Bread Book*. Nilgiri Press, 1976.

Rosicrucian Fellowship. *New Age Vegetarian Cookbook*. 8th ed. Rosicrucian Fellowship, 1979.

Rotondi, Pietro. *Vegetarian Cookery*. 2nd ed. Willing, 1948.

Shurtleff, William, and Akiko Aoyagi. *The Book of Tofu: Food for Mankind*. Autumn Press, 1975.

————. *The Book of Miso*. Autumn Press, 1976.

————. *The Book of Tempeh*. Harper & Row, 1979.

Thomas, Anna. *The Vegetarian Epicure*. Knopf, 1972.

————. *The Vegetarian Epicure, Book Two*. Knopf, 1978.

Vithaldas, Yogi, and Susan Roberts. *The Yogi Cook Book*. Bell, 1968.

Wiener, Joan. *Victory Through Vegetables*. Holt, Rinehart and Winston, 1970.

# INDEX